# Troublesome Behaviour in the Classroom

Why do some pupils behave badly in school? What can teachers do about it?

This thoroughly updated edition of *Troublesome Behaviour in the Classroom* is the most comprehensive and practical guide available on the subject of behaviour management in schools.

Discipline problems are frequently seen as a cause for increasing concern in schools. In this book, the author examines the full range of difficult behaviour from nursery age children to teenagers, and shows how it can be understood in terms of pupils' motives, their domestic peer-group and classroom contexts. He then demonstrates how it can be dealt with through teachers' skills, techniques and attitudes.

Distinguished by Mick McManus' lively and witty writing style, the book is very readable and is packed with practical ideas, activities, insights and solutions which will be invaluable to all student and classroom teachers.

**Mick McManus** has been a teacher for twenty years and is now head of secondary education at Leeds Metropolitan University. He is a regular contributor to school-based staff-training days.

# Troublesome Behaviour in the Classroom

## Meeting individual needs

## Second edition

## Mick McManus

ROUTLEDGE

London and New York

First published 1989
by Routledge
11 New Fetter Lane, London EC4P 4EE

Second edition published 1995

Simultaneously published in the USA and Canada
by Routledge
29 West 35th Street, New York, NY 10001

Phototypeset in Times by Intype, London
Printed and bound in Great Britain by
Mackays of Chatham PLC, Chatham, Kent

*British Library Cataloguing in Publication Data*
A catalogue record for this book is available from the British Library

*Library of Congress Cataloging in Publication Data*
A catalogue record for this book has been requested

ISBN 0–415–11360–1

To my wife June,
who has never been a bit of trouble,
and to our children, Sally, Jimmy, Maggie and Bob,
who have.

# Contents

# List of illustrations

**FIGURES**

**TABLES**

# Preface

This book began as an inquiry into why some schools exclude many more pupils than others. The results were unexpected. There was no support for the view that big schools had more discipline problems than small schools; that urban schools had higher exclusion rates than suburban schools; nor was there evidence that poverty and domestic disadvantage in a school's catchment necessarily led to more pupils being excluded for behaviour problems. Visits to schools gradually provided evidence that high exclusion rates were not a simple reflection of indiscipline, but were often the unintended consequence of taken-for-granted disciplinary procedures and teaching methods.

This book derives from the pre-service and in-service course that I have developed and taught to teachers from nursery, infant, primary, middle and high schools. There has been no difficulty finding common ground among this diversity, and it has often turned out to be a benefit; indeed, some of the most rewarding meetings were with teachers from a local authority that has long had a policy of grouping teachers from all sectors into neighbourhood pyramids. Others in the field have noticed this too (Hanko, 1985: 145). This is not to say that there are no differences in techniques and approaches between sectors, and where applicable these are specified in the text. It is my firm belief, however, that the skills of good teachers from nursery to university are more similar than disparate. In a major American study, Evertson and Emmer (1982) found that with primary and middle school age-groups effective procedures were broadly similar. The differences noticed were adjustments to age, subject and type of grouping rather than differences in 'qualitative principles'.

This book will be particularly helpful to school colleagues who now play a significantly larger part in preparing the next generation of teachers; some of the work has already been used with students on a wholly school-based training course. Each chapter is followed by a number of activities which are an integral part of the text. One way of conducting a series of training meetings would be for the staff-tutor to introduce each session with an outline and explanation of the theme of each chapter and use the activities as the chief learning aid. Generally, it is best if teachers or students have some time to consider the tasks alone before working on them in small groups and then sharing ideas in full session.

The course owes a lot to my twenty years' experience with troublesome teenagers in schools and units; but most of all I have profited from the help and friendship of teachers in schools, and colleagues and students in the university. Listing them all here would fill more than a page, and risk leaving some out or, worse still, including those who want nothing to do with it. I would like to mention, from the early days, Phil Simpson, Ted Bowskill and Gerry Vernon for the confidence they had in that aggressive young teacher I used to be; and those recent INSET students, Shoshana Angyalfi, Laura Detchon and Ben Rigg, who taught me as much as I taught them. As for the rest – friends, even if you read only this far, you can be sure you are on the list.

Finally, for this edition's more realistic cover drawing, thanks to Maggie McManus of City of Leeds School.

# Chapter I

# Concerns, causes and remedies

For playing truant he was caned. He tried to kick me, in fact he did kick me, and his mother then came to school and abused me in a most frightful manner.

(School Log of 1884, quoted in Porter, 1990).

## HAVE TIMES CHANGED?

The police believe themselves powerless before a rising tide of mischief and violence – particularly a recent serious increase in ruffianism among city youth. This sort of statement is made every day and commands wide assent, but it is a quotation from a complaint voiced in 1898. In the 1890s a government enquiry was launched into the rising crime rate among young people; a century later, similar concerns resulted in the Elton Report (DES, 1989), which was the most comprehensive study of school discipline ever conducted in Britain. The report contains 138 recommendations addressed to every conceivable audience. Employers, parents, the Broadcasting Standards Council as well as teachers and even pupils are all the subject of advice as to how they can contribute to reducing bad behaviour in schools. Elton, unlike some of the experts we will consider in this book, promised no miracles: 'Reducing bad behaviour is a realistic aim. Eliminating it completely is not' (paragraph 2/29: 65). The committee received extensive evidence, consulted research and commissioned some of its own, and came to the conclusion that 'any quest for simple or complete remedies would be futile'. Its own summary covers eight pages and the theme of the report is clear: discipline in schools is the responsibility of everyone and not only a matter for teachers. Nevertheless, it concludes that much indiscipline can be diminished by making teachers better at classroom management.

As the Elton committee discovered, the literature offers a bewildering collection of definitions, estimates of prevalence, claims about trends, historical evidence and speculations upon causes and cures. The popular view that disorder in schools, like disorder in society, is a recent phenomenon is easily contradicted by reference to historical sources. Curtis (1963) records some of the frequent disturbances at the ancient universities, whose students were in many respects the equivalent of present-day secondary pupils. For example, at Cambridge in 1261 there was a fight between scholars from the north and south; unlike twentieth-century two-nations disputes, this one led to plunder and burning. At Oxford, on St Scholastica's Day in 1354, a pub-fight ended with many dead and wounded; a similar riot broke out in Cambridge in 1381. School rules are a clue to what behaviour might be expected from thirteenth-century pupils: at Westminster, boys were forbidden to play tricks on townsmen and not allowed to carry bows, sticks or stones. The fifteenth-century Cambridge graduation ritual for a Master of Grammar, who sought a licence to teach, placed discipline on an equal footing with learning. After the candidate had 'argyude as shall please the Proctor' he was provided with a 'Rodde' and a 'shrewde', that is, mischievous, boy whom he then 'bete openlye in the Scolys'. In this way, says Curtis, 'the newly fledged master approved his ability to teach in a grammar-school' (1963: 65). Most sixteenth- and seventeenth-century pictures of school-masters, says Curtis, depict the master with a birch or rod. A number of serious disturbances followed the abolition of certain 'papist' holidays after 1565. In 1587, pupils used armed force to occupy Edinburgh High School, as had happened earlier in Aberdeen. In 1595, magistrates were called to regain control of the same school and a town councillor was shot dead in the process. Raikes was impelled to found his Sunday schools partly by the 'wild and mischievous behaviour' of children on their day of rest. Evidently some of it continued, for Raikes had discipline problems: in one incident, a badger was let loose in the schoolroom. The horrors of eighteenth- and nineteenth-century public schools have been described by Gathorne-Hardy (1977): for example, in an 1818 riot at Eton, pupils smashed the desk of their headmaster, Dr Keates.

It may be said in mitigation that these examples come from more brutal times, in which such incidents did not carry the horrifying implications that they would in the twentieth century. In the eighteenth century, Coram was moved to found his hospital to rid the streets of abandoned and dying babies, and even as late as the 1890s they were said to be a common sight (Schostak, 1986); there were twenty times as many child deaths then as there are today. However, there is evidence that past violence was not viewed lightly at the time. Concern about increasing disorder among the young led, in 1847, to the establishment of a House of Lords Select Committee to look into the operation of the criminal law with respect to children. Evidence included statistics showing a rising conviction rate among those under 21, and some witnesses blamed the ragged schools for it (Curtis, 1963: 302).

The Parliamentary Act of 1484, which invited Richard III to become king, described the state of the nation as chaos with 'murders, extortions and oppressions, namely, of poor and impotent people, so that no man was sure of his life, land, livelihood, nor his wife, daughter, nor servant, every good maiden and woman standing in dread to be ravished and defouled.' An earlier writer had even boasted that crime was evidence of the great courage of the English: 'There are more men hanged in one year in England for robbery and manslaughter than in seven years for such crimes in France' (Fortescue, quoted in Gillingham, 1993). In 872 at Malmesbury school, in an early example of violence towards teachers, the pupils of the unfortunate Scotus Erigena stabbed him to death with their pens. Confusion about the facts of the case commonly happens with twentieth-century incidents, and this ninth-century outrage was disputed too: Curtis comments that the report was the subject of controversy as to its trustworthiness.

## WHAT IS TROUBLESOME BEHAVIOUR?

Uncertainty about the amount of troublesome behaviour has always been a feature of the debate and is allied to the difficulty in arriving at a definition which all can agree is interpreted and applied consistently. Doyle says the key to understanding misbehaviour is to see it 'in the context of classroom structures'. He defines it, with a struggle, as 'any behaviour by one or more students that is perceived by the teacher to initiate a vector of action that competes with or threatens the primary vector of action at a particular moment in a classroom activity' (Wittrock, 1986: 419). In the effort to recognize the subjectivity and relativity of teacher perceptions, this definition makes anything potentially misbehaviour.

In a class which has been left to its own devices, so that the teacher can catch up with marking, a pupil who asks for some work to do would be misbehaving. Conversely, if the teacher does not notice the bored pupil cutting up his or her books, that is not misbehaviour. For, as Doyle's definition says, anything that interferes with the teacher's state of mind is misbehaviour. The definition of disruptive behaviour offered by Galloway et al. (1982) is similarly flawed: '. . . any behaviour which appears problematic, inappropriate and disturbing to teachers'.

Another attempt, which appears to remove the subjective element by defining disruption in terms of its effect upon (ordinary) teaching and the (normal) school, is that by Lawrence et al. (1977, 1984): 'Behaviour which seriously interferes with the teaching process and/or seriously upsets the normal running of the school.' As many teachers say when asked for examples of such behaviour: it depends what you mean by 'seriously'. Distinctions between maladjustment and disruption are similarly problematic. There is a popular view that maladjustment is a pathological medical condition and disruption is rooted in moral deficiencies. Individual pathology plays a greater or lesser part in each pupil's behaviour, but there is no line between those who are typed as maladjusted and those typed as disruptive. Similar errors were made in identifying pupils with learning difficulties prior to the abolition of categories of handicap following the Education Act 1981. For example, many came to believe that pupils could be sorted into remedial, ESN(M) and ESN(S) types, but these categories evolved from historical and administrative arrangements. They encouraged the view that problems were solved because they had been identified, and where a pupil proved unamenable in a particular placement there was a tendency to seek a fresh place rather than a fresh policy.

More than twenty years ago, Hewett and Blake (1973) wrote that 'the most pressing need is for a reliable system of definition and classification of emotional and behavioural disorders'. We still do not have one, and they were wrong. To rely on definitions and categories to suggest remedies is to divert attention from observation of the individual and his or her circumstances. There are no easy solutions, so we have to think.

In a survey described in Chapter 2, I asked fifty teachers to indicate on a list of thirty-eight items the pupil behaviours they thought were 'serious threats to good order'. There was total agreement on only one item: 'Hits teacher'. Five teachers ticked every item; five queried the meaning of 'serious' or declined to tick any. The difficulty of definition is captured in an autobiographical anecdote by Blishen (1980): 'There was a boy in class two who was, I had to conclude, an advanced delinquent – yet his offence was barely definable. The nearest I could come to it was to say that he turned sitting down into a comedy.' Becker (1963) was only slightly exaggerating when he wrote, more directly than Doyle, that: . . . 'deviance is not a quality of the act a person commits . . . the deviant is one to whom that label has successfully been applied; deviant behaviour is behaviour that people so label.'

Labels and classifications spring from theories, often held implicitly, and it is true that they may tell us as much about the labeller as about the labelled. This does not mean that labels, categories and definitions are purely arbitrary: the distinctions, especially if they stick, must have something to do with that which is being observed. As Pring (1976) says, words like 'cats' and 'dogs' tell something about the classifier, but they also tell us something about the nature of cats and dogs. Defining and measuring the seriousness of misbehaviour is not a matter of applying such a simple distinction: it is more like trying to decide which dogs are light grey and which are not. No objective definition which would reduce the measurement of disruption to a simple counting process is possible. This definitional obscurity, unsatisfactory as it may be, is an important clue to one of the ways in which the problem of troublesome behaviour might be tackled. There are at least two parties to any disruptive incident. Both contribute to its being defined as serious or not, or indeed to whether it becomes defined as a disruptive incident at all.

## IS TROUBLESOME BEHAVIOUR A SPECIAL NEED?

Under the terms of current legislation, children have special needs if they have learning difficulties or disabilities which prevent or hinder them from making use of ordinary educational facilities – unless special provision is made for them. The emphasis is not on the disability itself but on the child and his or her needs. It is possible for two children to share a disability, and to the same degree, but not to have the same need of special provision. For example, a child with a physical or sensory disability might be able to join in all the activities of a school through personal motivation, the welcoming attitude of other pupils, and the positive work of teachers to ensure full access to the school's provision; another child might have to face ignorance or unhelpfulness in a poorly adapted building.

Is it helpful to regard pupils who behave badly as having disabilities which hinder their access to the curriculum? As their behaviour usually impedes the progress of other children, perhaps there is a case for arguing that behavioural problems are not special needs in the same way that disabilities of sight, hearing, mind or mobility are. Unlike disabilities, where normally only the owner is hindered, behavioural problems create difficulties in learning for those children who have to share the same facilities and teachers. Arguments of this sort underpin the case for separation and separate provision for such pupils. To clarify the matter, we will look briefly at what might seem to be straightforward disabilities: visual impairment and blindness.

Very few people we think of as blind can see nothing at all. One of the official definitions of blindness is the inability to see at three metres what ordinary people can see at sixty metres; another is the inability to distinguish the fingers of one's own hand when it is held at arm's length. The majority of blind people have some residual vision of a restricted, blurred or shadowy kind. Tests of the degree of blindness control access to state assistance and benefits but do not completely inform us of a blind person's capabilities. They do not determine how mobile or competent a person is; they do not even tell us whether or not a person can read. Personal determination, help from other people, and access to appropriate technology are important influences on what can be achieved – even for people with extremely limited vision or none at all. This explains the many strange events that are usually treated with levity in newspaper reports: for example, a blind bank robber who escaped into the arms of the police, or a blind driver who claimed to be guided by his dog (which barked once for a green light and twice for a red). Both people probably had enough residual vision, and strength of will, to make them confident that they could cope.

The special needs of blind pupils will vary, and so will the provision necessary to meet those needs. The factors to be taken into account include the attitudes of those with whom they will be educated, the provision the school makes, and their own personal qualities and motivation. Let us suppose that all blind pupils attended ordinary schools and always had done. Some would have been welcomed and helped; others might have been rejected or isolated. Some would have settled down quietly and acquiesced whatever their experiences; others might have become distressed or aggressive. How would these varied responses affect the learning of those other pupils in the class? It is easy to specify the effect of open distress or aggression, but even where there is silent, passive acquiescence learning is affected. Pupils learn more than just the formal curriculum: in the hypothetical example here, they might learn that abandoning the afflicted in this way is an ordinary and acceptable policy. They might grow up to regard the blind in much the same way that slave-owners regarded slaves, as just another component of production – human resources and not human beings.

Three conclusions can be drawn. First, in what might have seemed a simple matter (someone is either blind or not) we find that the individual's personal qualities are but one of the groups of factors affecting the outcome: other people's knowledge, understanding and efforts are crucial. Second, individual disabilities affect the learning of others, and what is learned depends partly upon the beliefs and actions of those who do not have those disabilities. Only for a very small minority would provision in ordinary schools be ineffective and disruptive. Third, in deciding what is efficient learning and what is appropriate provision it is not enough to focus on one narrow aspect of school life. The whole social, emotional and moral context must be considered: education is an ethical not a technical activity.

These conclusions support the status of behavioural difficulties as individual needs and the rightness of trying to accommodate such pupils in ordinary schools. This book aims to provide the knowledge and understanding to help teachers improve pupils' behaviour, and to encourage the determination to succeed and the conviction that helping those afflicted in this way is the moral responsibility of members of the teaching profession.

## HOW MUCH MISBEHAVIOUR IS THERE?

Until the Elton report's research (DES, 1989) statistics on troublesome behaviour were conflicting and unreliable. The Pack Report (HMSO, 1977) on truancy and disruption in Scotland concluded as much. When figures are gathered they are disputed: if too low for the critic's liking, they are said to indicate teachers' unwillingness to risk censure in an atmosphere of hostility towards a beleaguered profession; or they may be dismissed as coming from a tainted source – headteachers covering up the shortcomings of their schools. If too high, then they are said to be the exaggeration of interested parties seeking additional compensation and resources. Hargreaves *et al.* (1975) recorded only one act of violence to staff during their research, as did Lawrence *et al.* (1977) during their work in a secondary school. In their four-year study discussed in Galloway *et al.* (1982), twelve of 266 suspensions were for violence to a teacher. A survey by the DES in 1975 (DES, 1980) found the level of violent acts to be 7.68 per 10,000 pupils, and the level of acts of rowdyism to be 3.81 per 10,000 pupils. With a school population of around eight million it is easy to see how a low rate of disruption could generate a daily supply of horrifying anecdotes. Reviewing research, Johnstone and Munn (1987) conclude that possibly one-quarter of teachers are worried by disruption but very few are seriously worried. Surveys by teachers' unions invariably produce more dramatic results, but it is difficult to know how to allow for sampling distortions: perhaps replies come only from those who are worried. The NAHT claim (reported in *The Times*, 17.6.88) that there are ninety-five assaults on teachers every day, if taken at face value, would indicate that the number had tripled since the DES survey in 1975.

The research conducted on behalf of the Elton Committee showed that serious trouble was rare in schools, but many teachers were under considerable pressure caused by the frequency of less serious indiscipline and its relentlessness. Primary and secondary teachers reported that the most common types of misbehaviour they had to deal with were such things as talking out of turn, idleness, distracting others and general unruliness. Surprisingly, actual violence to other pupils and staff was more frequent among primary than secondary pupils, but nowhere could it be said to be widespread – with no more than 2 per cent of teachers reporting physical aggression to themselves in the week prior to the survey. Physical aggression, it should be noted, did not mean assault. The researchers' interviews with teachers indicated that many did not consider themselves assaulted even when they had been pushed or hit by pupils. Some of the reasons for this apparently easy-going attitude, and its significance for the development of teachers' expertise with difficult pupils, will be explored in Chapter 4.

The term 'assault' is emotive, a legalistic category carrying the implication of serious harm; it distorts reality when applied to such things as pushing past a teacher to escape punishment, or being kicked on the shin by an infant in a tantrum. Lawrence *et al.* (1984) sought information from Europe on disruptive behaviour and uncovered a patchy but broadly similar mix of concerns and uncertainties as exists in Britain. The problems giving most general concern were bullying, vandalism, refusal to obey teacher, bad language and difficult classes (but not difficult schools). The type of offences that most often appear in the press – alcoholism and violence to teachers – were bottom of the list. Only in France was violence to teachers high on the list of concerns. Writing of the situation in America, where school violence is popularly believed to be widespread, Doyle refers to national surveys which show that serious incidents 'are generally rare in most schools' and most often occur out of classrooms (see Wittrock, 1986: 418). There seems to be no reason for Davies to modify his conclusion (quoted in Jones-Davies and Cave, 1976) that although much disruption is awkward and undesirable it is still a minority sport.

## COMMON-SENSE REMEDIES

The dip into past indiscipline with which we began this chapter was intended to put present problems into a less stressful perspective. It also prompts us to consider the value of the simple solutions that are popularly offered for indiscipline in schools. Brutal punishments are as old as history: 'A boy's ear is in his backside' wrote one ancient Egyptian scribe (quoted in Tyldesley, 1994). In more recent times, it is questionable whether such punishments were effective. While some pupils were being flogged at school, some of their non-attending peers might be awaiting capital punishment or transportation for non-violent crimes. Spooner (1988) recorded a case of a boy who had been caned on eighty-nine occasions in a year in which he had attended school on only eighty-seven days. Even in countries where violent offenders are still violently dealt with, there remain those prepared to offend and earn the punishments. Naturally, in assessing the efficacy of a punishment, most of us consider whether we ourselves would be deterred. This is a mistake. We rightly feel that we would not risk punishment for a crime, neglecting the fact that we make this decision from our present, comfortable perspective; and since most of us eschew crime and violence anyway, we are not able to understand the motivation of those who ignore rules and who would not be deterred. There are, of course, considerations other than the efficacy issue: for many people, and most western governments, repaying violence with violence is not morally acceptable and no amount of evidence that such a policy works would change that view.

Even if rigid and complete discipline in a school were achievable by force, it would not necessarily transfer with the pupil to fresh situations. Goffman (1968) has documented the varied strategies available even to asylum inmates to enable them to protect themselves from unwanted influences: for example, withdrawal, rebellion, 'playing it cool'. We can be sure that pupils are at least as inventive. Wills (1967) hoped pupils would devise a moral system of their own which was 'not unacceptable to society' and which they would stick to and value: 'It is possible for a person under discipline never to display a single symptom and go out into the world untouched.' Davies and Maliphant (1974) conducted an extraordinary experiment to measure the effectiveness of 'distinctly unpleasant' electric shocks in teaching 'refractory' pupils and ordinary pupils a simple skill. The refractory individuals received significantly more shocks than their more amenable fellows but the effects were short lived. The authors suggest that this is typical of the ineffectiveness of punishment upon them in ordinary life.

Discussing troublesome pupils, Laslett (1977) points out that the cause and source of punishment are easily confused. Punishment does not discourage misbehaviour but rather reinforces the pupil's view of adults as treacherous. In a research review, Topping (1983) concluded that punishment was ineffective and could aggravate problems. For a few distressed individuals, seeking punishment may be a part of their problem not a solution to it; others are denied the opportunity to make amends. Laslett therefore suggests that management is a more useful concept than punishment. A pupil is put in the care and under the close supervision of one person, perhaps a personal tutor or senior member of staff, where difficulties can be sorted out without the interference of an attendant audience: close proximity encourages a helpful exchange of information. Wills (1945) also thought punishment took away the valuable opportunity for the offender to make restitution. He also suggested that punishment led to the exclusion of moral thinking in favour of book-keeping calculations related to the possibility of being caught, and the likely price to be paid. This encouraged the attitude that misbehaviour could be paid for, the slate being wiped clean for fresh villainy. A similar claim is sometimes made about the function of the sacrament of confession and it is equally unconvincing; in any case, the argument applies as well to restitution as it does to punishment. At the other extreme from punishment, permissiveness is equally unhelpful. In a pioneer study, Jackson (1968) noted that to survive in classrooms pupils needed to learn turn-taking and patience: teacher as gatekeeper created the experiences of denial, interruption and distraction for pupils. Delamont (1976) produces the often-quoted figure of one minute of teacher's time per pupil per forty-minute lesson and comments that research is needed into how pupils spend their minute. Many pupils need help in learning how to use the other thirty-nine. Something of this sort is implied in Laslett's (1977) suggestion that troublesome pupils should be exposed occasionally to adults less tolerant than their teachers.

## COMMON-SENSE CAUSES

The advice in this book is intended to be useful in the teaching of all pupils, from the naughty to the seriously disturbed. No one should assume that classroom management skills, or the social and institutional pressures of classrooms and schools, are irrelevant to the treatment of pupils believed to be severely disruptive or maladjusted. Many teachers take it for granted that the treatment of pupils who have behaved very badly over a long period is a medical matter. Certainly, any other form of approach may seem hopelessly time consuming and uncertain in its effects: to listen, think and help can be an open-ended, unrewarding and exhausting enterprise. It seems self-evident that some pupils have something bio-chemically wrong with them, and common sense to leave medical experts to find the most soothing cocktail of tranquillizers. Teachers have grown accustomed to deferring to experts of various kinds and take it as axiomatic that medical advice is safe, scientific and objective. Doctors have only recently lost the right to decide whether a child needed special schooling or not. Teachers are rarely cast in the confident role of experts and do not find it at all remarkable to be told to consult specialists.

Much of the drift of a book on disruptive behaviour, written by two doctors, is in this vein (Holman and Coghill, 1987). Members of powerful professional groups are accustomed to having weight attached to their views on matters outside their specialism: for example, a scientist's opinion of religion, a doctor's views on parenting, a university teacher's policy for primary school maths. We defer too easily. Part of my argument is that teachers need to increase their confidence in their own expertise and therefore to give only what limited credence is due to members of other professions when they pronounce upon school matters. Much of what they have to say is pure tautology. For example, we are told: 'The prime purpose of schools as places of learning can be furthered by reducing impediments to learning, especially in children unable to learn' (Holman and Coghill, 1987: 220). In another inconsequential passage we learn: 'A teacher of 35, 15 years in the profession, when told by the head to get her hair cut saw this as a threat to her identity'; and well she might. However, a more serious threat to teacher identity is posed by politely accepting any kind of flim-flam from outsiders. A healthy scepticism is needed: the observations of those who have distinguished themselves in other spheres can be every bit as insubstantial as comments from any other person stopped on the street. To say that teachers should have confidence in their own expertise and not accept other specialists' opinions uncritically is not to say that teachers should regard their own medical and psychological knowledge as complete and sufficient. Laslett (1977) warns against teachers as amateur psychologists but notes that teachers' contact with pupils is greater in duration and variety than that of any other professional. That being the case, teachers are best placed to understand pupils' problems and should take a central role in assessing the advice of others, whose contact with the problem can seldom be other than peripheral.

The notion that problem behaviour can be attributed solely to chemistry, whether internal in the genes or external in food additives or petrol-lead, has a powerful hold over the imagination, comfortably placing the responsibility elsewhere and offering an easy solution. It is important to be clear about the relationship between biology and behaviour, if only to rid ourselves of impossible dreams in respect of miracle cures. Biology cannot cause behaviour. We use the word 'cause' in many ways and easily deceive ourselves about the reasons why of things.

To make the argument clear, consider the relationship of biology to behaviour in a larger context. For example, a news report may say that famine, resulting from a crop failure, is causing starvation and food riots. In the wealthy countries we see such reports as fitting a well-known pattern: some countries have too many people, climates that grow too little food, and inefficient governments – it is a natural disaster. It is nothing to do with us, but having been moved by television coverage we will contribute what we can. But is the crop failure the cause? We know that the world is over-supplied with food and transport as well as the necessary botanical knowledge. A famine is not a result of natural events but of social ones: food could be redistributed and resources reallocated but we do not choose this uncongenial solution.

Behaviour problems are sometimes thought about in similar ways: a pupil has got into a wild state and gone berserk again; she has too much aggression, too little self-control and ineffective parenting – one of life's losers. It is nothing to do with us, but we will try to make sure she takes her tablets. It is tempting to let nature take the blame, but biological conditions cannot be any more than a background feature: their behavioural outcomes are the result of being channelled by experience. There is a view that we all have an aggressive drive that is essential to our independence (Storr, 1968): repression is therefore disapproved of and the solution is said to lie in encouraging positive aspects of aggression. But this view assumes what it seeks to explain. Aggressiveness does not have to be an innate drive necessary for survival: many people survive, and even command others, without being aggressive. To postulate an aggressive drive and then prove its existence by describing any sort of personal effectiveness as aggression is a circular argument. Aggression in schools is better understood as a strategy that a pupil has learned to use as an effective method of expression or a way of achieving his or her goals. The focus needs to be on individual perspectives, relationships and situational constraints, not the supposed defects in individual pathology. This is not to substitute what Dyke (1987) describes as psychoanalytical determinism for the biological kind. Bastide (1972) notes how a psycho-analytical focus on individuals leads to a sociological interest in relationships: early-life influences are social; for traumas of infancy to affect the present they must be reawakened and maintained in the present.

No one is born with a predisposition to hitting teachers: in a life of parental neglect and societal indifference, one pupil may find that violence is effective, another that teachers are a safe target for the hate they feel for their family and themselves. There is no genetic configuration that causes a particular misbehaviour: misbehaviour is social and exists not as a natural entity but only in a relationship, or potential relationship. Bastide (1972) argues this point even for insanity. In chronic and serious cases the use of drugs may be the only feasible strategy. Tablets are less labour-intensive than straitjackets, and the alternatives – full preventive, social and financial support for families at risk, and ready assistance for those who get into difficulty – are unthinkable. Often enough, it is more comforting for the parent, too: the belief that one's child has a medical problem is less threatening than accepting that our parenting is at fault. Of course, all treatments have a cost. Passed from one expert to the next, defined as a psychiatric or mental health problem, prescribed first this and then that, it is not surprising that some pupils grow dependent and anxious; and every recurrence of their problem behaviour confirms their growing and reasonable belief that they are not as others are and must face a life of troubles, isolation and possibly madness. Their problem is as much a result of our omissions as their flawed inheritance. It matters very much that we avoid the error of assuming that pupils receiving medical attention are beyond the reach of teachers' understanding and skills.

Our beliefs about the nature of a condition have real consequences. Bastide (1972) describes how a religious sect, the Hutterites, interpret bouts of depression as a visitation by the devil. They stay with the afflicted person and give social support until, as they see it, the demon gives up and leaves. Of course, unbelievers will point out that the companionship of others has lifted the spirits, not driven off a spectre. But that is not a point worth worrying about. Whatever their reasons, the Hutterites have settled on an altogether better treatment for depression than anything available on prescription. Most important of all, their strategy reintegrates the sufferer into the community; much medical or quasi-medical treatment abandons the victim to treatment in isolation. Schostak (1986) likens some drugs to riots: one acts inwardly to destroy the self, the other outwardly to destroy reality. In the matter of troublesome behaviour, medical interventions are like charity concerts and fun-runs for starving countries: a temporary relief and a welcome distraction from fundamental moral deficiencies in the way we exercise our social responsibilities. As we shall see in the next chapter, some schools, like the Hutterites, view troublesome behaviour, and their responsibilities towards it, in ways that keep their pupils in their community.

Books and courses aimed at helping teachers manage disruption in the classroom generally fall into two groups: those that assume teacher skills are at fault and need remedying (for example, Chisholm *et al.*, 1984); and those that assume that disruptive behaviour can be unlearned through a programme of behaviour modification (for example, Cheesman and Watts, 1985). Some blend both (for example, Galvin *et al.*, 1990). Teachers can adopt the skills and strategies in these programmes without necessarily changing attitudes that may themselves be contributing to their problems and the stress they feel. Useful as these approaches may be, they are incomplete without consideration of the meaning of pupil behaviour and the hidden motives and anxieties that it may reflect. At a simple level, there is the testing of teachers' rules and resolution; the displaying and defending of personal identity; the establishment and maintaining of a place in a friendship or peer-group; and the straightforward relief of tedium and tension. Some teachers read these activities as personal attacks or as proof of a supposed rising tide of disorder. They may be disabused and reassured by the evidence in such texts as Beynon (1985), Denscombe (1985), Hammersley and Woods (1984), Schostak (1983) and Woods (1980).

At a deeper level, there are the influences of domestic and personal experiences which can dispose some pupils to unskilled and inappropriate strategies: struggles for attention, power or revenge; using the teacher as a safe target for feelings that belong to another person, place or time; seeking refuge from reminders of traumatic experiences in wild behaviour; camouflaged or inept attempts at friendship and destructive testing of any relationships that may be formed. Many teachers find themselves driven to pessimistic fatalism with severely disturbing pupils. Confrontations seem unavoidable and security may be sought in unbending and autocratic domination: pupils may be required to march in step or not to march at all. The result may be a synchronized but stressed and brittle atmosphere. Understanding may be gained through such texts as Balson (1982), Cronk (1987), Dreikurs (1957), Hanko (1985) and Stott (1982). Such knowledge permits a more dispassionate and analytical stance and can be used to produce an agenda for staff discussions focused on pupils or groups whose behaviour is causing problems. A possible list of tasks for such meetings might include: to retrieve and identify pupils' motives and strategies; to discover the sources of their need for attention or feelings of hostility; to uncover any teacher behaviour, classroom factors or school influences which may be unintentionally maintaining unwanted behaviour; to devise and agree a consistent, whole-school approach to particular problems.

This book is intended to provide a basis for teachers to begin their own casework discussions in their own schools. It is from a teacher and is addressed to teachers: the people who know and can help troublesome pupils. It is not intended to be a contribution from a 'tip and run' expert (Hanko, 1985). It is my hope that those who read it and begin to work in the ways described will integrate it into their practical experience: they should become unable to separate what they know from experience and what they read in the book. Sharing ideas, experiences and worries helps teachers become inured to and insulated from disruption; they may be less easily provoked and less likely to fall back on coercion and punishment. In a perfect example of the disarming approach, Kohl (1970) remarks: 'I like defiant, independent and humorous people and my preferences naturally come out in my teaching'. To be encouraged and enabled to use more detached and disarming strategies is to be able, should we so wish, to remain composed, dispassionate, impassive. And where such strategies predominate in a school the climate, ethos or atmosphere may be described as harmonious: many parts are played and varied tunes are possible. Pupils of every demeanour and disposition may feel valued in the care of serene and shatterproof professionals.

The deficiencies of explanations which rely on single causes are recognized in the more accessible guides that are now available – see Denscombe (1985), Docking (1980), Fontana (1985), Furlong (1985), Laslett and Smith (1984). Explanations for troublesome behaviour can be approached from two directions. On the one hand, we can begin with the pupil and his or her individual characteristics, personal perspectives and family circumstances; on the other, we can look at the social and cultural milieu in which schools and classrooms are maintained and teachers go about their work.

Whichever end we begin at, the quest for understanding leads us to glance towards, if not to travel to, the other. There is a similar range in the remedies offered for disruption in schools, but the fit is imperfect. Those focused on the pupil employ behavioural psychology, with its emphasis on straightforward rewards and punishments, or cognitive approaches which take account of the pupils' perspectives and motives. Those beginning at the societal end of the spectrum might emphasize the unequal distribution of chances in life, the social selection and allocation functions of schools, the shortages and competitiveness in the classrooms, and the resulting dilemmas and frustrations for teachers – many of whom see themselves as demoralized losers in a critical and unrewarding environment. Teachers stand on the boundary where pupils' problems and society's contradictions meet: to them falls the task of motivating those who have the skills that will be rewarded and mollifying those who do not. Some of the bad teachers blamed for indiscipline in schools are those who find this task beyond them. For some observers, confident that our social policies are fundamentally right, the weakness of such teachers renders them unfit for the profession.

In arguing for a broad and inclusive approach to problems in schools we are up against some terminology from which dangle simplistic theories and explanations. For example, the term 'disruptive' implies that the problem is caused by only one person. Sometimes the term is used in such a way as to suggest that it identifies a particular type of disorder – as distinct from maladjusted, delinquent or naughty. There is little to be gained in pondering these refinements. In general, I have used the phrase 'troublesome behaviour' and I do so, not to identify a specific syndrome, but in the hope that its neutrality carries no implications about aetiology or treatment. Worse still is the emphasis in many texts, and in the titles of some of them, on classroom control. Fontana (1985) suggests using the phrase in the sense of controlling an aircraft rather than a string of donkeys or a cage of lions. Another way of looking at it is to see virtue in increasing a teacher's power in the classroom: power is here understood as energy, a force from which pupils as well as teachers benefit. Davies (1984) claims that pupil deviance results when they are in danger of losing struggles in the classroom; giving the teacher more control may involve giving the pupil more power: absolute power and absolute power-lessness corrupt absolutely. Control of oneself and a feeling of empower-ment are important in social relationships: defensiveness distorts perception, isolates individuals and destroys relationships.

## TROUBLESOME GIRLS?

Just as this book applies to minor as well as serious forms of troublesome behaviour, it is also about both boys and girls. Girls are heavily under-represented in exclusion statistics and are commonly considered to create fewer problems in schools than boys do. If true, it may be a consequence not of innate temperamental docility but of strategic adaptation to the world as they see it. Aggression does not pay off for girls in the way some boys find it does for them. Other people's social and cultural expectations make other strategies more effective for achieving their goals. Although it is usual to deny that boys and girls are treated differ-ently, schools do seem to use sex as a basis for classification. King's (1978) infant teachers, asked why boys and girls should line up separately, were baffled by the question; Delamont and Galton (1986) recorded secondary pupils being classified by sex up to twenty times per day. During obser-vations in a nursery, I witnessed one of those points at which the teacher's unconscious teaching finally got through to the pupils:

Teacher (checking register): 'We'll call the girls first this morning.' (As each name is called the child stands.) 'Now let's choose a boy to count the girls. Sutpahl, you this morning.' (As he counts, each girl sits down again.) 'Now we'll call the boys' names. That's unusual, the boys are all together in a row this morning.'

In this way the biological category of sex is transformed into the social category of gender. This achieved, it is quite likely that goals and strategies will come to differ. Perhaps girls see education as a road to freedom or as an irrelevance in which failure is unimportant (Fuller and McRobbie, quoted in Furlong, 1985). Put simply, maybe our society teaches boys and girls that different strategies pay off, and then rewards them differentially. This would account for the common claim that when a girl is troublesome or aggressive she is more vicious and tenacious than a boy would be. As boys learn that aggression in males is rewarded, they may also learn ways of avoiding it and limiting its damage. For most girls, violence is taboo, and in not learning to use it at all they do not learn to use it with discretion. Perhaps those few who do strike out for independence, strike out more vigorously and strike out for longer. Other explanations centre on the different group sizes in which boys and girls find friends (Davies and Meyenn, in Woods, 1980a). The games boys are encouraged to play require large numbers, while girls are expected to engage in less energetic activities and are often found in groups of two or three. A boy who falls out with a friend will lose only a small percentage of his social circle; a girl may lose it all. In these circumstances, intense feelings are to be expected, and it is not surprising that some girls' friendship crises seem endless – to the despair and bewilderment of teachers and parents.

Davies (1984) argues powerfully for another view. She challenges the belief that girls are less deviant in schools and suggests that their deviance is as great but takes different forms. Both sexes seek to exercise power but they do so in different ways. Perhaps boys, like convicted persons, are not the only offenders but the only ones who are caught: the 'failed offenders' (Phillipson, 1976). Davies found girls to be conformist 'only in certain areas – the institutional rules of the school in terms of attendance, misbehaviour and damage, and the technical goals of achievement in terms of conscientiousness and presentation of work' (Davies, 1984: 14). That is a formidable list of areas in which to be conformist. Girls were said to be as bad as boys with respect to smoking and lack of uniform. In my survey of fifty teachers, reported in Chapter 2, covert smoking and inappropriate clothing were bottom of the list of teachers' concerns, which possibly accounts for girls not being regarded as serious problems. Davies says that girls were more deviant with respect to asserting 'more independence in the creation of personal time and space around the school'. Where bored boys might flick paper, girls would avoid work by pretending to write. Davies' evidence seems to confirm not her own argument but the popular view: girls cause less trouble in schools. Her list and examples clearly show this.

Deviating in ways that cause minimal annoyance and disruption to the routine is what is meant by conformist action. This does not imply intellectual conformism, but this is not seriously suggested, nor is it possible to imagine what possible evidence could be proof. If girls do choose to deviate in non-provocative ways, this may be a result of their different perceptions of others' actions and intentions. Girls may be the equivalent of deviance-insulative teachers, and boys closer to deviance-provocative (see Chapter 2). Davies' interesting Script theory seems to explain it all. Many scripts, or generally expected routines of behaviour, are for only male or female characters. Boys and girls can adapt or ad lib and they can act each other's scripts; but when they do, like drag artists and principal boys, they can get it horribly wrong. Further, if girls' scripts include the drama 'being more understanding than boys', then it may be that teachers offer them more honest explanations than they think worth the trouble with boys. Cronk (1987) argues convincingly that a lack of such explanations results in misunderstanding and misbehaviour. When pupils are persuaded that teachers are doing their best, they co-operate. Taken together, these two writers seem to have sorted out the mystery of the missing girls.

## OVER-EXCLUDED ETHNIC MINORITIES

Black pupils are over-represented in exclusion statistics. According to the director of the Institute of Race Relations (Bourne *et al.*, 1994), 'the number of black children excluded each month from schools in England and Wales is wildly out of proportion to their numbers on the rolls'. Figures from the DfE show that, nationally, 8 per cent of permanently excluded pupils are black, although black pupils make up only 2 per cent of the population. Since 3,000 pupils were permanently excluded in 1993, the DfE figures mean that 240 black pupils were permanently excluded; if black pupils had been excluded in proportion to their numbers in the population, then only 60 would have been excluded. This means that 180 black pupils were excluded unjustifiably – no more than one or two pupils per LEA. Shameful though this is, it can hardly be described as a figure 'wildly out of proportion'. The number of pupils temporarily excluded is, of course, much larger, but it is misleading to regard temporary and permanent exclusions as similar types of action. In some cases, temporary exclusion is an extension of a school's social work rather than a banishment: pupils are escorted home to cool off a potentially dangerous situation, parents are met, and conditions agreed for a return.

Searle (in Bourne *et al.*, 1994) says that 'there is a well-established tradition of black community resistance to the inequitable use of exclusion'. The DfE figures show that in 205 cases the headteacher's decision to exclude permanently was overturned by the governors or the LEA. In only 92 cases did parents appeal, and of these appeals only 14 were successful. This seems to suggest that over 90 per cent of permanent exclusions are supported by governors and parents – including the parents of black pupils.

It is important that the magnitude of the problem is not overstated. Searle goes so far as to suggest that there exist 'unprofessional and vicious practices among some teachers' which lead to pupils being provoked into violence; he makes alarming and wholly unbelievable comparisons with Brazilian horrors. Bourne (1994) describes twenty cases where black pupils were unfairly excluded (though not all permanently). In four or five of these, however, there seems to be a case for questioning her claim of clear unfairness: for example, one boy 'refused to work and when confronted by teachers became abusive'. Although it is helpful to expose examples of bizarre behaviour by individual teachers, however rare, such actions are not typical and generalizations should not be drawn from them. (The national annual total of all permanent exclusions amounts to fewer than one per secondary school.) With a school population of 8 million pupils and 400,000 teachers, some examples of disgraceful practice are inevitable. Certainly, it is no comfort for the victim and his or her family to know that their case accounts for a minute percentage of 1 per cent of the figures – if you are a victim, you are 100 per cent a victim – but to have unusual cases represented as the norm will not help identify solutions. There is not a single shred of evidence that schools discriminate against black pupils as a matter of routine. Many teachers feel helpless when confronted with the figures; as far as they are concerned, only pupils who have gone beyond the limits of acceptable behaviour are excluded – ethnicity does not come into it.

How can the problem be explained? In some situations, the strategies some teachers adopt are clues. Here is a black, special needs teacher talking:

> In my school we had a case where four boys set on another boy and hurt him so badly he had to have treatment in hospital. They got a one-week suspension. I *know* that if those boys had been black it would have been a much bigger thing – they would have been out (permanently).

Asked why she was so sure that black pupils would have been treated more severely, she replied:

> It would have been taken as a more dangerous thing – like, this is what these sort of kids do. For some teachers, it would have been frightening. Some teachers don't like even to talk to black kids. I can give you an

example. In our school we have trouble with gum – there is a rule, no chewing. I've had a teacher say to me, 'Will you ask x to get rid of his gum?' We'll be on break duty and all around are kids chewing gum, but a white teacher asks me to tell a black kid to stop chewing! Why don't they do it themselves? Why don't they ask me to tell the white kids? They're worse!

To be unable to talk freely and openly with another person is dangerous: it leaves that person in a category, and as a representative of it – a black child, a working-class child; we do not get to know and understand that person as an individual; what we do not understand we may suspect or fear. What is happening is hidden from those involved and unintended by them. It is easy to see how unfairness can result when well-meaning people respond to incidents in what seems to them a reasonable way, unaware that their own discomfort and ignorance are affecting the interaction. At best, such teachers will approach black pupils with feelings of ambivalence: on the one hand, they will be aware of the dangers of racism and anxious to show themselves free of prejudice; on the other, they will hold half-suppressed fears rooted in folklore and anecdote. Because the child is black, the teacher wants to show special concern, disassociate him or herself from racist views and be respected; because the child is black, the teacher is uncertain how to put these intentions into words and confused in interpreting the child's responses. This is a fertile ground for misunderstanding and the maintenance of fear and distrust on both sides.

From the black child's point of view, there may be deeper rooted problems caused by the way messages in society make their way into children's consciousness. Wilson (1987) assembles a compelling array of evidence in support of the view that black parents' knowledge of history and their own experience leave some of them in a state of ambivalence towards their children:

> The child may be loved on one level and hated on another. The child may be loved because it was desired for personal and social fulfilment, because it represents the hopes of its parents, and hated at the same time because it bears the mark of oppression – its blackness, since blackness is hated by whites.
>
> (Wilson, 1987: 53)

Wilson argues that this ambivalence can be compounded by guilt 'stemming from the parents' awareness of the degradation' to which the child may be exposed in the future, and their own responsibility for wittingly bringing the child into the world. This guilt can lead to uncertainty and inconsistency in upbringing: over-protectiveness, over-strictness, indulgence, indifference. The child, in an effort to adapt to his or her parents' behaviour, becomes confused and contradictory.

Perhaps this experience explains why some pupils are excluded for what seem to have been, on the surface, trivial reasons. An excluded black pupil, giving an example of the behaviour that had brought him to the exclusion unit, said: 'In lessons, when you have to clean up – after other people – I wasn't going to do that.' For the pupil, cleaning up signifies subservience – a role to which the pupil is particularly sensitive. For the teacher, the refusal is interpreted as straightforward defiance of authority. Both confront one another with more at stake than whether or not some desks are cleared. The teacher's request is taken as an attempt to force demeaning work upon a pupil who is already alert to the merest nuances of implied degradation. The pupil's refusal is taken as a danger-ous sign of rebellion, awakening fears that are related to stereotypes which the teacher has properly but perhaps incompletely suppressed. The fragile state of mind of such a black child would mirror that of any teacher with the sort of schizoid disposition that made them ask a third party to communicate for them. If my calculations and Wilson's argument are correct, there are enough encounters of this type to create 180 unnecessary permanent exclusions of black pupils in England and Wales each year. The complexity of the forces at work shows that those who look for evidence of overt discrimination in the day-to-day practices of schools are looking in the wrong place. Schools are where the symptoms of a wider and deeper set of historical problems appear. In many cases, the protagonists are no more to blame for the distressing outcomes than passengers on a train are to blame for a collision. Only by helping both parties to grasp the full context and take personal control can injustice be avoided.

## OUTLINE OF THE BOOK

The next chapter describes some of the research and other work with troublesome pupils that helped develop the methods argued for in this book. Where reference is made to real schools, teachers or pupils, their names, situations and peripheral details are altered. The material for this chapter was gathered over a period of several years: some of the schools have closed, some teachers retired, and many of the pupils are now adults.

Chapter 3 is a detailed account of teaching skills and qualities that are associated with freedom from troublesome behaviour in classrooms. The chapter describes ways in which this knowledge can be used to help teachers in difficulty and to improve the understanding of experienced teachers who are content with their classroom effectiveness. A major problem confronting those who see the solution to indiscipline in improv-ing teacher skills is the disagreement about what counts as a good teacher. Wragg quotes a review by Barr:

Some teachers were preferred by administrators, some were liked by pupils, some taught in classes where there were substantial pupil gains, and generally speaking these were not the same teachers.

(Wragg, 1987: 5)

In a profession where more than two-thirds now have more than twenty years' experience, it takes a reckless bravery to insist on colleagues following one's own prescriptions. Good teaching is difficult to quantify, because values intrude in a way they do not in more technical professions. And yet there is, as we shall see in Chapter 3, an abundance of research on good teaching. Much of it presupposes that it can be identified first and its characteristics listed later: we know it when we see it. Disagreements about teaching skills are similar to moral disagreements, in that arguments about low-level rules in specific contexts are confused with disputes about general principles upon which we all agree. For example, there can never be consensus on whether or not it is always wrong to tell lies. Faced with an armed desperado asking after the whereabouts of one's friend, most of us would apply a precept of higher generality and tell a lie. One of the exercises following Chapter 3 is an opportunity to think about general skill categories in teaching: discovering them is a task uniquely suited to the teaching profession. Success in this as yet unaccomplished work would form the foundation of a code of professional expertise. Empowering teachers in this way, far from weakening others, would enhance the knowledge, understanding and personal effectiveness of us all.

Chapter 4 considers the classroom scene from the pupils' point of view. The argument here is that pupils' attitudes, motives and strategies are invariably (some would say always) rational and reasonable with respect to their experiences and circumstances. Even apparently senseless activities, such as openly being drunk in school, have been represented as rational responses to an educational experience perceived as economically worthless (Willis, 1977). In a contrasting book, Robertson (1981) emphasizes the role of teachers' authority in combat with pupil motives, which he says are to seek excitement, attention, work-avoidance and peer-group status through brinkmanship. Different pupils will, of course, have different motives and this chapter considers all the possibilities. A dispassionate and developmental view is encouraged. Understanding the sources and motives of pupil hostility insulates the teacher from personal hurt and helps in the achievement of order and co-operation.

I depend heavily here on the writings of Balson (1982) and Dreikurs (1957). Their emphasis is on addressing not the surface behaviour of troublesome pupils but their underlying motives. This kind of reflectiveness is often scorned in favour of the behavioural approach (the manipulation of rewards and punishments) or even the common-sense tactic of 'shut up and do as you're told'. There is a feeling that reflection is misplaced on a battle ground: teachers would rather get their hands on something simple, effective and quick. I am convinced, and I hope readers will be too, that a reflective and analytical disposition does not preclude action nor necessitate relinquishing control. It puts depth and precision where there is often shallowness.

Interestingly, an American study of teaching styles and student behaviour concluded that there was some empirical support for approaches to discipline modelled on the work of Dreikurs. Discipline techniques were categorized as authoritarian, behaviour modification, common sense, instructional, permissive, intimidation, group process and socio-emotional climate. The latter pair were found to be 'positively related to on-task behaviour' (Wittrock, 1986: 422). Such studies cannot fully allow for differences in classes' original orderliness, however. The strategies recommended in Chapter 4 help teachers come to terms with the inevitable difficulties faced in classrooms. In this respect, they are effective irrespective of their effects upon pupils, and although empirical support is welcome it is not essential. I regard this chapter as the core of the book. Whereas the book as a whole concentrates on prevention, Chapter 5 focuses on responses in threatening situations of stress and confrontation. The advice derives from earlier chapters, so to some extent coping with confrontations and stress offers a relatively clear empirical test of the book's philosophy.

Chapter 6 describes two contexts, knowledge of which helps in the understanding of pupil behaviour. These are the classroom itself, which has its own particular dynamics and constraints, and the school – its climate, ethos and organizational arrangements. This chapter concludes with a case study which raises issues discussed throughout the book. The effect of schools' methods of allocating pupils to groups was first shown by Hargreaves (1967). The stigmatizing label indicating a low-ability stream is more powerful than anything actually spoken by a teacher, and many studies have confirmed this. Less rigid streaming seems to lead to less polarization of attitudes. However, Willis' (1977) work suggests that some pupils, whose opposition is more deeply and historically rooted, are able to see through organizational camouflage and educational myth. Others suggest that pupils can be kept in ignorance of their academic status until the time of year 11 examinations.

Chapter 7 discusses how teachers responded to the in-service work upon which this book is based, and explains how teachers and schools can teach themselves. It concludes with a number of activities that bring together the themes of the earlier chapters.

For explanations to be complete, and remedial strategies to have any hope of success, they must not depend on a single cause and a single remedy. This is often the first step towards abandoning responsibility. If a pupil is believed to be brain-damaged, hyperactive, or from a hopelessly ineffectual or irredeemably criminal family, then the school may see little point in trying to help, or may offer minimal help in a destructive atmosphere of pessimism. Pupils and classes vary in their behaviour: from 'a pack of hungry, half-starved wolves with the math and English teachers' to 'docile lambs with their science teacher' (Wittrock, 1986: 409). It follows that any explanation that rests entirely on them cannot be complete (Hargreaves, 1975). Similarly, it is futile to settle on explanations that blame capitalism, unemployment, television, the school or bad teachers. Pupils are not inanimate objects, malleable and ductible, responding in predictable ways to external stimuli: if they were, simple and effective treatments would have been found long ago. Pupils and teachers interpret the world of experience, both internal and external – a world of experience, not a narrow, solitary patch – and it is upon these understandings that they act.

Troublesome pupils cannot be understood without considering them in several spheres: individual, family, classroom, school, community and whole society. All these spheres have the individual pupil at the centre. In one sense we are all sociologists: thinking about ourselves and our position in the world is to be forced to consider relationships. What C. Wright Mills called the 'sociological imagination', exploring the relationships between public issues and private troubles, is essential in the understanding and management of troublesome pupils. To view problems from only one perspective is not so much incomplete as distorting (Andy Hargreaves, in Woods, 1980b).

Enlightenment is a valuable aid to seeing problems not as opaque and oppressive but as interesting puzzles to be solved – even if we conclude that on some levels no direct action is possible. Shedding light on the network of causes and social relationships makes them visible, accessible and less frightening than when they remain unseen forces in the darkness. Accepting and understanding our constraints is a form of gaining control of ourselves, a form of autonomy. In one sense, we are never powerless and no social or educational problem is hopeless. All teachers are part of the education system, and therefore no teacher should ever feel that decline is out of control and that nothing is being done about it. Pessimism is out of place. A teacher who is concerned about education is that part of the system that is thinking and is saving itself through him or her.

## ACTIVITY 1.1: A HISTORICAL EXCURSION AMONG NEWSPAPER CLIPPINGS FROM THE PAST

Consider for a moment what the nature of this eighteenth-century entertainment might be: Esther Showell versus Maggie the Nag, at Litchfield, on June 19th 1781. A race perhaps? A debate? Something associated with what we may imagine to be the womanly arts of that time, like baking or needlework? Both women had prepared themselves well, having consumed quantities of meat, bread, eggs and milk; they had run many miles and drunk pints of ale. Of Esther, aged 18, 'the fullness of her person about buttock and bosom' was remarked upon. Of Maggie, aged 30, it was reported that her 'buxomness was much greater and her muscles the more powerful'. Over 600 people gathered to watch the event. It was a fight, women's boxing being a popular activity at this time. The contest was eventually halted by a sheriff, but after both boxers had been stitched by surgeons the battle continued, until youth triumphed and Maggie was laid low by a savage blow to the throat. The victor had to be protected from those in the crowd who had bet against her and whose judicious attempts to kick her during the contest had failed to give Maggie the edge. There is no record of how these women's children behaved and we can only speculate about their attitude to compulsory schooling, had it been available.

Other pastimes of that century were as brutal. Jockeys included among their skills using the whip to knock out the teeth and eyes of rival horses and here, too, losers in the race often had to flee from losers in the crowd. Race meetings continued to be a cause of concern well into the present century. In the 1920s race-goers were considered easy targets for robbers, who were said to travel in organized gangs 'in luxurious motor-cars'. One report in 1924 said that there had never been 'so many rogues and rascals making a living by preying on other people as at the present moment'.

Slipping back a hundred years or so, those without money for racing could amuse themselves by bullock-chasing: 'An ox was furiously driven through Holborn to the great terror of the inhabitants. Above 50 Smithfield boys were in the chase' (1794). Or they might spend their time as 'idle and disorderly persons breaking off the arms of guide posts' (1814). As late as 1863, a women's journal, in an article advising on the organization of a picnic, warned of 'loungers and lookers-on of a doubtful class'. Picnickers were advised to secure the attendance of a police officer – if necessary by offering a tip.

The more enterprising loungers attacked mail-coaches. From 1784 such vehicles carried guards armed with two pistols and a blunderbuss. The Post Office's red livery was originally intended to simulate a military uniform. It later proved to be a means by which the public could tell whether or not properly authorized persons were opening pillar boxes; and letter carriers who neglected their work to loiter in ale-houses were readily identifiable. For their part, letter carriers complained that their distinctive uniforms made them easy targets for robbers, who would know that they would be carrying money, as letters were paid for on delivery. Theft from the mail was not prevented by all these measures. By a nice irony, John Howard, the prison reformer, had his baggage stolen from a mail coach when he returned to London from a tour of Asia in 1787.

Football violence, often taken as a barometer of social disorder, was at least as common in the past as it is today. Eighteenth-century football was described as 'a friendlie kind of fight' in which, with no enclosed pitch, the ball would be kicked about the streets by a rough crowd. The rural tradition of Shrovetide Football, which might involve the population of two rival villages doing battle over an area of a few miles, lasted until the middle of the nineteenth century in some parts of the country. Insurance companies used to include football among the activities for which compensation would not be paid. In the last years of the Victorian era, Arsenal, Sheffield Wednesday, Crewe Alexandra and Lincoln City were among the clubs closed because of crowd disorder. The fighting and destruction in the early years of the present century certainly exceeded any that has happened since. In 1909, for example, a Rangers and Celtic match ended with the goalposts alight, barricades ablaze, and over a hundred people injured. Although cricket fared better, 'Umpire retired hurt' was sometimes recorded – a consequence of rival teams fielding their own umpires; one was thrown into the Thames and there is a record of one being killed.

Enterprises and amusements that might have been expected to have a civilizing effect, diverting aggression towards more sedate pursuits, led to problems of another kind. Householders in the vicinity of Vauxhall Gardens frequently objected to the nuisance created by patrons. In 1794 a petition described how people were kept awake till three in the morning by 'fighting, singing, bell-ringing, window-breaking'. One gentleman spoke of his journey to church on Sunday morning being disrupted by 'women of the town, of the very lowest order, half dressed and more than half drunk, whose language has been too shocking for modest ears and whose behaviour has been degrading in the eyes of humanity'.

Riots have been a regular feature of life in British schools. Many reflected the lack of order and discipline in public schools and universities. The pupils of Eton caused a serious riot in 1729, and fifty years later their grandchildren were reported to have marched on the school after a drunken night out. The brutal but unfortunate Dr Keate, whose desk was smashed in 1818, sometimes had his sermons enlivened by the releasing of rats into the chapel. At Rugby, matters were just as bad. In 1797, the boys responded to punishment for vandalism by blowing up the head's office and burning his books and furniture. At Winchester, the final quarter of the eighteenth century produced a number of disturbances serious enough to require soldiers to be called out to restore order. The prevalence of vice, gambling, driving, hunting and riding at Oxford led to concerted efforts to ensure that students had enough work to do. Idleness was thought to be at the root of the problem: 'We must make study and not amusement the law of the university' wrote one professor in 1852; another, in a masterly statement of the obvious, declared that 'the most effective mode of preventing idleness is to interest the great body of the undergraduates in the studies of the university'.

Hooliganism was not a problem just within the schools and universities. In 1900, *The Times* led on what was seen then, as ever, as a new and growing problem: 'Our hooligans go from bad to worse; they do not starve and they do not work; they hustle and waylay solitary old gentlemen with gold watches; they hunt in packs too large for a single policeman to cope with'. School Boards and prisons were viewed as powerless to ameliorate the problem.

Hardly a decade has passed without some part of the country being in the grip of rioters. In 1780, during the Gordon Riots, one Justice of the Peace who read the Riot Act saw the mob disperse and set off to burn his house. In 1815 a mob composed of 'chiefly boys' was reported to have smashed windows in Baker Street. In 1842, many Chartist meetings were the focus of disorder. In one, a mob estimated at 15,000 gathered in Trafalgar Square; of these, at least a thousand were said to be young thieves 'who divided their time pretty evenly between leap-frog, pocket-picking and open robbery'. One observer remarked that the activities of juvenile predators were the most interesting part of the show – the speeches being dull and slow: 'Boys scarcely ten years old looted shops and openly robbed tradesmen.'

Outside London, Liverpool and Leeds provide more examples of youngsters at play. A hot August weekend in 1890 saw much of Leeds city centre wrecked and in the hands of drunken youths. In 1919, 'rough-looking women, out for loot' directed young boys to smash shop windows in Liverpool: 'The youths, fearless of pieces of glass, jumped in and made a lightening sweep of the articles.' Soldiers with fixed bayonets eventually regained control, leaving the roads 'littered with goods, from watches to costumiers' dummies'. In 1932, nearby Birkenhead saw the unemployed upon a similar enterprise. Pubs were robbed and police attacked by rioters as well as by the occupants of houses overlooking the mayhem: 'Even ambulances were attacked ... and special attention was paid to police vans, which had to run the gauntlet of showers of stones and pieces of metal.'

Respect for the great occasions of state seems to have been less plentiful in the past than now. There were five attempts on the life of Queen Victoria. In 1852, the scramble to get a look at the embalmed body of the Duke of Wellington cost some people their lives, and the police 'used their batons very freely' to restore order. In 1828, someone threw a dead cat into the carriage of the Archbishop of Canterbury as he processed from Lambeth.

Most crime has always been committed by the young. Writers regularly bemoan the 'relaxation in parental discipline'; it is claimed that 'the morals of children are tenfold worse than formerly'; parents are alleged to be 'not ashamed to confess that children of seven or eight years old are entirely beyond their control'; worse still, 'the hooligan knows more about sex perversions at the age of thirteen than most people know at the age of thirty'. These four quotations are from 1829, 1843, 1898 and 1932 respectively – but they are timeless. Small wonder that 90 per cent of nineteenth-century executions were of offenders under the age of 21 years. The feeling that things are always getting worse is as common as the view that young people have never been more wicked. In 1751, Henry Fielding, the novelist who treated rough-and-tumble bawdiness with such sympathy in *Tom Jones*, published his 'Enquiry into the Late Increase of Robbery'. He found idleness, easy luxury, tender-hearted prosecutors and bullyable juries to blame. There was in any case great difficulty in gathering evidence against robbers: 'The attack is usually begun by knocking the party down and depriving him of his senses . . . the innocent are put in terror, without any respect to age or dignity or sex.'

Lack of respect for the elderly is not new either, it seems. In 1274, Peter the Hermit wrote that 'young people today think of nothing but themselves. They have no reverence for parents or old age'. Matters were bad enough in 1710 for a popular schoolbook of the time to contain this verse: 'Adulterie good men defie; O 'tis a cursed evil: And such as to whore-houses go, Must perish with the Devil.'

Those who sought to extend education to the poorest children were not always thanked for their efforts. In 1864, the police were called to a West End school where they found the place in uproar: 'Gas fittings had been wrenched off and used as batons by the boys for striking the police, while the rest of the boys were pelting them with slates.' An inspector writing in 1866 recorded the difficulties experienced in some neighbourhoods: 'In one school visited there were 137 panes broken in the boys' school and 37 in the girls' at the time of my visit.'

As late as the 1940s and 1950s – a period widely believed to be a time of domestic peace – we find examples of youngsters' violence. A report from 1943 describes the practice, adopted by young soldiers on leave, of robbing waitresses carrying drinks: in one such case the woman was pushed over a hedge. In 1950, a date that epitomizes good order, Lord Justice Goddard complained that he could no longer order the flogging of young criminals. The cases before him included one where two youths, aged 15 and 17, had coshed, robbed and almost killed a woman on a train, and one where a young man had robbed with violence a woman of 60. Goddard's sentiments echo down the ages, though there were those who thought the punishments too harsh. In the 1860s, one writer drew attention to the fact that a boy of eight had received twenty-four lashes for stealing a piece of cutlery, and that boys of eleven or twelve could receive seventy-two lashes 'for repeated misconduct' – thus indicating, presumably, the ineffectiveness of this punishment with some offenders.

Outside the close supervision of the law, we can only guess at the scale of past ill-treatment of children that formed the context in which they grew up and developed. Certainly, supposedly modern ills like sexual abuse have been around for a long time. In 1922, Parliament raised the age of consent for females from 13 years to 16 as a result of a widespread belief that incest was prevalent. An attempt to make the age 17 was defeated in the following year. We now know from the diaries of such as the sculptor Eric Gill that children from comfortable families were not necessarily safe. Those women who told Freud of their experiences were not, as he was persuaded to conclude, making it all up. The overcrowded poor left few literary reminiscences. We have to rely on Dickens, Mayhew, Smollett and Fielding to imagine what life was like for them; and we need to remember that the National Society for the Prevention of Cruelty to Children was formed in response to a need identified more than a century ago.

**Points to consider**

1 History repeats itself and we do not seem to learn from it. What can be learned from this trip through the history of juvenile trouble?
2 How does a historical perspective help or hinder teachers' work? If it encourages teachers to be dispassionate, how is this different from being tolerant and complacent?
3 What practical implications are there for teachers? Does an understanding of historical precedents necessarily affect practice in helpful ways? Is it as likely to lead to fatalism and hopelessness as to resilience?

Those interested in more of this sort of evidence should read Pearson (1983) and Rose (1991) and refer to Gathorne-Hardy (1977), Curtis (1963) and Sturt (1967) – or look through the back files of any local or national newspaper.

**ACTIVITY 1.2: A PARENT'S VIEW**

This passage is a summary of the experiences of a parent of a boy of twelve with behavioural problems. In reading it, it might be helpful to have in mind the distinction between disability and handicap. Disability is a given, but the extent to which it becomes a handicap depends on social and environmental factors, hence the slogan 'disability is physical, handicap is social'. Issues for discussion would include the role of all members of a school community (including pupils) in minimizing the needs of pupils with behavioural difficulties, and the responsibilities of teachers for this, as well as for the wider social and cultural ethos of the school.

My boy was always trouble, but I knew he wasn't bad. When they came and said he should go to a special school for behaviour, I didn't want that. I've seen the kids there and I didn't want him mixing with bad kids. He's not brainy but he's not dumb and he's not bad – but he can be trouble, tumbling around like a bag of puppies, but he's only a little boy. He's no bigger than his sister and she's only eight!

I went up to the school and promised them I'd back them, and I made my boy promise too, and so for a while – a year and nearly a term – he stayed in the normal school. In the first term he was suspended two, no three, times. I had to take him back up and I made him apologise for his behaviour to the teachers. The reasons were always the same – refusing the authority of the teachers. If I asked what he did, what exactly he did, it never seemed to me to be too bad. It was not taking out his book, or answering back, or going to the toilet without permission. But I never said anything about that. It was their school and they had the right to set rules.

One thing I did not like was they would not let me near the classroom. I wanted to see what sort of things they did in there but no, the head kept me in his room and I wasn't asked to look round or anything. I know some other parents have been shown round, but not me. Maybe they thought I'd make trouble too! I kept on trying to make it work out. I tried not to let it get me down. I wanted him to make good and I didn't want him in bad company. I was determined to keep him in a school with decent children.

What decided me to take him away and let him go to the special school was one day when I saw him in the yard. He was just back in that morning from another suspension. I was kept waiting to see the head, and in the end all I saw was the deputy. As I'm leaving, the children came out into the yard for break, and I saw my boy and he didn't see me, so I thought to myself, I'll just watch him – see how he behaves in the yard, see what sort of friends he's taken up with.

He tried to join in the football, but they kept him out. I watched him trying to join in, and him laughing when they kept the ball away from him – but he wasn't really laughing. He was trying to force the smile to stay on his face. I knew that smile and I knew he was hurt. He gave up after a bit and walked round on his own and then he saw me and I could tell from his face that he knew what I was thinking. I had never seen it from his point of view until then. He had never told me. The teachers never said anything. I didn't know. If he was acting up in class – no wonder!

I went to visit the special school. They were very nice to me and very open with me. I told them I was worried about him following bad characters. They didn't try to cover up and they agreed it was a problem and they told me all the things they do to make the children toe the line. So I agreed to him going and that was it. I must be truthful and say I am not happy about it. One of the boys there is covered in gold and they let him. Where does a boy like that get gold? But my boy, he's working and he isn't suspended any more, and he comes home happy. I just have to hope that he doesn't take up with some of the bad ones. I did the best I could to keep him in the normal school. I have asked myself a lot of questions, like what if he'd been a white boy and have I done right by him? In the end you just have to do what you think is best for your child.

## ACTIVITY 1.3: DEFINING MISBEHAVIOUR

Review the definition of special needs given in this chapter and, in the light of the definitions offered by various authors for misbehaviour, produce your own definition of misbehaviour. Your attempt, and those of colleagues if you are working in a group, should address the contributions of other people and the setting, as well as the part played by the misbehaving pupil. Examine definitions critically to see that they do. For those who have not reflected on the matter, this exercise is easy; those who have followed the themes of this chapter may not be able to complete the exercise to their satisfaction.

## ACTIVITY 1.4: SHORT STORY

Suggested points to consider after reading this story are listed at the end.

### Spiritual needs

'For a blind man, he was doing pretty well,' said Michael. His companion made no reply as they continued along the softly carpeted corridor.

'I mean, apart from changing lanes every couple of minutes,' continued Michael, 'it was not too bad an effort. He didn't hit anything and he stopped at the lights.' He waited, as if expecting a reply. None came. 'He was safe, wasn't he?'

'He had a lot of help from the dog,' said Gabriel. They had reached the meeting room.

'But he had the dog trained – don't you see? That was *his* effort: it barked once for a green light and twice for a red.'

Gabriel looked at him sceptically. 'I thought dogs were colour blind,' he said, pushing open the door with some difficulty. 'Beats me why we need automatic closers up here,' he added, almost to himself. And then, with a sly smile, 'It isn't as though there was any fire risk.'

'If dogs are colour blind, it's even more supportive of my case for having his efforts recognised: credit where it's due.'

They entered the room and took their seats as the Chair shuffled papers and peered at a pile of computer printouts. The Chair addressed the meeting:

'I think we are all present, so we'll make a start. May I remind everyone that this meeting is solely concerned with a review of persons who have special needs: that is, such needs as are significantly greater than those of the majority of people, and for whom we have previously determined that special provision should be made.'

At these familiar phrases, Michael and Gabriel looked towards the Chair and found the next remarks addressed, pointedly it seemed, at them.

'We are not concerned with anyone else, and especially not with those whose needs are minimal.' Satisfied that everyone's attention was engaged, the Chair continued: 'The first case today is a Chief Education Officer.' He ignored the murmurs of mild protest that went around the table. 'It was a severe problem from the start, but is now a great deal worse. I regret to say we are now dealing with the ultimate . . .' He searched for a word and was interrupted by Gabriel.

'Not killing?'

'No, not the level of difficulty we had with the doctor.'

Michael whispered to Gabriel: 'What doctor? I wasn't at the last review meeting.'

'Abortion. He'd been terminating those we held the highest hopes for – those we very sparsely equipped with intellectual abilities.'

Michael bowed his head and for some moments was not able to speak. The Chair was distributing papers around the table.

'Did they have to go back?' said Michael.

Gabriel nodded. 'I'm afraid so. Their spiritual standard was high – which was why we had given them such limited abilities: they were in need of very few in order to perfect their souls.'

'But their souls were not perfect?'

'No. Only a short life would have been needed, but they were denied it.'

'Gabriel,' said the Chair impatiently. 'I have already reminded the meeting that we are reviewing only those with special needs: you are again discussing those who were manifestly close to spiritual completeness and perfection; and when you came into the room you were talking of the blind.'

'Michael and I were talking of the blind because we were uncertain whether attempting to drive a motor vehicle constituted a step forward in the perfection of the soul, or a step back.'

'A step back, I should think,' said the Chair, 'but, as I have said, this is not the time for discussing those who are blessed; let us return to the Chief Education Officer.'

'I hope we are not proposing to divert further resources to him,' said Gabriel sharply. 'He has been lavishly supplied already: sufficient ability to get into Oxford – if that's not enough to allow him to perfect his soul, I don't know what is.'

'Gabriel, may I remind you,' said the Chair, patiently, 'that we are concerned with meeting his individual needs and not with the husbanding of our resources.'

'It looks like a case for separate provision to me,' said Michael, putting his papers down. 'We have tried integration with the support of substantial intellectual ability; he has engaged in the activities of the world together with those who do not share his spiritual difficulties, and now he is depriving others.' He flicked through the papers in front of him. 'There's every offence possible here: delays on assessments, refusing to let statements quantify the provision to be made, pressure on educational psychologists. That can hardly be described as efficient from our point of view, nor from that of those he has deprived of the opportunity to develop spiritual perfection.' He sat back in his chair with arms folded. 'Managers are all the same,' he added, bitterly.

The Chair spoke quietly. 'Michael, you are right to raise the question of the efficient provision for those with whom he associates, but you are wrong to say that managers are all the same. You know perfectly well that we are concerned with *needs* not *categories*: we created individuals not classes.'

The Chair folded over the computer printout and read extracts from it. 'He was identified as having selfishness, arrogance, greed and cruelty. We supplied high abilities in the arts and sciences together with team sports. He had some initial success – respect for teachers and some pupils – worked hard – joined a caring profession – took a special interest in those with learning difficulties.'

'If that's the aetiology,' said Gabriel, 'then I agree with Michael: the prognosis is hopeless. Separate provision.'

The Chair looked around the table. 'We seem to have disposed of this case. Are there any other comments?'

There were none.

'In that case, can I leave this one to you two?' he said, glancing from Michael to Gabriel. 'Alert those below to make the usual arrangements.' They nodded assent.

A few days later, one of the tabloid papers carried a characteristically tasteless headline: 'Blind Driver Blames Dog for Death-Crash.'

**Points to consider**

1 You should relate the story to one of the themes of this chapter and be able to identify the evidence and theory on which the story draws.
2 Consider, at a practical level, what policies and practices would be in keeping with the argument and spirit of the story.
3 Adopting a more reflective stance, consider the ethical and philosophical issues at stake, and clarify your own position in relation to them.
4 If this story has led you to modify your beliefs and attitudes – or encouraged you to hold them with more prudence and caution – consider how you might pass on these benefits to others.

# Chapter 2

# Exclusion from school

> I would there were no age 'twixt ten and three-and-twenty, or that
> youth would sleep out the rest; for there is nothing in the between but
> getting wenches with child, wronging the ancientry, stealing, fighting.
>                    (William Shakespeare, *The Winter's Tale* III. iii. 58)

In this chapter we will consider the phenomenon of exclusion from a
number of perspectives. We will look at the nature of excluded pupils
themselves, the contribution made by the organizational features of
schools, the role of pupil–teacher relationships, and some unexpected
factors that studies of schools reveal.

Many studies over a long period have found correlations between
disruptive or delinquent behaviour and domestic deprivation, family disorder, erratic parental discipline, poor attainment or ability, as well as
being male, teenage and working class. Furlong (1985) and Galloway *et
al.* (1982) contain summaries of this work. Looking specifically at
exclusion, York *et al.* (1972) found excluded pupils to be 'severely disturbed psychologically and have serious educational handicaps'. They also
noted family disruption and parental delinquency and located the cause
of exclusion firmly in the pupils, their domestic circumstances and their
failure 'to meet the demands of school life'. Teachers and headteachers
were explicitly excluded from the equation. York's pupils did not include
any short-term excludees and almost all had already been referred to a
hospital psychiatric department, making them untypical of troublesome
pupils in general. Galloway *et al.* (1985), while agreeing that there is a
'high rate of psychiatric disorder in excluded pupils and their families',
notes the 'strong evidence for the importance of school variables in
determining exclusion rates'. In his Sheffield secondary schools, five out
of the thirty-nine accounted for more than 50 per cent of excluded pupils
over a three-year period. In a similar survey, I found that five out of
forty-nine schools accounted for 30 per cent of excluded pupils in one
year.

Although Galloway's research did not identify any specific school factors responsible for differing exclusion rates, he concluded that policies on exclusion were idiosyncratic to each school. He suggested that the practice of pastoral care, as distinct from its formal organization, was a possible factor: this proved to be the case in my survey. Longworth-Dames (1977) found no significant differences between the personalities of excluded pupils and their peers, as measured by Cattell's High School Personality Questionnaire. However, Stott's Bristol Social Adjustment Guide showed a higher level of hostility and failure to inhibit impulses (in consequence) in excluded pupils. Pupils who had changed schools did not always exhibit the same extreme behaviour in their new setting, which the author puts down to the pupils' modification of their behaviour in a new school. This may be so, but it could also be accounted for by a difference in the perceptions of a new and more resilient teacher filling in the questionnaire.

That the domestic cultural environment may help or hinder school attainment patterns is generally regarded as self-evident. It is a simple explanation, readily illustrated to the satisfaction of many teachers (Chessum, 1980). The theory of social learning proposed by Bernstein (1971) has made its way into teachers' thinking in various forms. Brice-Heath (1986) described the educational consequences of a mismatch between domestic adult–child interaction and that between teachers and pupils in the classroom. An interesting feature of this case-study was the clear evidence that, for first-grade pupils, the home environment was richer and intellectually more complex than the classroom. In the domestic environment adult questions referred to whole objects, events, causes, effects, comparisons. At school, the teachers asked only the names and features of things. This is similar to the distinction Barnes (1969) makes between closed and open questions. There are likely to be behavioural consequences where there is misunderstanding: pupils, baffled, may withdraw or, feeling resentment, assert themselves in unwanted ways.

In this chapter we will examine two attempts to identify the features of schools' provision which are associated with high and low exclusion rates. The first enquiry involved fifty high schools in a large city. The first thing I became aware of was that schools' rates of exclusion are no guide to the degree of disorder or harmony to be found within them. In all my visits to schools I saw no sign at all of the disorder and decline that outside commentators sometimes claim characterize the system. Whatever the relationship between exclusion and disorder, a school's ability to retain its pupils is a significant achievement in itself, and differences in effectiveness in this respect are themselves worth investigating. Raw exclusion rates alone are insufficient for comparing schools, because it is usually supposed that some school catchments contain more pupils presenting problems than others. However, schools which were comparable in many factors turned out to have widely differing rates of exclusion.

*Table 2.1* Correlation coefficients

|  | Excl. % | Free meals % | Number on roll |
|---|---|---|---|
| On free meals % | 0.47 | | |
| Number on roll | −0.35 | −0.45 | |
| Poor attendance | 0.45 | 0.80 | −0.29 |

Table 2.1 shows the correlations among all the data. The outstanding correlation is between poor attendance and the proportion of pupils qualifying for free meals. In this table, poor attendance was a measure of the percentage of pupils attending for less than 80 per cent of the required time – that is, missing an average of one day a week. A correlation of 0.8 means that approximately 65 per cent of poor attendance can be explained by this free-meals statistic. In a similar study, Galloway *et al.* (1985) found a slightly higher correlation between poor attendance and free meals. They found a correlation of 0.89 with the percentage of pupils missing more than 50 per cent of their schooling. That is to say, poor attendance on this scale seems to be 80 per cent attributable to poverty in the school's catchment, as measured by free meals. There was, however, no strong relationship between school processes and attendance. This suggests at first sight that a school's attendance rate is a given, over which school policy can have little effect. The lack of relationship may be a statistical artefact, however, produced by the fact that school attendance policies differ less than catchments do: almost all the schools visited had rigorous attendance policies and regular checks on absentees. Attendance rates are normally taken as outcomes of school policies in measures of school effectiveness. It is worth noting that if attendance is, in fact, more properly a measure of catchment, then differences in attendance would partially explain differences in other outcomes.

The correlation between free meals and exclusion of 0.47 indicates that only about 20 per cent of a school's exclusion rate can be attributed to catchment poverty. This leaves a large margin that must be explained by something else. More importantly, these other factors, unlike local poverty, are more likely to be under the school's influence, if not its total control. Behaviour in school is known to be related to the general atmosphere, ethos or climate of the school, irrespective of catchment (Reynolds and Sullivan, in Gillham, 1981; Rutter, 1979). Reviewing research, Graham (1988) notes that in Gray *et al.*'s research (1983) 'intake explains behaviour in school the least, and academic attainment the most'. One suggestion that I sought to investigate was the role of the school's referral system for discipline problems. The procedures used by a school may unintentionally escalate minor problems into major confrontations, in which the authority of the school may be perceived to be at stake. This is documented in Lawrence *et al.* (1977), who described 'a fast route which, started at the level of exclusion from class . . . could lead to . . . exclusion'. Further examples are in Galloway *et al.* (1982). The most unexpected correlation was between school size and exclusions. It is often suggested that larger schools create an impersonal atmosphere which leads to disaffection, disorder and exclusion. The figures show exactly the opposite, although this may be partly a result of there being two types of school in the sample: those taking pupils at age 11 (larger schools) and those taking pupils at 13 (slightly smaller schools). Schools with a higher proportion of older pupils might reasonably be expected to have a higher level of disaffection with which to cope.

It is one of the arguments of this book that fewer exclusions and less disorder follow from the decentralization of authority and distribution of power within schools. Studies of industrial organizations have suggested that increased size can have precisely these results (Pugh and Hickson, quoted in Dunkerley and Salaman, 1986). There is anecdotal support for this being a difference between large and small schools, which perhaps helps them keep down their rates of exclusion. When supervising teacher-training students in large schools one scarcely ever meets the headteacher and almost never needs to, the responsibility for students, as for many other features of the school's life, having been delegated. This is not the case in small schools, where there is a tendency for the headteacher to be directly involved in all aspects of the daily routine.

*Table 2.2* Comparable schools

|  | Roll | Poor attendance | Free meals | Excl. | Excl./ frees % |
|---|---|---|---|---|---|
| School A 11–18 | 840 | 3.6 | 9.1 | 3.7 | 39.8 |
| School B 11–18 | 1,040 | 3.1 | 9.7 | 0.2 | 2.0 |
| School C 13–18 | 900 | 38.0 | 55.0 | 0.8 | 1.5 |
| School D 13–18 | 1,100 | 41.0 | 30.0 | 3.9 | 13.0 |

Table 2.2 shows four sample schools. Schools A and B are suburban comprehensives, comparable in all respects except that one has an

exclusion rate eighteen times higher than the other. Schools C and D serve poorer urban areas, yet the school in the least favoured situation has an exclusion rate of only one-fifth of the other. A standard, if crude, way of allowing for domestic disadvantage is to use the schools' percentage of pupils qualifying for free meals. Surveys have shown free meals to be a measure of catchment deprivation comparable to census records of social class and headteachers' estimates of social and economic disadvantage. In the city under investigation, the proportion of pupils taking free meals varied from under 4 per cent to nearly 60 per cent, with a mean of 21 per cent. There are two ways of combining these figures in order to judge how well schools are managing to contain their number of exclusions.

Figure 2.1 Scatterplot of free meals against exclusion rate

The first method is to draw a scatterplot (see Figure 2.1). By inserting the mean values for exclusion and free meals, it is possible to identify four groups of schools. Two of these groups are of particular interest: group A comprises schools whose free meal rates are above average but whose exclusion rates are nevertheless low; group B comprises those schools whose free meal rates are low but whose exclusion rates are above average. It seems reasonable to suppose that school X is managing very well in potentially difficult circumstances; school Y, on the other hand, seems to have an unnecessarily high rate of exclusions, despite its favoured catchment.

The second method of comparison is to use a simple formula. In my 1987 survey, schools whose exclusion rate was less than one-tenth of their free meal rate were doing better than average. However, the validity of such a formula depends upon many factors which are not easily measurable: local variations in recording exclusions; the local average rates; the actual take-up of, as well as policy changes in entitlement to, free meals. The method of recording exclusions continues to mask information. For example, in one of the schools, one-third of the instances of exclusion registered over a one-year period were attributable to one pupil. Table 2.3 shows four schools ranged in order of exclusion rate and apparently, therefore, of effectiveness in this respect. When free meals are taken into account the order of effectiveness is reversed.

Table 2.3 What is a high exclusion rate?

|  | Free meals % | Exclusion % | Excl./frees % |
|---|---|---|---|
| School P | 39.1 | 4.0 | 10 |
| School Q | 24.1 | 3.0 | 12 |
| School R | 9.7 | 1.4 | 14 |
| School S | 3.7 | 0.8 | 21 |

Having found a fair way of comparing schools, and a method of identifying schools with very high and very low exclusion rates, the task was to identify the positive and negative factors at work. It is not easy to discover how a school's stated policies are applied in practice. For example, all schools have group tutors and some sort of system for dealing with disciplinary problems. Almost all schools claim that the form tutor is the key person in the system and that they try to ensure that group tutors retain responsibility for a class during its four or five years in the school. Most schools provide comprehensive policy statements on their pastoral and disciplinary organization. I found that, when presented with examples, heads and senior teachers responded in ways which were not congruent with their own policy documents. It was in their responses to examples that differences in practical policy emerged. Three factors seemed to be most important: the way in which group tutors were used in practice; the extent to which preventive rather than punishing approaches were employed; and the list of offences earning exclusion.

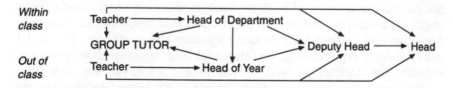

Figure 2.2 Referral routes for discipline problems

In some schools the group tutor's role is nominal. When a crisis occurs, he or she is bypassed as the difficulties are referred rapidly up through the hierarchy. In other schools the year team acts as a considerable barrier, either holding pupils at the year-teacher level or referring them back down to group tutors. Two examples were presented to heads: if a teacher has persistent difficulty with a pupil in class, what does he or she do? If a teacher discovers a serious incident out of class, what does he or she do? In almost all schools, difficulties within class are referred first to the head of department and difficulties out of class to the head of year. It is what happens next that appears to be crucial (Figure 2.2 shows the possibilities). Schools with lower than expected exclusion rates tended to give the group tutor a more significant and responsible role. There was an expectation that problems would be dealt with at the lowest level in the school's hierarchy. Group tutors were regarded as significant and important, and decisions were not taken without consulting and involving them. In some schools the year team actively resisted attempts to refer pupils to higher authority. Schools with higher than expected exclusion rates tended to have a rapid referral system, where even the head of department or head of year might be left out of decision making. In these schools, pupils could find themselves outside the head's or deputy's door for such everyday trivialities as dropping litter. Not surprisingly, these senior staff sometimes felt overwhelmed by a seemingly ever-rising tide of disorder and disruption. Delegation, or sharing, might have lifted their burden and reduced the number of pupils being rejected by their schools.

In schools where there was a positive and preventive approach to troublesome behaviour there was a lower than expected rate of exclusion. Some schools had a special area or set of rooms where pupils causing difficulties could be taught by particularly expert staff and then supported on their return to the ordinary timetable; others had integrated their support teachers into ordinary classes. This usually involved teachers in considerable planning for what was, in effect, a specialized form of team teaching. It was not regarded simply as adding a remedial teacher to an ordinary class; the lead role in lessons was exchanged or shared and in some cases rendered unnecessary through careful preparation of resources and self-programming learning materials. Whether the support was wholly or largely within the ordinary class, there was an emphasis on tackling the problem in its original context; teachers were not encouraged to refer pupils to specialist staff in the expectation that responsibility for these pupils would be transferred. Working together was an effective and practically relevant type of staff development and training. Teachers could support one another as well as the pupils; whatever the difficulties, teachers were sure of a colleague's support in discipline, teaching and the maintenance of personal esteem. All the pupils, irrespective of their needs, benefit from this integration of the pastoral and academic curriculum. It has costs in terms of staffing levels and the additional time teachers need to spend in planning.

The extra noise caused by more activity, discussion among pupils and between pupils and their teachers is also a discouraging factor. No school thought these costs outweighed the benefits. In contrast, schools with higher than expected exclusion rates tended to respond to problems after the event. If they had units they tended to be regarded as a punishment and there was not the emphasis on supporting return to the ordinary classes. Teachers came to believe that their responsibility ended once the pupil was referred. In extreme cases, troublesome pupils were exiled in an empty classroom and supervised by a rota of teachers; some were made to work outside the head's door. Not surprisingly, few pupils with serious problems responded positively to this punitive treatment. Schools with lower than expected exclusion rates had a restrictive policy with respect to exclusion and used it only for serious cases of bullying and intimidation. There were attempts to prevent decisions being made in the heat of a crisis and the procedure was deliberately slowed down to give time for reflection. Interestingly, a pupil's past history was not allowed to influence decisions about guilt and innocence unduly. Some schools were also concerned to prevent pupils manipulating the system in order to be released from school; where it was suspected the pupil and his or her family welcomed exclusion, alternatives were looked for. Schools with higher than expected exclusion rates tended to have a list of exclusion-worthy offences. After bullying, the most common offences for which pupils were excluded were verbal abuse to staff and disruption of lessons. Some schools automatically excluded in certain circumstances: for example, being caught smoking three times or setting off a fire-alarm. Some reasons for exclusion seemed bizarre but were not, in fact: one school excluded pupils who failed to use the proper crossing point on a nearby dual carriageway notorious for fatal accidents. Other reasons seemed bizarre and perhaps they were. One pupil had been excluded for leading a pupils' strike against the teachers' strike; discovering the gap between practice and precept can be a punishing, if educational, experience.

Three other factors emerged, but less strongly. There tended to be lower than expected exclusion rates where unruly classes were reorganized and pupils exchanged with other classes; where teachers in difficulty received help in their classes by being teamed up with an experienced teacher; and where headteachers believed that the social and non-academic side of school life was worth spending funds on. Asked if they would use school money to support a trip to the coast, some said there would have to be an educational input but others responded along the lines of 'money well spent' or 'how wonderful'. These factors may be clues to other aspects of school climate that I found difficult to measure. For example, pupils can be exchanged and classes reorganized only in schools where groups are of similar ability. Such fundamental strategies are not possible where there is relatively rigid streaming or where setting is widespread. It may therefore be the relatively uncompetitive atmosphere that is contributing to fewer exclusions, and the freedom to reorganize classes is a symptom of this. To support teachers in difficulty by teaming them up with experienced colleagues indicates a degree of openness and collegiality that may itself reduce stress and help the staff as a whole cope in difficult situations. The relationship between each of the six factors and schools having higher or lower than expected exclusion rates is given in Figure 2.3.

*Figure 2.3* Exclusion rates and school policies

Each of the factors identified may seem trivial in itself, but the figures indicate that modifying policies in line with these findings could reduce a school's exclusion rate by about half. Taken together, they indicate a significant difference in atmosphere between schools. In those where few pupils are excluded there is a greater degree of shared responsibility, a willingness to face up to and prepare for difficulties that arise, and a determination to accommodate and cope with the vagaries of adolescent demeanour.

Distributing authority to tutors lends support to the view that giving people responsibility makes them act responsibly. Perhaps the effect is more fundamental. Schutz (1972) distinguishes between consociate and contemporaneous knowledge of others. To know a person as a contemporary is to know him or her only as a member of a category of people; to know a person as a consociate is to know him or her as an individual, in the way that members of a family know each other. Empowering tutors gives them the incentive to get to know their pupils as consociates. Tutors who know that their views will be listened to and given weight will see some purpose in seeking to understand their pupils, however unacceptable their behaviour. It may be thought that some pupils' behaviour is so unacceptable that it is beyond the reach of even the most well-disposed teacher, but there is evidence that this is rarely so. I have yet to meet a case where there was not at least one teacher prepared to speak on behalf of a troublesome pupil; and it is a common experience, in the adult sphere of deviance, to find apparently balanced (and often distinguished) people eager to plead on behalf of people known to them but guilty of distasteful crimes. David Goode's chapter in Barton and Tomlinson (1982) provides support for the view that no human being is beyond our understanding. He describes a number of cases where severely impaired people, whose disabilities engendered horror in strangers, were nevertheless known, liked and communicated with by parents, nurses or companions. When pupils realize that their tutor has real power to represent their point of view, however idiosyncratic, then genuine communication can take place. Teachers and pupils can get to know one another as individuals and not merely as typical members of groups, imperfectly understood and possibly distrusted. In such low-key and unglamorous ways as this can real democracy and understanding enter schools.

## HARMONIC OR SYNCHRONIZED?

The school is threatened because it is autocratic and it is autocratic because it is threatened.

(Willard Waller 1965)

This section generalizes the findings on school policies and in so doing tries to account for variations in schools' exclusion rates. The discussion relies on two theoretical ideas: the concepts of mechanical and organic solidarity introduced by Durkheim in a classic work (1893/1933), and the concepts of classification and frame described by Bernstein (1971).

Durkheim argued that social cohesion depended upon one or other of two types of solidarity and that the nature of the law in a society served as a barometer of solidarity type. A school's declared policies and written documents are imperfect indicators, since schools do not always act in accordance with their stated policies. There is normally a gap between word and deed. A school's rate of referral for permanent exclusion is the equivalent of the law's actual disposals and may be taken as a reasonably reliable indicator of its true threshold of tolerance. Mechanical solidarity, which Durkheim found to be prevalent in what were then thought of as primitive societies, is 'born of resemblances ... and directly links the individual with society'. He called it mechanical because it was analogous to the links between 'molecules of inorganic bodies'. The division of labour was undeveloped, and beliefs and sentiments were largely shared by all members of the group. Cohesion was strong where ideas and tendencies common to all members of the group were stronger and more numerous than individual ideas. In the terms used by Mead (1934), each person's 'Me' eclipses his or her 'I'. In this type of society, individuality does not develop and the collective conscience acting within us envelops our personal conscience. As individuals depend upon the collective they 'become dependent upon the central authority in which it is incarnated'. In such a society, law was essentially repressive; as social cohesion took its source from similarity, individuals were relatively dispensable.

Organic solidarity arose from the division of labour and depended not upon resemblances but upon differences among individuals. The term 'organic' was used because it was analogous to the links between the different organs of higher mammals. The unity and capacity for action of society increased in proportion to the increasing individuation of its parts. Members of society depended upon one another because they depended upon one another's specialisms. Solidarity of this type derived its strength from individuality; law was characteristically restitutive; in Mead's terms, each person's 'I' was greater than his or her 'Me'.

Durkheim proposed these two types as analytical tools and was not suggesting that they could be found in their pure form in reality. He proposed to take the ratio of repressive to restitutive law – criminal to civil – as a measure of the importance of the collective conscience to social cohesion. Punishment served to maintain cohesion in mechanical societies and only secondarily, if at all, to deter or correct. 'Inversely, commensurate with the development of individual types and the specialisation of tasks, the proportion between the two types of law ought to become reversed.' The concepts of mechanical and organic solidarity may be adapted and applied to schools. The argument will be that schools with high exclusion rates exhibit the characteristics of mechanical solidarity and that those with low exclusion rates exhibit the characteristics of organic solidarity.

Durkheim's ideas can be expressed in terms of Bernstein's concepts of classification and frame. In Bernstein's (1971) paper, classification refers to the degree of insulation between curriculum contents: the strength of the boundaries between subject disciplines. Here I shall use classification to refer to the strength of the boundaries between individual actions, the degree of discreteness of individual acts, the certainty about the meaning of acts. Where classification is strong there will tend to be agreement about the significance of pupil behaviour. Where classification is weak there may be hesitation and uncertainty about the meaning of pupil behaviours: they will be individuated and pupils' histories may be searched for mitigating evidence. For example, with strong classification, verbal abuse to a teacher will signify the same, irrespective of the pupil and the circumstances: it will admit of no other interpretation but will be a piece of behaviour that could be entered on a behavioural questionnaire.

Where classification is weak, verbal abuse may be interpreted in many ways: it will be seen as an act having many possible meanings rather than an example of a questionnaire category. It may be taken as an insult; it may be seen as an insecure pupil's strategy to win approval from a peer-group; from a pupil with a history of domestic ill-treatment, verbal abuse may be seen as a way of testing the sincerity of a teacher who has shown interest and concern. Analyses of the sort described by Dreikurs (1957) and Balson (1982), and used in Chapter 4, imply weak classification. Where classification is strong, such reflection appears as indulgence; for example, swearing is swearing and there is no excuse for it.

In Bernstein's (1971) paper, framing refers to the degree of control teacher and pupil have over what may be taught: the strength of the boundary between that which is permitted and that which is not. I wish to use framing to refer to the strength of the boundary between types of behaviour which the school regards as containable and those which it does not. Where framing is strong there will be a number of types of behaviour which earn exclusion and a reluctance to make exceptions. Where framing is weak there will be fewer, and a willingness to allow the uncertain line to be crossed and recrossed before a pupil is finally excluded. Where there is strong framing, deviant behaviour is seen only as an impediment to the teacher's proper task; where framing is weak, coping with deviant behaviour is included in a teacher's professional responsibilities and is not seen merely as grit in the machine.

Figure 2.4 School type matrix

Figure 2.4 shows the four school types that result from combinations of weak and strong framing and classification. The harmonized type most fully exhibits organic solidarity and the synchronized type, mechanical solidarity. Both may be relatively stable, but the synchronized type is perhaps more vulnerable to change. For example, relatively inflexible standards and brittle distinctions would be threatened by increasing diversity in pupil intakes. The flexible and assimilative ethos of the harmonized type may allow it to accommodate change without danger.

All schools have rules on such things as dress, hair-styles and deportment, but synchronized schools will state them more inflexibly and apply them less sensitively. The range of offences meriting exclusion will be wide and include many offences against collective norms; offences against people will tend to be described in a collective-referenced vocabulary, as will reasons given for exclusion. Authority will tend to be centralized and referral to it relatively swift; responsibility will be vertically distributed. As the school seeks to achieve behavioural uniformity it is likely that some segments will be perceived as threatening, and there may be a corresponding anxiety about any possible increase in the diversity of the intake: for example, a rise in the number of pupils with special needs following the integrationist tendencies of the 1981 Education Act. There will be a moralistic and judgemental view of deviance and more vigorous attempts to suppress it. A pupil's record or school history may be used to redefine an otherwise trivial act as more threatening, and subversive motives may be attributed.

Harmonized schools will tend to have fewer rules on dress and personal appearance, and they will be sensitively interpreted and enforced with discretion. Offences earning exclusion will be few, and such as there are will be offences against people. Authority will be laterally distributed, power and responsibility shared, teachers will have considerable discretion in their dealings with pupils, and the headteacher will not normally be directly referred to in disciplinary matters. Such sharing may reduce the gap between the formal and informal systems within the school's organizational structure. Staff will have greater discretion to be flexible, to permit a degree of non-compliance in the longer-term interests of co-operation, respect and goodwill. Reasons for exclusion will tend to employ a person-related vocabulary. Since the school accepts a wide range of individual differences in demeanour there will be no areas where subversive groups are perceived to be sedimented. A pragmatic and utilitarian approach will predominate over a moralistic and judgemental attitude and there will be a correspondingly relaxed attitude to increasing diversity of intake. There should be evidence of positive and energetic attempts to repair breaches in relationships between pupils and teachers before any pupil is excluded. Where a pupil's history or record is referred to, it will tend to be as mitigating rather than incriminating evidence.

These types are, in effect, opposing extremes of a scale: it is not suggested that any schools are actually like this in reality. They are similar to the incorporative–coercive school types proposed by Reynolds and Sullivan (1979). Moving from the macro (or meso) level of school organization to the micro level of individual interaction, they are paralleled in Jorden's concepts of insulative–provocative teachers (see Hargreaves *et al.*, 1975: 260–1). For example, there should be a higher proportion of deviance–insulative teachers in schools of the harmonized type. A school might, therefore, be typed as harmonized or synchronized by discovering the stated policies with respect to behaviour and by assessing the teachers with respect to their degree of deviance–insulativeness or deviance–provocativeness.

The grid generates two other types which might be regarded as intermediate forms but which will not be used here. It may be that in the type labelled as retreatist, much is permitted but not approved of: for example, in the case of a synchronized type's staff losing the power to control aspects of their pupils' behaviour but continuing to believe they ought to do so. Were they to adopt the individualized view of pupil action found in the harmonized type, they would arrive at a more comfortable perspective and be able to negotiate. In the irresolute type there might be a realistic perception of pupil behaviour but a lingering attachment, perhaps ritualistic, to unsustainable norms and standards as regards what a school should accommodate. A wider professional view of a school's responsibilities would resolve their conflict and reduce their stress. Exclusion rates should be high, if somewhat arbitrary, in the irresolute type but may be low in the retreatist type, at the cost of considerable internal disorder.

Typing teachers according to a dominant perspective, and schools according to a dominant ethos, can be too gross an over-simplification of reality. Referring to school types conceals the fact that schools as such do not have rules, policies and attitudes. Individual members of schools create and maintain rules and thereby influence the overall atmosphere or ethos according to their individual power and commitment. Furthermore, teachers themselves do not use a consistent perspective: in one situation, provoked; in another, insulated. Simple dichotomies give clarity at the expense of validity; attempts to increase validity result in cumbersome typologies which confuse rather than clarify. Compare, for example, Hammersley's (1986) complex teacher-perspectives scheme with simpler typologies such as Esland's (described and discussed in Woods, 1983).

## CONTRASTING CASE STUDIES

The argument will be illustrated by describing two schools, one of the harmonized type, which will be called St Matthew's, and one of the synchronized type, which will be called St Luke's. These two examples, and the policies and pupils described, are constructed from data gathered from several schools through interviews and questionnaires. We move, as Schostak (1986) puts it, away from soft statistics towards hard social facts; but St Luke's and St Matthew's are real only in the sense that the characteristics of people and places in novels are real, and they serve some of the same purposes: protecting real people and highlighting only those aspects that are relevant to this book. This technique has been used by some writers in attempts to evaluate educational innovations and will be discussed in Chapter 7. Senior teachers or heads were interviewed about their policies on disruption and exclusion, and other members of staff were asked for their reactions to common disciplinary incidents. Similar incidents are presented for discussion in Activity 3.1 at the end of Chapter 3. All the strategies offered by teachers aimed at achieving some degree of co-operation, but some responses were direct and confrontational, whereas others seemed more impassive and disarming. Particular teachers varied from situation to situation as to which sort of approach they said they would use. For each example, the strategy offered was assessed as either confrontational or disarming – these terms being adopted in preference to those used by Hargreaves and Reynolds. A confrontational strategy is one where the teacher's response is autocratic and unbending: demands are made and the aim is compliance through domination. A disarming strategy is one where the teacher's response is less direct and more dispassionate: the teacher is unruffled and seeks to maintain order through mollifying and humouring. The questionnaire responses were categorized by two people and only those upon which there was agreement were counted. It was clear that few teachers approached every incident with the same perspective and most varied their strategies in different situations: of fifty teachers replying, only three were assessed as confrontational, and only one as disarming, in all five situations. On the whole, teachers tended to confront problems directly. Even in schools exhibiting the highest degree of organic solidarity, and closest to the harmonized type, most responses were confrontational.

St Matthew's serves an area of poor housing and high unemployment: two-thirds of the pupils qualify for free meals, but its exclusion rate is almost the lowest in the district. The headteacher describes the school's policy as follows:

> To be excluded from this school there would have to be not just one but a whole catalogue of serious offences and the catalogue would have to include a number of attacks, or at least swipes at staff, teachers hurt in prising pupils apart and so on. The final straw in one case was a very vicious attack on another pupil; in another, a girl thumped a teacher four times – she was protecting another pupil. In both cases

there had been a series of offences before that and we would have to think carefully before having them back. Before we exclude a pupil the staff have to feel that we have tried everything and not been any help to the child. We have the usual list of detentions, report cards, attachment to senior staff and contracts between pupil and school. We try to mend situations before excluding. After an incident we try to give teacher and pupil time to reflect. There are no instant decisions. Staff might think about what had happened and think, yes, well, that's maybe provoked by me. We would not take the pupil's part against the teacher, we would arrange for the teacher and pupil to speak somewhere quietly. Not all the staff agree with this approach, it is not a unanimous view. Some say we might act more swiftly, but not many.

My argument is that we must make special allowances for pupils who are socially disabled. Some pupils have physical disabilities and so we excuse them from some activities, let them be late for some lessons, for example. We have to accept that those whose relationships with others are disabled need special consideration too. One thing we have tried is to allow pupils to withdraw from situations which they feel are threatening their temperamental equilibrium. They are told that if they know they are going to blow up and do something they will regret, they should withdraw from the situation: either count up to ten or leave the classroom. I have given some extremely unstable pupils notes authorizing them to do this. It helps to keep the pupil in the school community and it is a rather skilful way of colonizing and making legitimate the flight reaction many people have in situations where they cannot cope. In this school, walking out of a class and away from potential conflict can be a way of avoiding disruption. In most other schools it would make matters worse and itself become the target of punishment. It is seldom abused: most pupils go to the agreed place rather than wandering the school shouting abuse through doors. That can happen, though. We are prepared to go to great lengths to keep hold of a disturbed pupil. We will accept a very basic minimum of co-operation as a negotiating baseline. We feel that if we can get them to school and keep them there we have a chance of improving them. If we exclude, we are not just admitting defeat but passing our responsibility for a pupil on to someone else. There is even less chance of success for others because the pupil is carrying the badge of failure already. We are always trying to find new ways, we try everything before even considering exclusion. You've got to be prepared for things to fail, you've got to accept failure. It is like diagnosing faults on a car that will not start. You learn to resist your first impulse, which is usually to kick it. It is just as ridiculous to kick the pupil out of the door. You have to see a difficult pupil as a problem to solve not as a personally insulting challenge. Sometimes a crisis can be a turning point for the better: an opportunity for a teacher and pupil to form a more rewarding relationship. The pupil would see that they had upset someone and perhaps do something to make amends.

We are a very democratic institution: we believe in sharing the power and authority. To all intents and purposes the year heads are headteachers. I would never overrule them. They have a lot of autonomy; they have to have, as there isn't always time for consultation, but they would try to consult the year team. I have to be responsible for exclusions, of course, but I am guided by my year heads. Before the law changed, I delegated exclusion to them. I see delegation as a means of staff development and education. If a teacher made frequent referrals to me I would see that the teacher was kept on the case, let them see what work was involved. In general, I don't touch discipline. If I had a problem with a pupil I would refer it to the pupil's tutor. I do not think it would be proper for me to be judge and jury in my own case.

We have few rules written down and I cannot think of any off-hand. They tend to lead to silly situations. We have requests not rules. For example, we have no rules about uniform but we ask the pupils to dress reasonably. If a pupil came to school in wholly unsuitable clothing then we would certainly not send them home or show them up in front of others. The pupil's tutor might compliment them on the outfit but point out that it was not suitable for school. They would have shown it off to friends and to us and not got into trouble. They would usually leave it at home the next day.

There are no full school assemblies but occasionally year groups assemble together. From time to time, pupils, parents and staff meet for a sort of celebration evening. It is a bit like a speech day but it is individualized and non-competitive. Parents see individual teachers and pupils may receive one of our awards. We have a very wide curriculum and pupils of all sorts of abilities manage to get an award for something or other.

St Luke's, on the other hand, has a very high exclusion rate but very few pupils qualify for free meals. The school is pleasantly situated, popular, has a good reputation and is proud of its high standards. The head does not think the exclusion rate is unnecessarily high and puts the school's policy as follows:

Some pupils make it impossible for their teachers to teach. For example, we had one pupil who broke our rules from almost the day he came here. In his first year he broke the uniform rules on eight occasions: these included wearing the wrong jumper, having no tie, and coming to school dressed in a jean suit and wearing a hat in school. In the end we had to suspend him when he came to school with a shaved head.

It may seem a minor matter in itself, but we feel we have to get compliance in the small things or we find ourselves in battle over things that should never be challenged by pupils. Defeat on the issue of uniform will lead, domino style, to defeat in total.

We have a formal system of referral. A pupil would have to go through several tiers before getting to me. However, there are usually one or two pupils referred directly to me every day and if I do not get a satisfactory response from them I might well suspend them. I regard the school's discipline as my province and would certainly not want every class tutor involved. That would threaten standards. We do place a high priority on personal and social education, however. Tutors remain with the same class as it travels up through the year groups, but they are not involved in matters that are properly the head's responsibility.

I am aware that our exclusion rate is thought to be high; but we do have some very difficult groups of pupils. There are some pupils for whom there is no alternative to exclusion now that the cane has gone. I am thinking of older boys, probably in the bottom half of the ability band, aiming for a low GCSE grade or none at all. Of course we take a pupil's record into account: for example, if a boy was badly behaved in a lesson, and he had a history of bad behaviour, then he would be quite likely to be excluded for it. Another boy might get a reprimand. We do not let troublesome pupils take up time that properly belongs to others. Some situations are calmed down by having the pupil stand outside my door. I do not think the staff would be very impressed if I held meetings and called in a counsellor or something of that sort.

The teachers at both St Luke's and St Matthew's are generally inclined to confront disciplinary problems directly: their confrontational responses outnumber their disarming ones. However, fewer than half of the responses from St Matthew's staff are confrontational and more than one-third are disarming. In St Luke's case, two-thirds of responses are confrontational and only one-fifth are disarming. This suggests that one school has a wider and more flexible range of strategies than the other. In addition, St Luke's staff are twice as likely to say they would refer problems to senior staff and much less likely to express doubts or add qualifications to their answers.

In the harmonized type of school like St Matthew's, exclusion tends to be restricted to cases of violence, group tutors have more significance and responsibility, and within-school exclusion units tend to be preventive rather than punitive; there is a diminished tendency to see particular categories of pupil as more productive of problems than others; a pupil's history, if used at all, has a mitigatory rather than an aggravating influence on the responses to their behaviour. The meaning of exclusion itself is also different in the two types of school. In the synchronized type, like St Luke's, it is a punishment and even an abandonment; in St Matthew's it forms part of the school's reparative policy: pupils are taken home rather than sent and there is an attempt to avoid the impression that exclusion is a final break.

## WHAT SCHOOL INSPECTION REPORTS REVEAL

So far the analysis has depended heavily on the relationship between features of schools' internal referral systems and exclusion statistics. The second phase of the work explored a larger group of school factors in a more widely dispersed sample of schools by exploiting the data available in published reports from school inspection teams. As a research exercise an Ofsted (Office for Standards in Education) team's inspection of a school is a major activity. A typical secondary school inspection will involve a dozen people in these activities: the pre-inspection review of several hundred pages of information and statistics; a one-day meeting of about one-third of the team to discuss the documents and formulate hypotheses (or issues requiring attention); a full week observing and interviewing in the school; around thirteen hours of after-school team meetings during that week; and the draft report, checked with the school's management team and other key members of the staff. As a source of data for researchers the published report has a number of benefits: the team know the context well and follow good research practice, checking their findings with each other and with those whose work is being investi- gated; the conclusions are built on a substantial evidence base; and the findings are presented in a standard format, written up in relation to specific, published criteria. The comparison and synthesis of the work and findings of differing teams ought, therefore, to be easier, and more secure, than that of other individuals or groups reporting on their research work in schools.

A random sample of sixty reports was collected and analysed to provide data listed in a numerical form under fifteen headings. As before, school roll, free meals, attendance and temporary and permanent exclusions were recorded; added to these were the figures given for the percentage of pupils gaining one or more bare pass at GCSE, as well as the figure for those gaining five good GCSEs (that is, grade C or better). These last two give a measure of schools' educational standards and perhaps of their success with their lowest achievers. To this set of figures I was able to add information (in numerical form) about aspects of schools' teaching and learning quality, ethos, and religious and moral education.

Although numerical data on these features is not included in the reports, they are susceptible to translation into numbers because of the grade-referenced criteria used: the choice of language used in the reports is guided by the criteria attached to each grade. Full details can be found in HMSO (1993). In summary, the key words are as follows: grade 1 quality is described as very good, excellent or outstanding; grade 2, good; grade 3, satisfactory or sound; grade 4, unsatisfactory; grade 5, poor. The paragraphs of the report normally detail examples of the sort of work that was seen and further elaborate on the overall judgement. HMSO (1993) contains amplifications of the criteria, and these help in transferring text into grades. Not all aspects of all reports are susceptible to this analysis: some pay insufficient attention to the criteria or are ambiguous in some way. Only thirty-seven of my original sample of nearly sixty reports could be used in this way, but these gave information on aspects of schools that are almost impossible for most researchers to tease out. The seven factors are as follows:

1 The quality of oracy, as observed across the curriculum as well as in English lessons. In reporting on oracy, or speaking and listening, inspectors are looking for coherent speech, suitably adapted to the purpose, the ability to explain, hypothesize, analyse and question, and the willingness to attend to others and respond appropriately. Inspectors are required to report on general, cross-curricular standards of literacy and numeracy, too, but most of the reports studied contained insufficient data or, in the case of numeracy, consistently recorded that it was not evident as a cross-curricular skill.

2 Provision for pupils with special educational needs. This measures a school's commitment to coping with pupils in difficulty and the appropriateness of that provision in raising standards of achievement without socially isolating pupils or restricting their opportunities to have access to the main curriculum.

3 The quality of religious education in a school. This is included to test the prevalent view that it is crucial to pupils' moral and behavioural development.

4 The quality of behaviour and discipline. This part of the report records such things as the degree of compliance with rules, the sense of responsibility exhibited by pupils, and the orderliness of the school community.

5 The quality of pupils' spiritual, moral, social and cultural development. This is an important indicator of the atmosphere in a school and measures both the standards achieved by the pupils and the extent of the opportunities and teaching provided by the teachers. This area covers such things as the understanding of religious beliefs and other cultures, values and the functioning of society.

6 The quality of teaching. This records the team's overall judgement of teaching in the school, looking at the provision across the curriculum as a whole. Reports also contain a judgement about the quality of learning, an aspect which overlaps to some extent with the cross-

curricular skills of oracy, literacy and numeracy. I used the factor for which there was most evidence – oracy, the first item on this list.
7 Worship. Schools are required by law to have a corporate act of worship daily. Few secondary schools fully comply (under 20 per cent of the sample under study), and it seems likely that the requirement is not, in fact, legally enforceable (Bibby, 1994). I recorded the number of such acts of worship taking place weekly.

Correlations among all the fourteen variables showed that attendance and free meals had the highest association with other selected variables. High levels of attendance are associated with low levels of exclusion (permanent and temporary), good standards of oracy, good behaviour and good teaching. High proportions of pupils taking free meals are associated with poorer examination results, poor attendance and high levels of exclusion – particularly the temporary kind. These figures are broadly in line with the work described earlier in this chapter and with similar studies (for example, Galloway *et al.*, 1985; McManus, 1987). The highest correlation is between the two types of exclusion: schools with high levels of temporary exclusions will tend also to have high levels of permanent exclusions. This might seem unremarkable, but the 0.79 figure contrasts with one of only 0.41 found in my earlier (1987) study.

Looking particularly at variables measuring internal school factors, we find some interesting variations. The strongest relationship for temporary and permanent exclusions is with oracy: there are fewer exclusions in schools with good standards of oracy. This relationship is stronger than that between exclusion and behaviour. The strongest relationship for behaviour is with oracy, suggesting either that schools with good behaviour can develop good speaking and listening, or that developing good standards of oracy can develop good behaviour. Another possibility is that good standards in both are related to something else. Variables weakly associated with exclusion and behaviour include the quality of religious education, the number of assemblies with acts of worship, and the quality of provision for spiritual, moral, social and cultural education.

Using regression analysis, I found that, for each type of exclusion, free meals (and the other type of exclusion) predominate when all the variables are included. Two of the four best three-variable groups (most strongly associated with temporary exclusion) include free meals, permanent exclusion and oracy; the other two groups replace oracy with behaviour or religious education. The results suggested that almost 80 per cent of schools' temporary exclusions can be explained by these few variables. For permanent exclusion, no strong pattern emerges.

An additional analysis was carried out with free meals, roll, attendance and the other type of exclusion removed. As with the work described earlier, this allowed the programme to concentrate on those school factors which are most under teachers' control. For both types of exclusion, the best groups of three or four variables included oracy and the percentage of pupils achieving at least one bare pass at GCSE.

As the percentage of pupils qualifying for free meals is so closely related to exclusion, a school's exclusion rate is not in itself a fair indicator of its efforts and success in managing difficult pupils. Poorer catchments are likely to produce more children with difficulties and children whose domestic and neighbourhood experience has weakened the messages schools transmit about the importance of education. Using the methods described earlier in this chapter, the best and worst five schools on this criterion were identified for further analysis. Both groups were similar (and better than the national average) in free meals, attendance, behaviour and examination results. For internal, school ethos factors, one significant difference appeared: the best and worst schools had markedly differing scores for oracy. On the one-to-five scale, the low-excluding schools scored two (or good) compared with four (unsatisfactory) for the high excluders. This is further confirmation that exclusion rates are not simply a response to catchment difficulties nor even to behaviour problems in schools; other factors than actual misbehaviour are an influence. This is supported by, for example, DfE (1992) and Galloway et al. (1985).

Discussion with teachers and pupils in a school with a high exclusion rate added some support for the importance of the factors identified so far, as well as clues to reasons why some schools have high rates of exclusion irrespective of their catchments. The school recorded 194 instances of temporary exclusion in one year (22.4 per cent); all curricular and ethos aspects were satisfactory or better, except RE (which scored 4, or unsatisfactory) and oracy (which scored 5, which is poor).

The disciplinary procedures made heavy use of senior staff through a pupil report and referral system. The written policy was that misbehaving pupils were required to carry around a report card, which each class teacher signed and wrote comments in. The head of year then checked report cards at the end of each day. In practice, pupils were often sent to more senior staff. The head of year 10, whose pupils accounted for nearly half of the exclusions, said: 'The system is frequently bypassed and they don't come to me at all. If there are a lot of negative comments it goes to [the deputy head].' Asked what he himself did with pupils whose cards carried negative comments: 'Detention, and I'd send them to [the deputy head]'. Rapid referral has been identified before as a contributory factor in high exclusion rates (Lawrence et al., 1977; Galloway et al., 1982; McManus, 1987). The Elton Report noted the evidence that 'schools make a difference' and suggested that 'exclusion rates could be reduced in some schools by reorganising their internal referral systems' (HMSO, 1989: 88, 191).

It would be stretching the evidence perilously thin to say that such swift processing of pupils left little time for talking things through or modelling and developing the skills of oracy that seem to be associated with low exclusion. However, a class teacher in the same school was asked to talk about a typical or recent incident leading to exclusion. He described how he had been ticking off a disruptive pupil in his lesson when the deputy head came in.

> It was just coming up to break and I told [the deputy] I was keeping him back. After the class had gone, [the pupil] just burst into tears – it was a real shock – anyway, it all came out about his mother dying, I think it was a drugs case, lighter fuel, something like that. I tried to calm him, by telling him that he hadn't to go on at the girls as he had been. End of break, [the deputy] walks in and says: 'Out, my office.' With the kids coming back in I couldn't very well tell him what I'd just heard. I didn't see him after school. Next morning, excluded – notice up in the staffroom.

Asked whether he had wanted the boy excluded, he firmly denied it. If the teacher had managed to explain about the boy's problems, would that have stopped the exclusion? He thought not. Why was that?

> Scared, basically. They feel threatened. He looks hard and he isn't, basically he's soft. [The deputy], the head, they don't see him as he basically is. He was seeing this dangerous hooligan and he wanted safety. He went for safety and excluded him.

A second teacher present commented that the referral system in her view did not work: 'You never get any feedback.' Evidently oblivious of her colleague's implied criticism of the exclusion-prone system, she elaborated:

> It has got better this last term. I had trouble with a boy who wouldn't hand over a picture he'd got out of a newspaper. I sent him up to [a member of the senior management] and he was excluded for the rest of the day. It wasn't just for that – there was bad language and never ever any homework.

Her view, stated repeatedly in the short interview, was that there should be 'standard action'. Standard action would certainly seem to rule out the need for discussion, but perhaps we are seeing here an example of the over-speedy referral rather than a lack of commitment to oracy.

A group of pupils in the school were asked to list its rules. They managed eight, all of which were low-level prohibitions: for example, no running, no earrings. When the question was turned around to elicit their views about how pupils should behave, the results were remarkably different. All the guidance offered was positive and related to relationships among pupils: for example, treat others like your own, be kind and considerate. Perhaps these pupils, who had not been involved in formulating the school's rules, were capable of positive contributions. The possible link between exclusion and the skills of oracy and the opportunities to use these skills in contributing to school policy is tantalizing.

The comments in a low-excluding school's Ofsted report on behaviour and oracy are an interesting contrast. The school was said to have 'a high standard of oral work ... pupils excel in expressing their ideas with clarity and in responding thoughtfully and articulately to the contributions of others ... those with learning difficulties are able to discuss their work with confidence and fluency'. Behaviour was described as 'excellent with pupils demonstrating high levels of responsibility'.

## ORACY AS A COUNTER-EXCLUSION STRATEGY

If it were the case that working to improve standards of oracy might improve schools' internal relationships to the point of reducing exclusions, this would be a new focus for preventive work. Hughes (1988), discussing cognitive behaviour therapy, outlines some techniques derived from the cognitive focus: teachers spend more time in interaction, explaining programmes, encouraging pupils to talk themselves through their problems, and commenting on their feelings and reactions. One of the teachers of difficult pupils interviewed by Lovey *et al.* (1993) stressed that 'counselling involves listening', and he went on to say that ex-pupils often returned after many years 'to talk'. Gillborn *et al.* (1993) regard dialogue as central to making pupils feel they matter as individuals. The study of a residential placement by Cooper (1993) contains ample evidence that even some of the most intractable pupils are capable of reflection through talk.

A piece of film from the National Oracy Project Packs, 'Learning Together Through Talk' (Baddeley, 1992; Kemeny, 1993), is significant. Both packs contain ample evidence of the value of talk in learning but one of the primary school scenes gives clues as to how oracy might affect behaviour. The children are discussing the relative talents of boys and girls, and on first viewing the conversation seems stilted and scripted. In response to contributions we hear such things as 'not necessarily ... only sometimes ... not always'. Later, we realize that they are implementing rules of discourse that have been formally taught; they are not concerned simply with the substantive topic of discussion but are monitoring their own behaviour and the process of orderly interaction itself. The rules of orderly discourse have parallels in the rules of orderly behaviour. For example, in one school, rules for talk formulated by pupils include: 'All have to have their say without being interrupted or laughed at; no one has to go on too long.' These might be said to parallel, or be derived from, school-wide rules of behaviour: 'We must show courtesy to others and respect their right to work in a friendly atmosphere.' In learning to work together in the classroom, perhaps pupils are also learning to co-exist with each other and their teachers. The relationship between teaching and behaviour is the focus of Chapter 3.

## PERSONAL HISTORIES OF EXCLUDED PUPILS

In this section I shall discuss data on some typical pupils who were thought to be beyond the reach of ordinary schools. These pupils had been excluded from secondary and senior special schools and in some cases from schools for the maladjusted and units for excluded pupils. These cases are therefore extreme ones. That the pupils are largely unremarkable in their behaviour, certainly in comparison with other troublesome pupils, is further support for the argument that where there is the will to cope with problem pupils, teachers can do so.

My first major post working with excluded pupils required me to find and visit them at home in order to arrange home tuition or attendance at my special centre. Before setting out to meet my new clients I looked at their files, from which I expected to learn all about them. Invariably they were little help, and it soon became clear that reports were not the simple records of events and explanations that I had naively expected. A similar problem confronted Garfinkel (1967) in trying to discover the selection criteria employed to choose applicants for hospital treatment. He found records to be so poorly completed that they were useless for his research project and he was led to ask why it was that the records at his disposal were so uniformly bad. He concluded that the hospital staff did not see the time involved as justified, and that the marginal utility of additional information was nil in circumstances where the use to which it might be put was unknown. Reporting carried risks to personal careers. For clinic staff, the chief function of the records appeared to be to provide evidence of the proper fulfilment of a therapeutic contract. They were compiled as insurance against the possible need to portray the clinical relationship as having been in accord with public expectations: 'Speaking euphemistically, between clinic persons and their clients and between the clinic and its environing groups the exchange of information is something less than a free market.'

Cicourel (1968), studying police reports on suspected offenders, found them to be constructed in such a way as to justify police interference, locate the suspect in a legal context and map the event in legally relevant categories. Appropriate 'prior information' was used to support statements, including past record and family problems. Reports and records are not straightforward, actuarial accounts; they are compiled for various reasons and always with an eye on their possible audiences – parents, colleagues, superiors. Even after the Education Act 1981 it is rarely possible to draw up a statement of a pupil's special educational needs without having regard to the resources likely to be available, the reactions of the various parties to the document, and the need to protect the pupil's teachers and school from appearing to be ineffective or unconcerned.

The reports I received had usually been assembled after a crisis and when the reporting institution had already decided that the pupil was beyond their control. Psychologists have noted that some schools refer to them not for advice about a pupil but after a decision that the pupil must be moved has already been reached (see Welton, 1982). Often, teachers had not filled in the official forms fully, preferring instead to write statements in their own way. It was not uncommon to find a folder with up to fifty headings but almost all of them blank. The primary school report on one pupil included brief biographical details, a reading age, and the words 'don't let him out of your sight'. In the records the principal concern seemed to be to show that the school had done all in its power with the pupil. All had tried everything they knew. A scent of failure hangs about any admission of inability to control a pupil, and this is particularly the case where the referring institution is itself meant to be a specialist resource for difficult pupils. One example shows the exasperation: 'I can assure you that everything possible has been done. We have tried to educate him in the normal way but he has made it impossible for his teachers to teach. We can no longer accept responsibility . . . disastrous days lie ahead.' Some reports evidenced the reluctance to admit that a pupil is being excluded or expelled: 'It is not that we do not want him. It is not that at all. The problem is that this school is not suitable for him.' At another case meeting a teacher said: 'We're sorry to do it, we don't want to lose him.' All the members of the staff present agreed that they did not want to lose him. Nevertheless, he was excluded the following day and sent to me.

Teachers were uncomfortable about expressing dislike of a pupil. The passive tense was used: 'Not a very likeable character.' Hargreaves *et al.* (1975) quote a number of teachers at length and an extract from one shows a similar discomfort: 'I must confess that I can't like him, you know. . . . I like them all really, even the ones who hate and irritate me, I do like them.' Nash (1973) suggests a taboo is in operation and Becker (1952) quotes a teacher who evidences guilt at his own harsh words: 'They're a bunch of bums, I might as well say it.' Some referred to a pupil's personal appearance as unattractive, unhealthy or odd looking: 'unprepossessing appearance – Gollum like'. Hoghughi (1978) writes about the unattractive appearance of so many of his pupils and suggests that this may have set in train a series of hostile reactions of dislike and avoidance. Stott (1982) makes a similar point. Attractiveness depends, to some extent, upon health, personal care and self-esteem, but it is far from an objective quality that some pupils may simply lack. Goode (in Barton and Tomlinson, 1982) describes his work with Breta, a massively disabled girl whose drooping gait and excessive salivation had led one of her teachers to compare her to a slug. Her mother viewed her differently but, aware of others' opinions, told Goode, apologetically: 'I know you won't understand this but we think Breta's beautiful really.' During his time in the home, Goode came to understand Breta as a person with likes, dislikes, expectations, routines and 'a beauty that was visible to the heart rather than the eye'. The lesson to be learnt here is that familiarity is needed: the opportunity to become acquainted with pupils as persons, not merely by description as they pass from one treatment agency to another.

Explanations and speculations on the causes of a pupil's behaviour, where they are offered, invariably do not refer to matters within the school. Home background or, more rarely, personal psychopathology are blamed. One school had compiled exceptionally comprehensive and detailed reports on a troublesome pupil, gathering in the process reports from the fourteen teachers who contributed to his timetable. Only one phrase in the collection referred to scholastic abilities or interests: 'a nearly complete lack of scientific awareness'. I did not notice at the time, nor did anyone else, that having fourteen teachers might have been one of this pupil's handicaps. There was much description of and speculation about the pupil's home background – there had been inconsistencies in his upbringing, mother was said to be ineffectual, father had been in prison, a neighbour was being paid to look after the boy. Attributing school problems to home background, and sometimes to inaccurate perceptions of it, is common among teachers (see, for example, Nash, 1973; Sharp and Green, 1975). The most sweeping example comes from a writer whose sympathy and dedication to working with difficult pupils was undeniable: 'I have come to the conclusion that where the parents seem quite normal it is only because we do not know enough about them' (Wills, 1967).

It has become customary to advise teachers to pay no heed to background factors and to concern themselves only with the rewards and punishments of the immediate classroom environment. Certainly, background information can engender a climate of despair, a feeling of powerlessness, and the abandonment of effort and responsibility. Yet it is well established that troublesome pupils do tend to come disproportionately from unhappy or unstable homes (Furlong, 1985). Hoghughi (1978) found only 5 per cent of the children in his assessment centre to have stable families. Chronic rows, divorce, alcoholism and psychiatric disturbance characterized most of the rest. The home situations of the pupils in my unit were varied – some were dirty and bare beyond belief; others were comfortable and well appointed. All the families had some degree of difficulty and some were in tragic states of disorder. Most blamed the schools for their children's problems. Some seemed to be excessively indulgent of their children while others were openly hostile, comparing them unfavourably with their siblings. Discussions with parents showed, however, that scarcely one had deliberately treated their child cruelly, permissively or inconsistently. The damage had been unintended. Parents had found themselves helpless in the face of seemingly uncontrollable and growing difficulties, with their efforts to regain control seeming to make matters worse. Teachers often feel the same way. In Chapter 4 we will see how this information can be used positively as a source of strength.

Sometimes referring institutions found themselves in a dilemma. To have a pupil moved they had to show that he or she was ungovernable, but in so doing they ran the risk of making the pupil appear unacceptable to the target special school or unit. This is another of the hidden functions teachers had to have in mind when compiling reports. This feature has been present from the early days. Wills (1945) writes: 'We usually find when a boy has been with us for a little while that there are other symptoms not mentioned by the referral agency.' In Wills' experience these other symptoms frequently included bed wetting and soiling as well as temper tantrums and 'dirty habits'. In one bizarre case a special school had transferred a pupil to an ordinary school after reporting on the telephone that he was not maladjusted as had been thought. When the boy's new school received the records, sure enough they stated that he was 'not maladjusted'. The report continued: 'He is a delinquent and must now face the consequences of his actions.' Not surprisingly, he did not remain long in his new school and was sent to me. I visited his original placement to discuss him. When I mentioned his name the teacher held both hands to his head, as if shutting out a painful noise, and uttered a long groan. Theatrical, but unambiguous, at least; and we shall see in Chapter 4 how such responses are an important clue to the nature of the pupil's problems.

That special schools and units, like some ordinary schools, find some pupils unacceptable is not evidence of irresponsibility. Centres were not opting for pupils who were in any general sense easier to cope with. For example, one unit tried to refuse pupils who were 'psychiatric problems, or low IQ'. This centre expressed a preference for tough pupils who were straightforwardly violent, and it managed them very well. In a survey of units for disruptive pupils, HMI (DES, 1978) quoted heads of centres who saw the need for 'control over the composition of the group'. Some recalled their early days when they had taken every school's most difficult pupils – their nominal purpose. They had found the work more congenial, and themselves more effective, with some sorts of problem rather than others. They now wanted the right to select and reject.

In an ordinary school which had set up a support system for trouble-some pupils, a similar phenomenon was observed. A pupil was eventually excluded, partly because he had not conformed to the school's view of a troublesome pupil's appropriate role. A personal counsellor had been made available whom the pupil had made use of, but not in the appropriate way: 'He comes here four or five times a day on some pretext or other. He does not discuss his problems with the counsellor or respond to the support systems – rather, he takes advantage of them.' Here we see limits, unintentionally hidden from the pupil, on how counselling may be used: some reasons for visits are defined as pretexts or as taking advantage of the system. A possible complicating factor might be that some pupils do not discuss relationships readily, nor are they coded to operate on them (see an early paper of Bernstein in Halsey *et al.*, 1961). Another example comes from the children's ward of a mental hospital: 'We have a very free regime here, we believe in letting them act out.' This free regime had unstated limitations, however, for the pupil under discussion was said to have taken advantage of it and to be more suitably placed with me. Bastide (1972), discussing the history of mental disorder, sums up this phenomenon as follows: 'Society plays as great a part as the sick person himself, who, to be recognised as sick has to make his behaviour conform to the behaviour traditionally expected of the madman.' To put it another way, 'how hard it sometimes is to recognise a madman' – a remark that is more profoundly informative than intended: it was attributed to Adolf Hitler (Speer, 1970).

Not one of the pupils referred to above was utterly beyond reach. Most of the time, most of them worked at much the same sort of materials they had failed to settle to elsewhere. In a small unit they, and I, were free from the many pressures of an ordinary high school. One of my pupils said he preferred to be in a school where 'there was not too much people'. In another unit the same sentiments were expressed in almost the same words. Asked what was different about the unit, one pupil said: 'Less pupils, there's less teachers, you get more attention, it's quite good. Not much people.'

It is undoubtedly easier to stay cool and disarming when critical audiences of colleagues and conforming pupils are absent. It is easy to arrange what Reynolds calls a 'truce' and others regard as 'simply a pretentious term for teachers not bothering anymore' (Musgrove, 1979). Pupils in the unit certainly notice a difference. Asked about any differences in the teachers they had now compared to those in their former school, several were eager to respond: 'At this place, they're a bit better – they understand kids like us. They've taught kids like us for years and years'; 'At my other school the teachers were too stressed out.' These teenagers had identified an attitude of understanding and a capacity to stay cool in their unit staff. How others can develop these characteristics is explained in Chapter 4.

HMI (DES, 1978) considers the possibility that small units enable the development of personal relationships, a freer atmosphere and greater flexibility. Lovey *et al.* (1993) found that the most popular programme of work in units consisted of basic mathematics and English, together with informal counselling and club-type games and activities. Significantly, in the light of the evidence for the importance of oracy, one of Lovey's respondents stressed that informal counselling 'involves listening'.

All this may be close to suggesting that behavioural units can be a soft option for both pupils and staff. This is not the view of some unit pupils, however: 'Teachers are more strict here. At my old school, if you didn't do your work they didn't do nothing, but here they make you get on with it'; 'If you talk in a lesson, or if you go to the toilet without permission, you get punished.' As it is clear that the teachers in these pupils' former schools had not 'done nothing' to make them behave, it must be that the pupils themselves were voluntarily co-operating. No doubt they had more respect for teachers they perceived as more under- standing: 'You can have a laugh with them here.' For many, being in a smaller group of people protected them from humiliation. Talking about why he had been permanently excluded, one apparently tough youth could not conceal the pain in his expression when he said, in a soft voice: 'I'm not that good at reading and writing.' An interesting feature of many units, in the light of the importance of oracy in ordinary schools, is the stress put on negotiating rules, routines and punishments. If apparently ungovernable pupils in exclusion units can engage in rational discussion perhaps the opportunity should have been made available (or seized) earlier. There are no compelling reasons to believe that the favourable aspects of small units cannot be reproduced in ordinary schools. Examples of effective high schools have already been described. We have also noted the difficulty in finding agreement upon what sort of behaviour is so serious as to necessitate permanent exclusion from school. This is not to say that no such behaviour exists, but only that it is exceedingly rare and certainly insufficient to justify a large and growing behavioural unit sector. From only a handful in 1973 there are now several hundred and possibly as many as a thousand (DES, 1978; *Where?*, May 1980; Graham, 1988). The proliferation of units and assessment centres increases the uncertainty for some pupils. What from the administrative point of view is a series of specialized assessments, trial placements and treatments is subjectively experienced by the pupils as a career of rejection. Hoghughi (1978) notes that circulating pupils in this way can only increase their feelings of confusion and rejection; he mentions a pupil who had been in almost twenty placements. There is also an inherent illogicality in trying to re- adjust pupils by removing them from that to which they are not adjusted. The existence of separate provision is itself a discouragement to schools to find ways of accommodating their difficult pupils. The more complex the education system is as a whole, with respect to types of institution, the more likely it is that each institution will be able to specialize. Ordinary schools may find it easier to reject unwanted pupils rather than cope with them, and each special unit will find it easier to specialize, too: only the withdrawn, or only the dull and violent, or only the intelligent truants. All will be able to become more restrictive and increasingly closed to the full range and variety of pupils, to the long-term detriment of comprehensive education in all its senses.

Three tests have been proposed for behaviour that is certain to be universally regarded as abnormal in all cultures and at all times: gross unpredictability; permanent inaccessiblity to communication; and consistent lack of minimum control of impulses (Kluckhohn, quoted in Bastide, 1972). Whatever allowance is made for interpretation and ambiguity, few pupils in any type of school or unit cross these barriers. Inaccessibility to communication depends partly upon the skill and persistence of the other party. Whether a person is grossly unpredictable or lacks impulse control (which is another way of describing unpredictability) is also dependent upon the observer. In any case, everyone's behaviour is, strictly speaking, unpredictable (incomprehensible is closer to what is meant here). Looking too closely and for too short a time, as in physics, makes events look random and inexplicable: viewed in context and over time, patterns and explanations emerge. In support of this it is worth noting that in all the cases discussed there was always at least one teacher who found the pupil amenable. Sometimes it was a confident, almost arrogant, statement: 'He was all right for me.' Others seemed to be genuinely puzzled: 'I could never understand it. Every staff meeting there was somebody saying what a horrendous character she was but she was no trouble in here. She was all right for me.' Hargreaves *et al.* observed this phenomenon and noted its significance for understanding pupil deviance: 'Given that the conduct of the same class varies enormously with different teachers, any explanation which rests exclusively at the pupil level must be deficient' (Hargreaves *et al.*, 1975). Whole classes vary in their behaviour from 'hungry half-starved wolves ... [to] docile lambs' (Wittrock, 1986: 409). Where there is the willingness, reflected in organizational flexibility and personal professionalism, schools can cope with troublesome pupils. There is no good reason for despair in ordinary classrooms.

## CONCLUSIONS

Some value assumptions are implicit in the argument of this chapter. First, that teachers' strategies and school organization affect pupil behaviour, and not the other way round. Second, there is an underlying implication that harmonized schools are superior to synchronized: values intrude here, as it may be said they do in Reynolds' (1985) notion of coercion–incorporation and Hargreaves' (1967) description of insulati-ve–provocative teachers.

My particular interest is in factors affecting rates of exclusion and methods of reducing those rates, for there is evidence that exclusion itself is associated with later offending, irrespective of the severity of the reason for it. For example, in England, school reports influence magistrates' sentencing policies and excludees are twice as likely to receive custodial sentences; in Scotland, all the excludees in a sample of 678 offenders were referred to hearings (Graham, 1988). Excludees may be simply more serious offenders but in a London survey, most excluded pupils claimed their behaviour was no worse than that of some of their friends who escaped exclusion (Mortimore et al., 1983). This does not clear up the matter, however, for troublesome pupils are at least as inclined to blame others for their problems as anyone else. But it does seem reasonable to conclude that schools which can hold on to their clients are more likely to keep them from a criminal career. It may be not just failure at school but the school's response to that failure that is significant for pupils' future careers: delinquency is 'at least partly contingent upon rejecting or being rejected by the school' (Graham, 1988). There may be no simple, one-directional cause. Teachers may feel constrained to be confrontational or disarming; they may feel that they are reacting to circumstances (rather than initiating them) by the pressure of pupil behaviour or parental and societal demands. Even infant pupils are able to constrain teachers' roles in classrooms (Bruner, 1980). Some pupils probably feel similarly caught up in situations which seem to leave them no alternative. It may be the case that confrontational strategies are less likely to lead to higher exclusion rates in schools with favoured catchments. A policy may be ineffective in some circumstances and effective in others. Reid et al. warn against applying generalizations to all schools and note the 'hints in the literature – little else – that some schools do particularly well for low-ability pupils but not for high-ability pupils' (Reid et al., 1987: 35). This cautions against the uncritical adoption of policies seen to be favourable in another environment. Teachers' strategies are, and I would add ought to be, individually motivated, interpersonally adapted and situationally adjusted (Woods, 1980b). The evidence discussed here suggests that change is needed at both the organizational and personal level: schools must attend to behaviour and referral policies, and also to methods of teaching and learning, as well as to the personal developmental needs of staff.

The organizational change that is needed is that group tutors and year teams need allocations of time, delegated responsibility and the encouragement to use their autonomy to work co-operatively with difficult pupils. To make this latter possible, some teachers will need to increase their understanding of, and ability to analyse and cope with, pupils'

motives and strategies. This will involve embracing philosophies and practices consonant with the harmonized type of school described earlier:
discipline becomes restitutive; individual voices are listened to and valued
for the information they give about individual needs; pupils' talk is
valued because it aids teachers' understanding and interpretation of
pupils' actions; and it is valued because it helps identify the positive
contributions that might be expected and secured from pupils who are
presently disaffected. Schools like St Luke's, where talk is constrained by
a one-sided expectation of a 'satisfactory response' and staff are 'unim-
pressed by meetings', need to move towards the outlook typified by St
Matthew's, where consultation, reflection and talk are respected.

In formulating policy on behaviour it is not enough to determine a list
of rules and attach rewards and sanctions. Addressing the issue requires
four phases: rules, opportunities, support and pedagogy. In the first, class
teachers discuss with their pupils five or six rules. If the pupils produce
a list of prohibitions (as they might in rule-bound, difficult-to-discipline
schools), they can be invited to consider how rules can be formulated in
positive and encouraging ways. This exercise can be tailored to the particular needs of each school. For example, if bullying is an issue, then
specific methods of monitoring, support, punishment or restitution can be
formulated. Lateness, litter, graffiti, neglect of homework or any other
matter can be given emphasis. The rules and policies so generated can
be collated at school level through joint meetings of pupils and staff
through, for example, a school council. The results are then communicated
or taught where necessary.

The second phase involves ensuring that pupils have enough opportunities to demonstrate self-discipline and exercise responsibility. Securing
conformity to reasonable behaviour is only the start: pupils must be able
to grow into responsible, independent people who value good behaviour
for its own sake and not merely because it avoids punishment and brings
rewards. Opportunities might be to support staff through prefect roles, to
help younger pupils or lower attainers, to organize lunchtime or after-
school clubs or to represent fellow pupils at school meetings or councils.

The third phase requires staff to review the means by which pupils are
guided and supported. This includes such basic matters as ensuring that
absentees and latecomers are monitored, and impediments to attendance
and promptness addressed: to be careless of pupils' attendance will
encourage some to believe, perhaps correctly, that their presence is not
welcomed or valued. Support also includes a wide range of provision
from ordinary day-to-day safety and welfare to careers guidance. It should
not neglect those intangible aspects of school life in which we aim to
impart civilized values: an appreciation of spiritual values and religious
beliefs; an interest in moral issues and a reasoned approach to them; a
sense of social and personal responsibility and the rights and duties that

society incorporates; and an openness to and understanding of the variety of cultural experience available within and beyond pupils' own locality.

Finally, schools need to ensure that pupils' classroom experience is congruent with the school's wider policies and ethos. Teaching and learning are the subjects of Chapter 3, but we have already identified an important aspect of classroom experience – oracy and its relationship to rates of exclusion. If pupils are to take discussion in relation to behaviour seriously it must be apparent in all aspects of schools' provision. Pupils learn to respect others and behave reasonably when they take turns in discussion in classrooms. In practising their German conversation, or talking through a mathematics problem, or arguing the moral issues in women's suffrage, they are learning courtesy, respect for others and their duty to act responsibly under the rule of law.

## ACTIVITY 2.1: WHAT TYPE ARE YOU?

This exercise is derived from the work discussed in this chapter. Therefore, it may not be of interest to schools which have no reason to be concerned about the issues raised in it. The purpose is to explore how helpful it is, if helpful at all, to apply theoretical types to one's own situation. The first two tasks are necessarily crude but they serve, by bringing some elegant ideas down to earth, as a stimulus to discussion. First, look at the ten statements below and decide whether you agree with them or not. Second, tick those types of behaviour on the list that you think would seriously threaten your teaching or control. Third, spend a few minutes looking at the summary of types and strategies before sharing your thoughts in groups of three or four. Do not feel constrained to hide any reservations you may have about this exercise; they indicate the complexity of the task of teaching and the need for a critical approach.

### Opinions on troublesome pupils

 1 They like fair, firm and clear rules.
 2 They are determined not to conform to rules.
 3 They work when teachers organize properly.
 4 Improvements do not last, they do not change.
 5 If I punish them I let them 'save face'.
 6 They should not be in the classroom. Refer them.
 7 I like them all really, share a joke.
 8 Basically they are not interested in work.
 9 I think they are all potentially winnable.
10 I show who the boss is, warn then punish.

**Types of pupil behaviour**

Arriving late
Tapping other pupils
Asking to go to toilet repeatedly
Missing lesson, absconding
Smoking in toilets
Rude remarks under breath
Pushing past teacher
Refusing to do set work
Playing with matches in class
Running on corridor or stairs
Cheeky remarks to teacher
Talking when meant to be writing
Keeping coat on in class
Open abuse to teacher
Fighting others in class
Chasing round room
Setting off fire-alarm
Throwing pencil across room
Talking when teacher talking
Packing up early, as if to leave
Unauthorized drawing on book
Taking pupil's property
Failing to bring homework
Unruly on way to school
Taking teacher's property
Graffiti on corridor wall
Damaging classroom fittings
Bizarre clothing, make-up
Rocking on chair defiantly
Hitting teacher
Fighting in yard
Threatening teacher
Swearing at pupil in class
Attempting smoking in class
Refusing punishment
Leaving class early
Comments on exercise

For the first task, insulative or disarming teachers would probably agree with the odd numbers and disagree with the even ones. Most people have difficulty deciding without having a particular pupil, event and situation in mind. This illustrates the point made about the validity of strategies as opposed to styles. In the second task, on average, about half the items are ticked. A low score might indicate that you are unflappable, or that you have iron discipline; again, more needs to be known about the particular circumstances.

*Teacher style/strategy and school ethos/climate*

| | |
|---|---|
| *Deviance-insulative* (Hargreaves et al., 1975) exemplified by: | *Deviance-provocative* exemplified by: |
| Allowing face-saving and avoiding confrontations | Contest view of interaction, ultimatums/confrontations |
| Avoiding differential treatment | Neglect and denigration of deviants |
| Optimistic, defence of deviants | Expects trouble, punishes inconsistently |
| Belief that they really want to work, encouraging any sign of progress | Pupils don't want to work, apparent improvement is deceit or cover for hostility |
| Informal relationships, respect, humour, sympathy | No outside contacts, ready referral to authority |
| leads to (?): | leads to (?): |
| *Incorporative ethos* (Reynolds, 1985) exemplified by: | Coercive ethos exemplified by: |
| Minimum institutional control or 'truce' | High level of control and punishment |
| Hesitation in enforcing rules likely to cause rebellion | Strict enforcement |
| Participation by both pupils and parents | Low pupil and parent participation |
| Underestimation of degree of social deprivation (optimistic) | Overestimation of degree of social deprivation (pessimistic) |
| High expectations of pupils' ability | Underestimation of pupils' ability |
| *Disarming strategy* leads to: | *Confrontational strategy* leads to: |
| Harmonious atmosphere, where teachers are: | Synchronized atmosphere, where teachers are: |
| composed | autocratic |
| impassive | unbending |
| dispassionate | dominant |
| serene | formal |
| unruffled | stressed |
| shatterproof | brittle |
| and | and |
| many parts are played and many tunes are possible (minuets, modern jazz) | there is only one tune and we keep in step or we do not march at all |

## ACTIVITY 2.2: EXCLUSION AND DISCIPLINE QUIZ

### Local Education Authorities

1 If the Local Education Authority (LEA) asks a school to allow an excluded pupil back in order to complete coursework and take examinations, how should the head respond?

2 The LEA insists that an excluded pupil be readmitted, but the head knows that governors and staff will object. What action should the head take?

3 The parents of a pupil excluded from another school, who has a conviction for assault, is seeking a school place and is supported by the LEA. What possible responses does a reluctant school have?

4 Can an LEA insist on being represented at all meetings and sub-committees of the governors where exclusions are considered?

### Governors

5 Headteachers are the only members of school staff permitted to exclude pupils, but when the head is absent can the chair of governors exclude?

6 When the governors express the view that a school's discipline is too harsh or too slack, what are their powers and what are the duties of a headteacher?

7 If a governor feels that behaviour problems are arising out of the weakness of a particular teacher, should the head yield to a request to visit the teacher, observe the teaching and gather his or her point of view?

8 A governor, who is a local shopkeeper, wants action to be taken about unruly pupils who gather around his shop at lunchtimes and after school. The shop is half a mile from the school. How should the head respond?

### Headteachers

9 Should the head be on the sub-committee of governors considering a parent's complaint about an exclusion?

10 What should be in the letter sent to the parents when a pupil is excluded?

11 Is a head right to insist on permanent exclusion whenever a pupil is guilty of an offence which, for an adult, would carry a prison sentence?

12 In a struggle to detain a pupil after school for disciplinary reasons, a teacher breaks a pupil's arm and collar bone. The police are to pros-

ecute for assault. Should the head act and, if so, how should the impending prosecution be weighed?

## Teachers

13 In breaking up a fight, a teacher punched a pupil, causing superficial bruising. Does this contravene the law against corporal punishment?
14 Does a teacher have the right to refuse to teach a pupil who has been reinstated after being excluded for assaulting her?
15 A parent has written expressing a wish to meet a teacher who is alleged to have used excessive force in disciplining her son. The parent is a solicitor by profession. What should the teacher do?
16 On lunch duty, a teacher is called to a fight by the school gate. One pupil is unconscious on the ground. By chance, a police officer is passing and he begins to question the pupils about the incident. Should the teacher prevent this until parents can be called?

## Pupils and parents

17 The parents of a family of two difficult children have been advised by the head to seek places in other schools. Meanwhile, both children have been told to remain at home pending transfers. What are the parents' rights and responsibilities?
18 A statemented child is refused admission to a school on the grounds that it lacks the expertise to cope with the emotional and behavioural difficulties identified. The LEA has already indicated that additional funds will not be made available, although 'appropriate support' is mentioned in the Statement. What can the parent do?
19 A pupil has been excluded for fifteen days in each of three terms. All the proper procedures have been followed, but do parents have any redress when their children are excluded repeatedly?
20 The parents have received a letter informing them that their child is to remain at home until such time as they attend a meeting to discuss the child's behaviour. After many fruitless attempts to make an appointment outside working hours, it becomes apparent that the head expects attendance during the school day, thus involving financial loss. What rights do the parents have?

## Answers and comments

What follows is merely guidance and does not constitute authoritative legal advice. The particular details of incidents can result in different outcomes, and the law is subject to modification by parliament and through decisions in particular cases. Full details of procedures are available in 'Exclusions from school' (DfE circular 10/94) and 'Misconduct of teachers and workers with children and young people' (DES memorandum 3/82).

1 Loss of the opportunity to take an examination is a serious matter and LEAs can insist on schools permitting pupils to return for that purpose. The DfE circulars do not mention coursework, but as it contributes to examination results schools should consider reasonable requests to allow it to be completed. Where excluded pupils abuse these concessions, for example by disrupting an examination, then, of course, they can be instantly excluded again.

2 LEAs can direct reinstatement in cases of permanent or fixed-term exclusions of more than five days or where a public examination might be missed. They must first consult the governors.

3 If there is room in the school the pupil must be accepted. Natural justice demands that the pupil be given the opportunity to make a success of the new placement.

4 No. DfE circular 10/94 expresses the hope that all concerned will bear in mind the need for close co-operation, but this does not give the LEA powers of representation. It must be informed when a pupil is permanently excluded or when a pupil might miss a public examination.

5 No. In exceptional circumstances a deputy head can act in the head's absence. Heads should always satisfy themselves that exclusion is appropriate and not rubber-stamp the recommendations of others.

6 Governors are responsible for approving a school's disciplinary policies, so they can influence it by setting general guidelines. Their role is strategic, and day-to-day operational matters are the responsibility of the head.

7 An individual governor has no rights or powers of any kind. If the governing body as a whole has concerns about a particular teacher, then it should raise the matter with the head. Although governors often are encouraged to join in the school's activities, this does not extend to assessing the performance of individual teachers in the classroom.

8 As in question 7, governors can only act as a body. If they feel the complaint is based on fact, then the head can be asked to act upon it. No reasonable head, however, would decline to intervene in such a clear case as this – irrespective of how he or she learned of it. In such cases, the difficulty is how far the school can be held responsible for the behaviour of its pupils out of school hours and away from the site. Cases have determined that it is reasonable for the pupils to be subject to school discipline when travelling to and from school, reason-

ably near it, and when they are identifiable as being from the school (by uniform, for example).

9 Certainly not. The head is the person with the sole right to exclude, and he or she cannot act in a disinterested way. The governors should ensure, when parents exercise their 'right to make representations', that the environment avoids intimidation and excessive formality. The minimum sub-committee of three should normally be enough, and governors would be wise to ensure that this committee includes a parent-governor.

10 The letter, prompt and backed up by a telephone call or a visit if appropriate, should state the exact length of the exclusion, if it is not permanent, make the specific reasons for it clear and inform the parents of all relevant circumstances. Parents must also be notified of their right to make representations to the governors or LEA. If the exclusion is permanent, details of previous warnings, disciplinary action and exclusions should also be notified and parents informed of their right of access to the school's curricular and other educational records on their child.

11 No. In deciding an appropriate punishment the head should take account of the individual(s) concerned, the school's behaviour policies and the severity of the impact upon the life of the school – in addition to the law, if appropriate. The DfE circular stresses that exclusion should be reserved for serious misbehaviour and full account taken of mitigating factors, such as domestic trauma, peer pressure and previous record. Research evidence discussed in Chapter 2 indicates that an inflexible list of offences automatically earning exclusion is likely to result in a high exclusion rate and injustice for some pupils.

12 The head in conjunction with the governors will have to make a judgement in the light of all the circumstances, which include the effect of any decision on the life of the school. The decision made by the police is a separate one – a factor to be considered but not a constraint. The force might be construed as reasonable: for example, where a strong and violent pupil was detained in order to prevent him or her from assaulting a weaker one on the way home. Even the outcome of the court case does not require the school to follow any particular action. Police are required to inform the Department for Education of convictions for some offences including violence, but employers must inform the Department only of dismissals for misconduct (irrespective of whether a criminal offence occurred).

13 As before, the individual circumstances determine the answer. A punch might have been necessary to prevent injury to another party, perhaps where a pupil had a weapon. If that intention can be proved, then no offence occurred. If the punch was a teacher's angry or

disciplinary response, then the law was broken. The head and governors must consider all the factors, as in question 12.

14 If the teacher feels it is unreasonable to have to teach such a pupil,
and the head disagrees, then the normal grievance procedure will have
to be activated and the matter judged on its merits.

15 The teacher should pass the letter to the head. If both agree to such
a meeting there is no problem: it is good policy for parents and
teachers to meet to solve problems, as long as neither side is intimidated. The head can decide to meet the parent – particularly if the
teacher refuses. A teacher could not be compelled to meet the parent,
nor could he or she be disciplined for refusing a head's instruction to
do so, unless it could be shown that the head's request was reasonable.

16 The teacher should summon the head immediately. Parents should be
present, but in emergencies the head is able to take the parents' place.

17 This is quite wrong and an allegedly common way of circumventing
the exclusion procedures. The parents should continue to send their
children to the school. If they are excluded the parents have the right
to make representations to the governors and the LEA.

18 The school cannot refuse the pupil on such grounds. Schools have a
responsibility to provide for their pupils' needs. The Statement should
specifically state the amount of support to be allocated and this is
then a legal entitlement.

19 The DfE circular says that when a child's behaviour repeatedly war-
rants exclusion the school should be actively looking for ways of
breaking the cycle. It is not expected that single exclusions of fifteen
days will be normal. If the parents suspect their child is being unfairly
treated, and neither governors nor LEA accept this, then an appeal
can be made to the Secretary of State or the Ombudsman: the grounds
would be unreasonable conduct and failure in a duty.

20 This is not permitted and is an example of the indefinite exclusion
that is now abolished. Even where parents refuse to attend the school,
and deny visiting teachers access to their home, it is wrong to exclude
as a means of bringing the parents into line. The interests of the child
are not served by exclusion being used in this way.

## ACTIVITY 2.3: WHICH HEADTEACHER FOR YOU?

Look back at the statements by the headteachers of St Luke's and St
Matthew's. Both convey a flavour of life in their schools, as well as
informing us about their own particular style of management and
leadership.

Consider which school you would prefer to work for. Specify the criteria
you have used and discuss how these relate to your own view of the
professional responsibilities of teachers. Think about what the conse-

quences might be for the education system as a whole if in choosing for yourself you were choosing for all teachers.

## Comments on the activity

This task raises a number of issues, from the relatively simple matter of securing a congenial post to the wider moral and social implications of educational policies. These issues will be developed further in subsequent chapters.

## ACTIVITY 2.4: THE EXCLUSION

At the end of the following short story some points for reflection are suggested.

### The exclusion

'It seems a rather excessive punishment to me,' said the Chair. She looked at the headteacher and waited.

'There is a rule,' said the head flatly, taking off his glasses and rubbing his nose.

The Chair looked exasperated. She made an effort to sound patient. 'Permanent exclusion for stealing an item of such little value.'

The head shrugged. 'Rules are made to be obeyed.'

'Yes, I know, but what I'm asking is whether you don't think, with hindsight, that it is rather a harsh rule, rather inflexible. It isn't as though the young person had been previously troublesome.'

'Persons,' corrected the head.

'Persons, yes. And that's another thing. Surely the boy was not to know – the girl deceived him didn't she?'

The head sighed. He reminded himself that he must keep calm if he was to have any chance of having the appeal against his action thrown out. It was a challenge to his authority, just as the theft had been.

'The rule had been made quite clear and explicit to both of them. He must have known what he was doing. It was a direct challenge to the rule – the only prohibition I might point out – and it was therefore a clear challenge to my authority. If you want me to run the place, I have to have authority.'

'I don't wish to challenge your authority, but I do think the rule should be reconsidered.'

'It's irrelevant now,' said the head, 'unless I am compelled to let them back in.'

The Chair looked around the table. No one spoke.

The head, taking the silence as acceptance of his last statement, looked encouraged. 'The inspectors' report said that behaviour was excellent. Are you suggesting that it would improve if this theft – as you call it – were to be overlooked?'

The Chair looked tired. 'I'm simply saying that there are other responses short of permanent exclusion that might have been satisfactory in this case. I seem to remember the report saying that there were insufficient opportunities for the pupils to exercise self-discipline and individual responsibility.'

'That's nonsense,' said the head, momentarily losing his patience. He recovered himself. 'They were given sole charge of the garden area and the animals. They were trusted and given every encouragement, but they abused that trust. They broke a clear rule and I took that as a direct challenge to my authority.'

The Chair held up a hand and interrupted. 'Please. Your authority is not at stake. It is a simple matter of a minor theft.'

'It is not minor,' said the head warmly. 'I made a rule and it was broken. I made a decision to exclude and it is challenged. Perhaps you'd like to run the place yourself?'

'We have every confidence in your ability,' said the Chair wearily. 'But we return again to the precipitate nature of your actions; after all, you had been in the post only a week when this occurred.'

'Six days,' corrected the head.

'Six days,' repeated the Chair. They seemed to be deadlocked again. She looked over the papers, and then, as if noticing it for the first time, 'It says here that they were naked when you found them. Is that true?'

'Almost naked,' said the head. 'They were not excluded for that – though it was related to the theft, of course, as they were hiding from me. They had absconded in effect – I had to look for them; they were not where they were supposed to be.' He looked at his watch.

The Chair sat back and placed her hands on the table. They were getting nowhere, she reflected. This was what happened when you put men in charge; they stood on their dignity and saw every trivial transgression as an attack on their authority.

The head moved forward in his chair as if to get up. 'I told them to leave the fruit tree alone but they defied me. That's the issue: defiance of authority, not theft of fruit.'

The Chair smiled; his obsession with his authority was faintly ludicrous. The head smiled back; maybe she was not entirely incapable of seeing his point of view after all. He had put his case and that was that. Few others had accomplished as much as he had in such a short time. If they overruled him it would be their loss.

He stood up. 'They're outside. Shall I send one of them in?'

The Chair nodded. 'We must get on.'

The head strode to the door. Outside in the passage sat a boy and a girl. The boy's clothing was rough and dirty; his face and hands were grimed, the nails blackened with soil like a farmworker's. He looked worn out and he sat with his head in his hands. The girl stared boldly up at the head, and he noticed without surprise that she was obviously pregnant; she was eating, noisily and with obvious enjoyment, a large apple. God knows what their children will be like, he found himself thinking; and then he smiled to himself.

'The appeals committee will see you now,' he said. 'One at a time. You first, Adam.'

## Points for reflection

1 You should be able to relate the theme of this story to the discussion and research in this chapter and identify the argument it seeks to support.
2 At a practical level, identify the policies and actions that would be supported by the argument of the story.
3 In a more reflective stance, identify the ethical issues raised, consider your responses and clarify your own position in relation to exclusions.
4 If this story has led you to modify your attitudes – or to hold your views with more caution – consider how you might pass on these benefits to others.

# Chapter 3

# Teacher qualities and classroom management skills

> Those actors who say a dull audience is a challenge and all that crap know nothing about the theatre. They are only voicing their own inadequacy.
>
> (*The Kenneth Williams Letters* [Davies, ed., 1994])

If acting is the art of stopping people coughing, teaching is the art of stopping them throwing things about. For hard-pressed teachers of difficult children the whole concept of classroom management seems to embody an unattainable ideal. Children whose behaviour is predictable only in its unpredictability can effortlessly thwart attempts to plan and implement any goal-directed activity. In reviewing their lesson planning, many teachers often find themselves in the same position as the British Surgeon General in the Crimean War. Asked why the medical services had collapsed, he is said to have replied: 'The medical services would have been perfectly adequate if it had not been for the casualties' (Taylor, 1969).

Silcock (1993) seems to challenge the idea that effectiveness in the classroom can be taught, suggesting that preparing trainees for the social encounters is work enough. Those of a therapeutic disposition might wonder whether management should even be a goal with difficult pupils. Control, which is what is often meant by management, has already failed – and dogged attempts at imposing it might even have contributed to pupils' problems. Control might itself be part of the problem. Laing and Chazan (1986) suggest that organizational routines that compel ordinary young children to participate can themselves create incentives to opt out and disrupt. Many disturbed children treat themselves more aggressively than they do others. Rose (1991) noted that many of the children he cared for in a residential setting were unable to differentiate between well-meaning adults and those they had met first – 'their frequently exploitative parents'. Such children easily mistake management (with the aim of securing education) for coercion towards a sinister if undefined objective. As Cooper (1993) puts it, 'teachers' control strategies can some-times exacerbate rather than alleviate problem situations'.

This sort of talk makes no impression on teachers faced with ungovern-able pupils. Whatever the antecedents and the ideal might be, someone has to cope with day-to-day responsibilities. Before we consider what skills might be effective we can draw one conclusion from the discussion so far. Teachers' personal qualities as well as their technical skills are vital. Teachers have to be good in two senses of the word: they must be good in the sense of being effective in the skills of classroom management; and they must be good in that they must be morally good, possessing natural virtues. In teaching, the concept of professionalism needs perhaps to incorporate the older notions of vocation and selfless service that have been displaced by a twentieth-century focus on functional expertise (Kimball, 1994).

Interestingly, Cooper (1993) gathered a list of complaints about teachers from disaffected, difficult boys in a residential school and contrasted this with the qualities the head looked for in staff. The head spoke of the need for approachability, a commitment to comprehensive education and the ability to make good relationships with children. She was not asked to elaborate on what she meant by a commitment to comprehensive education, but it is reasonable to assume that this encompassed respect for individual needs and a concern that all pupils, irrespective of ability, should make the best of themselves. The last criterion she mentioned was academic breadth. The teacher characteristics disapproved of by the boys included being 'stuck up, unfriendly, humourless', indicating that they shared their headteacher's views on the essential personal qualities of teachers.

These notions have a long history in education. When, in 1699, The Society for the Propagation of Christian Knowledge set about establishing Charity Schools, it listed the criteria to be met by teachers. These included: 'Good government of himself and his passions, of a meek temper and humble behaviour' (quoted in Sturt, 1967). Earlier still, George Snell wrote of the need for teachers to have 'a gentle demeanour, a pious qualitie, unwearied industrie and invincible patience' (quoted in Sturt, 1967). Perhaps (if we modernize the language) we should give Thomas Arnold more credit than is customary for his nineteenth-century exhor-tation to the pupils of Rugby School: 'What we must look for here is, first, religious and moral principles; secondly, gentlemanly conduct; thirdly, intellectual ability.'

The view, once common, that education was not a priority with trouble-some children no longer commands much assent. In a standard text on the education of maladjusted children, Laslett (1977) wrote that 'edu-cational needs are not foremost' and described schools for the mal-adjusted as 'a preparation for learning elsewhere'. A later work, however

(Laslett and Smith, 1984), provides a comprehensive and concise guide to teaching skills appropriate for all pupils and includes advice on coping with more serious problems in the classroom. Wills (1967), a pioneer of residential maladjustment therapy, came to the view that perhaps he had 'underrated the importance of the education factor'. Brennan (1979) takes the educational requirements for granted in a heavily critical report. HMI (DES, 1978) commented upon the inevitably restricted curriculum of disruptive centres. At the time of its report, these centres were increasing in number and it was becoming possible for some pupils to spend the whole of their school lives in them. Warnock (DES, 1978) drew attention to the recognition of educational failure as a factor in maladjustment and noted that, although some still perceived a conflict between education and therapy, schools increasingly emphasized the quality of the education they provided. Warnock found it necessary to justify the provision of education for the full range of pupils with disabilities, and it is easy to underestimate the magnitude of this achievement; education in the ordinary sense, not therapy and treatment, is now taken for granted.

The teacher skills and qualities required by teachers of troublesome pupils are often those that any teacher might need. The classroom management focus of the materials in Chisholm *et al.* (1984) is an example. Research upon which such programmes may be based is reported in Fontana (1985), Wragg (1984) and Walter Doyle's chapter of Wittrock (1986). A recent summary (Wragg, 1993) shows that, although detail is constantly being added, the catalogue of teaching skills is much as it has been for many years. (Compare, for example, Wragg, 1984.) Robertson (1981) emphasizes, among an abundance of ideas and suggestions, the importance of the teacher presenting as an authority figure. It is easy to criticize this particular aspect as being irrelevant to the situation in schools. Perhaps this is so, or ought to be so, and in secondary education unsubtle forms of control are usually less effective. However, it is worth noting some remarks by Kohl (1986) in this respect. A liberal advocate of openness and democracy, he nevertheless found the need to assert his authority from time to time:

> In one short week I went from informal Herb, with an open collar and sweater, to Mr Kohl with a suit and tie, a very controlled manner and an unnatural, stern look. My students had taught me that I had to establish my authority before I could teach them anything.
>
> (Kohl, 1986: 38)

Hoghughi (1978) draws up a demanding list of qualities for those working with troublesome children: teachers must be stable, compassionate, sensitive, intelligent, resilient, mature and, ominously, physically fit. Laslett (1977) prescribes predicability and reliability but with exposure to less tolerant outsiders too. Wills (1967), with characteristic elegance, says, 'to live with maladjusted children you must be able to live without them and indeed without anyone – a whole complete person entirely sufficient unto yourself'. Hewett and Blake, reviewing the literature in Travers (1973), suggest that teachers of troublesome pupils do not need to assume a unique professional role: 'A competent teacher is a competent teacher whether working with disturbed or normal children.' This is true in so far as all teachers must be teachers of groups, able to cope with the unpredictable demands, the overlapping activities and the dynamics of maintaining public order in classrooms. Classroom management skills, by definition, primarily encompass the task of orderly management, but that is not co-terminous with the task of managing disorder. Classroom management is an essential basis, but controlling and helping troublesome pupils require other skills and insights, which will be described in Chapter 4.

## BASIC CLASSROOM MANAGEMENT SKILLS

There are fundamental difficulties in trying to describe classroom teaching skills. These difficulties are related to those encountered in attempts to teach, or persuade others to teach, using behavioural objectives. The act of teaching is something more than the sum of its parts, and attempts to define it closely seem doomed to destroy that which they would describe. To a considerable extent, human activities are beyond complete description: accounts, tape-recordings and films cannot capture the amount and complexity of events; some things are missed, changed or destroyed in the act of data gathering. In the example given by I. Reid (1986), watching a video of a football match is not the same as being there. In addition, observers have attempted to quantify the complexity of teaching: for example, Jackson (1968) estimated more than 500 interactions in a typical teacher's day.

Teaching is rarely apprehended as the putting of skills into practice. When a lesson is going well it may be experienced as an energetic blend of interaction and involvement, varying pace and tempo, new insights and explanations, and unexpected outcomes. Teaching skills are difficult to get a purchase on because they are dynamic rather than mechanistic in character (Eisner, 1982). The skills used in a successful lesson, and the objectives achieved, are easier to think about after the event. This does not contradict the argument that a description of teaching skills cannot completely capture the reality of classroom life. Reflecting on the characteristics of a good lesson can help identify techniques for use in future encounters; this is a long way from claiming that the success of future lessons can be guaranteed if certain skills (or objectives, for that matter) are used. This chapter and the three following should be read with this caution in mind.

These chapters constitute the substance of the in-service work that I hope teachers will be able to replicate in their own schools. In translating a course that was conducted in seminar rooms and teachers' own schools into a textbook some things are inevitably lost. I have tried to resist the temptation to write just another academic thesis, although many references are given here that appeared only in supplementary handouts to the course. There is a convention, to which Eisner (1985: 158) alerts us, that 'the less expressive a description is, the truer it appears to be. Yet if there is an absence of emotional or qualitative content, the description risks leaving out more of what is important in the classroom.' As far as possible, the text is faithful to the pre-service and in-service courses on which it is based, and the intention is to convey something of their atmosphere.

It often appears that experienced teachers have trouble-free lessons, not through knowing how to cope with troublesome behaviour, but simply because it does not seem to arise in their classrooms. The skills of classroom management become part of a taken-for-granted procedure, and often neither the practitioner nor the inexperienced observer is able to identify them. The ability to control pupils is regarded as so vital a part of a teacher's personal identity that many continue to suffer in the isolation of their classrooms rather than admit weakness and seek advice. When advice is sought it is seldom easy to give without conveying personal criticism. Part of this problem is the tendency for teachers to be accustomed to working unobserved and to feel uncomfortable if called upon to work in teams.

Hargreaves (1980) remarks that many teachers regard their teaching as an activity in some respects comparable to sex: being watched interferes with the performance. Watching teachers in difficulty is certainly embarrassing, and it is difficult to know how to offer advice without implying insult, as this observer's note shows:

> The lesson is now out of control totally and I am embarrassed. The quiz goes on – some boys are singing. It is hopeless and embarrassing. Mr Wolfe asks me, Are they always like this when you're in? The answer must be no.

> (Delamont and Galton, 1986)

The aim of this section is to describe and discuss the teacher skills that have been observed to be associated with freedom from pupil disruption in expert teachers' classrooms. The skills discussed are listed in a summary at the end of the chapter and constitute a relatively objective agenda for teachers to use in helping less experienced colleagues improve their classroom control.

Lessons conducted in the traditional style often fall into phases to which varying rules and expectations are attached. Hargreaves *et al.* (1975) noted an entry phase, settling down, the lesson proper which included teachers' exposition and pupils' work, clearing up and, finally, exit. The amount of movement and pupil talk varies from phase to phase and some pupils seem to have more difficulty than others in adjusting to this. It is therefore necessary to give explicit directions and clear warnings when a change of phase is imminent. These warnings have been called 'flags' (Marland, 1975) and 'switch signals' (Hargreaves *et al.*, 1975). Some of the signals and cues observed by Evertson and Emmer (1982) included a real switch signal: 'moving to a specific area of the room, ringing a bell, or turning on the overhead projector'. If the lesson is planned, or the teacher can see its unfolding form if it is extempore, then it is relatively easy to make changes within the lesson clear and to prepare the pupils for them. For example: 'In two minutes we will stop and read the first paragraph.' The amount of class time occupied by transitions has been estimated at up to 15 per cent, with the associated finding that these are peak times for misbehaviour to occur. Despite the common belief, external interruptions from visitors are responsible for only 10 per cent of classroom distractions (Wittrock, 1986: 406).

The traditional form of lesson, the recitation or question-and-answer type, is by its very nature vulnerable to disruption. Ironically, it is a form of teaching that was intended to put voice and life in place of the deadness of print. Stowe, an early teacher trainer of the 1840s, called it 'picturing out' (quoted in James, 1994). He described how the teacher was to engage the attention of the class by interrogation, suggestion and ellipsis – which would nowadays be called the cloze procedure (see Curtis, 1963: 216). A basically similar style of teaching in America appears to have evolved from a different activity: having individuals recite lessons privately to the teacher (Hamilton, quoted in Wittrock, 1986: 403). The teacher conducts an inquisition, attempting to involve the whole class and keep silent the non-attending parts of it. Observations of such lessons, for example Barnes (1969), indicate that questions are typically closed, that is, admitting only of the answers in the teacher's mind, thus limiting and constraining the range of contributions from pupils. Although recitation has the appearance of a joint teacher-and-pupil search for understanding, in reality the teachers hold most of the cards and the pupils are reduced to guessing them. What masquerades as an inquiry after meaning and truth may become a game of 'guess the word I'm thinking of'. An example from a primary school of learning degenerating into a guessing game is analysed in MacLure and French (1980). Teachers give information, elicit answers, direct who shall speak, decide whether an answer is acceptable or not, and evaluate publicly both the answer and the pupil's effort. Pupils are limited to seeking permission to speak and reacting or replying if called upon. Perhaps some procedure of this sort is sometimes inevitable in crowded classrooms where teachers' knowledge has to be shared in some sort of interactive way; few school teachers consider straightforward lecturing to be appropriate or possible.

Approximately one-third of classroom time is said to be occupied in this way and, in general, observers note a high degree of pupil attention, as compared with other classroom activities. Where the questions are closed and admit of only limited answers, participation is limited to the more able pupils; where the emphasis is on ideas and opinions, and almost all answers are acceptable, lower ability pupils take a greater part and some of the more able tend to withdraw (see Doyle's review in Wittrock, 1986: 402–5). Class discussion sessions in which all answers are apparently accepted have been noted in infant schools (MacLure and French, in Woods, 1980a). However, although teachers seemed to accept all answers, this was only a surface feature of their remarks to the class, and the authors show that pupils' logically derived responses were, in fact, rejected in favour of the single answer in the teacher's mind. There is no doubt that the whole-class recitation method generates a considerable number of easily breakable rules. A pupil need only speak to a neighbour upon the topic under inquiry to create a disruptive event. Mehan (1979) notes that the rules of turn-taking, and the ways of displaying knowledge which are appropriate to the classroom community, may remain implicit. Some pupils need these rules and expectations to be made explicit.

The traditional teacher control of the classroom does not necessarily evaporate in open, resource-based environments. Whatever the limitations and difficulties of recitation as a classroom strategy, the traditional teacher presence is still necessary from time to time. Edwards and Furlong (1978) reported on a school organized along open, resource-based lines, where pupils had fewer restraints and more opportunity to follow their own learning paths. To some extent, they were able to create their own 'local' curriculum, to work at their own pace and to have a wider range of their knowledge and interests valued. Nevertheless, the authors observed no marked reduction in teacher control of knowledge – booklets were a substitute for teacher talk – and teachers retained some of their directive role, though in response to pupils' demands rather than on their own initiative. Where possible, therefore, it may be strategically appropriate to avoid the recitation (or teacher-versus-the-class) style. Using a varied menu of learning and teaching styles is the first step towards pre-empting control problems in the classroom.

### Early encounters

One of the most frequent observations made by researchers and experienced teachers is that control is easier to establish if the teacher is in position ready to receive the class. It is not an auspicious start to have to calm an already disorderly group. Rutter et al. (1979) reported that where teachers were waiting for classes and able to supervise their entry there was less school disorder. Research reported in Wragg (1984) showed that experienced teachers, when compared with students, were more likely to greet the pupils, occupy a central position in the room, wait for silence before speaking, issue directions authoritatively and use eye contact. They did not rely on voice alone to convey their requirements: posture and expression were relaxed and confident. Goffman (1968) has observed that impressions given off, as distinct from those deliberately given, are normally taken as a more accurate guide to a person's inner state. Naturally, if a troublesome class is expected there is a temptation to cut short an unpleasant encounter by arriving late. Similarly, one is more likely to find oneself shouting and less confident about taking a position forward of the desk while looking pupils in the eye. Many years ago, a teachers' newspaper published a cartoon showing a teacher standing in front of a class, arms folded, impassive. The pupils are depicted in a state of dis order: paper aircraft and chair legs fill the air; cobwebs stretch from the teacher to the walls and ceiling and the caption is: 'I'm still waiting' It takes courage to try non-verbal control skills and few teachers are completely free of the fear that they, too, may find themselves still waiting.

Laslett and Smith (1984) convey the briskness associated with effective teachers in their summary of the entry rules: greeting, seating, starting. They and Marland (1975) point out that a straightforward start to lessons, with something that occupies pupils in their desks, allows the teacher to cope with interruptions and late-comers. Where this advice seems uncongenial or inappropriate, perhaps where pupils are engaged in group projects, interruptions can still be prevented from becoming disruptions. For example, late arrivals can be briskly and amiably greeted and directed to the topic without shifting one's attention from the rest of the class. There is no need to express annoyance or begin an interrogation; any necessary enquiries can be conducted later.

One way of proceeding with classes that are already out of hand is to draw up jointly a short list of rules and make some sort of bargain with the class. This is especially effective with primary age pupils. When asked to suggest three rules for the class, both teachers and pupils tend to express them in negative terms – for example: no shouting; no wandering about; no spoiling other people's work. It is more effective to express the rules positively, so that the pupils know what they have to do rather than not do. The three rules mentioned would therefore be written up on the board as follows: we must talk in quiet voices; we must stay in our own places; we must be helpful and polite to each other.

Having established some simple and achievable rules in this way, the teacher may then offer a reward. This can be tangible or not, according to the particular circumstances; some classes are happy just to show they can keep bargains. In a primary school, a teacher might say something like this: 'I will look around the class every few minutes – that will be about twenty times this lesson. If everyone is obeying our rules on at least half of those occasions then there will be extra story time this afternoon.' The required success rate must be set at a realistic level that is likely to be achieved. The target can always be raised on future occasions – it is a bad idea to be too ambitious and begin with failure. Bull and Solity (1987) note the importance of stressing to the class the natural consequences of keeping the rules; this makes it easier gradually to withdraw the artificial system when a co-operative and productive atmosphere is established. A similar procedure was found to reduce disruptive behaviour in a study of two secondary school classes (McNamara, in Johnstone and Munn, 1987).

It may be the case (difficult to prove) that some populations of pupils are more amenable to these techniques than others. Rutter remarked that it was very difficult to be a good teacher in some schools. Calderhead (1987) reports on an experiment to discover the influence of the class on teachers – in this case two trainees. One who appeared to have established order of a precarious kind through a good deal of shouting and threatening was exchanged with another, who kept control using a quiet voice and positive, rewarding behaviour. The students altered their behaviour, so that the former became quieter and the latter began to coerce and shout. This is, however, no reason to surrender a skills approach: if pupils are such powerful constraints upon teacher behaviour it can never be too early to begin re-educating them.

Wragg's team reported that experienced teachers tried to present a brisk, hard image on first meeting a new class: they would be resistant to enquiries, keep their 'mystery', or perhaps play on their eccentricities if these were known, respected or feared. Many used their first lessons to explain their rules, which related to territory, property, work, talking and safety. However, Fontana (1985) warns that teachers should limit their continuous talk to no more than one-and-a-half minutes for each year of the average class age. Many teachers convey their extensive ownership of the classroom by specifying how pupils must use and keep neat their books, materials and desks (Evertson and Emmer, 1982). Rules were precisely stated and continually reiterated. This does not necessarily lead to confrontational situations if, once established, teachers are prepared to allow them to be discussed. For example, in one behavioural unit I visited, the chief rule in operation was: 'We don't lay a finger on you and you don't lay a finger on us.' I witnessed a discussion on this rule arising from a complaint by a pupil who claimed to have been poked in the chest by a teacher. The group decided by vote that being poked in the chest did not infringe the rule; a pupil who had flapped his hat in a teacher's face, however, was found guilty and ordered to apologize.

Whether this sort of discussion is genuinely free varies according to each situation. Wragg noted that some teachers would allow rules to arise in discussion, but it was clear that rules were not negotiable and the discussion was little more than a way of involving the pupils in the exercise. On this theme, Delamont (1976) reports Torode's observations on teachers' use of the consensual 'we'. Too much can be made of such refinements, however, and it is not necessarily the case that all aspects of a successfully dominant style can be simply transplanted. In using a discussion format for emphasizing rules, perhaps teachers were doing no more than exhibiting those personal characteristics of effective managers for which Wragg (1993) gives examples: Mrs Abel used praise and good humour extensively and had a benign but firm manner, with warm and positive relationships; Miss Baker, by contrast, was harsher, more negative in her comments and made few references to good work.

Where the first lesson was related to the curriculum, experienced teachers tended to plan something simple and undramatic. In contrast to these intentions, students aimed to be friendly, approachable and to identify with the pupils. Rules would come out naturally 'as problems arose'. Students often intended to begin their encounters with something interesting and active, though many chose a less risky start on the day. In one class a student chose to demonstrate a chemical reaction which simulated a volcano: an event which came to symbolize the lesson. In contrast, effective classroom managers tend to begin with activities that have 'a simple, whole-class instructional structure, and the work was familiar, enjoyable and easy to accomplish' (Evertson and Emmer, summarized in Wittrock, 1986). Often, the teaching of the rules and procedures was the substantive lesson.

Evertson and Emmer (1981, 1982) found significant differences between more and less effective teachers in their behaviour at the start of the school year. They conclude, as others have (Ball, in Woods 1980b; Doyle, in Wittrock, 1986), that the beginning of the year is crucial for establishing effective classroom procedures and advise that planning should be done before school starts. Effective teachers had 'a better behavioural map of the classroom and what was required for students to function within it'. This map would not omit the basic precautions mentioned by Fontana (1985): no dead tape-decks, illegible visual aids or stiff glue. The teachers of younger pupils placed more emphasis on teaching their rules, and for all teachers the time spent on this activity varied from a few minutes to over forty minutes. Time did not appear as significant, however; effective teachers were more explicit and more likely to give out copies of the rules or have pupils write them in their books. In addition, 'more effective managers tended to have more workable systems of rules, and they taught their rules and procedures systematically and thoroughly' (Evertson and Emmer, 1982: 486). This seems to be stating the obvious, and in some respects all observational studies are vulnerable to this charge: effective teachers are found to do the things that effective teachers do. In this study they were more vigilant, tended to use more eye contact, responded quickly to inappropriate behaviour, checked and gave feedback on work, maintained contact with the full class and set appropriate, clearly explained tasks. They kept better track of progress and had 'stronger and more detailed accountability systems'. They were better predictors of pupils' concerns and difficulties and were able to see the classroom 'through the eyes of their students'. Doyle, too, reported that effective teachers maintained vigilance over the whole class and kept individual contacts brief (Wittrock, 1986: 402).

It is possible that those teachers typed as less effective are merely those unfortunate in their classes. Evertson and Emmer dismiss this possibility with the claim that classes did not differ in misbehaviour levels during the first week. However, the graph they give in support of this shows that less effective teachers had almost 30 per cent more 'unsanctioned off-task behaviour' during the first week of term (4.5 per cent compared with 3.5 per cent); this difference was not, however, statistically significant. Even if no differences in initial behaviour are noticed this does not mean that classes are similar in their potential for disruption. Teachers often find there is a honeymoon period before groups and individuals settle down or 'find their feet'; this has been documented (for example, Ball, 1981; Beynon, 1985; Wragg, 1984).

The concept of effective management shares a ragged border with effective teaching, professionalism and common sense. Some ineffective teachers returned no marked work to pupils during the first three weeks of term. Another instructed a low-ability English class to 'write an essay from the perspective of an inanimate object'; this would be a difficult if not inherently impossible task for anyone, but 'the problem was compounded by an unclear explanation of the term, "perspective" '(Evertson and Emmer, 1982: 488). In Wittrock (1986: 398–401), Gump estimated that 65 per cent of pupils' time was spent working at their own desks; Rosenshine reported that pupil attention was lowest in deskwork activities, especially when these were frequent; and Silverstein and Kounin found deviance during deskwork to be four times as high as in teacher-directed, whole-class activities.

These findings clearly underline the importance of interesting and appropriate work but they also suggest that the rules bounding deskwork activities may need review. Deskwork is usually conducted individually and teachers find themselves periodically calling for silence. Classmates who help each other find themselves accused of copying or cheating. If co-operation were a more frequent requirement in deskwork, there would be fewer rules to break, less disciplinary intervention and, possibly, more learning.

## The main part of the lesson

Giving the pupils an outline of the lesson's planned form helps to minimize interruptions and expressions of surprise at a later and possibly more vulnerable time. Similarly, to start with some deskwork ensures that all the pupils have the books and materials they will need for the lesson. This is particularly important with disorderly and forgetful groups. It is sometimes difficult to maintain a fresh and vigorous demeanour with topics repeated from year to year, but some extra reading or resequencing the material can help. Laslett and Smith (1984) refer to the Henson and Higgins view that pupil motivation can be engendered by taking an interest in pupils, knowing their names and treating them courteously. This involves being generous with praise, and Laslett and Smith suggest preparing a number of synonyms for such tired words as 'good' and 'nice'. Bull and Solity (1987) advise 'full praise statements': gain attention, show approval, specify the progress, point out its benefits and challenge them to do better. Balson (1982), however, distinguishes between praise and encouragement; certainly, older pupils do not always respond gratefully to praise and this advice must be used with discretion. It is equally important to convey enthusiasm for the lesson topic and thereby communicate to the class that it is something in which it is worth taking an interest.

Partington and Hinchcliffe (1979) noted that effective class managers prepared effectively and extensively; as well as the content, they planned for organizational matters such as movement, time and the tasks of particular pupils. To make a brisk beginning, explaining the relationship of the lesson's work to the course or to pupils' present concerns and future interests, is preferable to wrangles about the last lesson's leftovers or missing homework. These can be attended to later when they do not keep uninvolved pupils waiting. A variety of activities and tasks is more likely to engage the pupils than a monotonous period of listening or writing. Gannaway (1984) found that pupils were less likely to co-operate in lessons, especially ones judged boring, if there was too much writing. Some pupils regard writing as the only activity that counts as work and resent lessons where no writing is done at all. Teachers need judgement in this matter.

Attempts to introduce new learning methods and groupings sometimes collapse into disorder because pupils are unused to autonomy and unclear as to what is expected of them. They may pester the teacher with questions or occupy their time in unwanted activities, hoping that some other group will come up with an answer that they can reproduce. Where pupils are set to solve problems in pairs or groups it is necessary for the task to be explicit. It may even be necessary to specify a number of words, or the headings for lists under which appropriate results may fall. Pupils sometimes fail to co-operate in open-ended paired work because the teachers' evaluation criteria have previously indicated that only some results are valued. This repeats one of the problems encountered with whole-class question-and-answer sessions, where questions which appear to be open to several answers are in fact closed and admit of only one answer, which is decided by the teacher. Where the task set is open, and therefore to some extent ambiguous, it is necessary for teachers to reduce the risk of pupils incurring negative evaluations, that is, low marks and criticism. Failure to take account of pupils' perception of the teacher's evaluation criteria may result in pupils declining to co-operate: they may pester the teacher for the answers or turn their attention to something safer. Wrong answers may be pupils' attempts to transform tasks into something they can achieve or they may be a clue to the pupils' perception of the teacher's requirements (Posner, 1980).

Doyle and Carter (1986) analyse classroom tasks in terms of their degree of ambiguity and risk. They observed pupils pressing a teacher for additional guidance with a written assignment until they had transformed the work into something easier than the teacher had intended. She also made available extra marks in an apparent attempt to meet the pupils' anxieties. This opens the possibility that teachers might systematically present easier, low-level work to keep pupils occupied and reduce management problems. HMI has complained over a long period that pupils are not set sufficiently demanding work. For example:

> Usually expectations are too low ... almost invariably the tasks which are set are too closely directed by the teacher ... pupils need to be encouraged, and expected, to take more responsibility for their work.
>
> (DES, 1984)

> In poor lessons ... work lacked pace, was over-directed by the teacher and was often dominated by worksheets that made unduly limited demands on the pupils ... with less-able pupils, expectations are often too low.
>
> (DES, 1989b)

> Areas which give particular cause for concern are ... the persistent underachievement of pupils in many primary and secondary schools, particularly in inner city disadvantaged areas.
>
> (DES, 1992)

The work by Doyle and Carter suggests that it is not low expectations that are the primary cause but the demands of crowd control in busy classrooms. Three solutions seem possible: teachers might use control and management techniques that are strong enough to withstand the disruption that high-level academic tasks seem to involve; methods of group working might be adopted which free the teacher from a barrage of pupil questions; and, associated with this, a noisy and talkative class would no longer have to be seen as evidence of poor teaching. Doyle quotes work suggesting that, in open activities, teachers' talk is more positive and related to learning rather than control; and that group work, when carefully structured and rewarded and where individuals are accountable for performance, has positive effects on 'achievement ... race relations and mutual concern' (Wittrock, 1986: 400). Denscombe's paper (in Woods, 1980b) suggested that noise is overrated as an efficiency indicator but described, in an open classroom environment, pupils using subtle strategies of friendliness in order to take rests from work. However, if Doyle and Carter are correct, many busy and well-ordered classes are far from completely engaged in worthwhile learning.

Caspari (1976: 20) shows how a teacher's presuppositions about how supposedly open-ended tasks should be completed caused her to overlook valuable and revealing contributions from pupils: expecting a descriptive essay, she failed to see the value in an imaginative and fantastic account. Mercer and Edwards (1981) use the concept of 'educational ground rules' which are the hidden or implicit cognitive frameworks to which pupils must have access in order to complete tasks successfully. These may be related to particular modes of expression or presentation integral to the nature of a topic: for example, the conventional way of presenting a letter or describing an experimental observation. They may be idiosyncratic: for example, 'creative writing' or the insistence on hands being raised before contributions will be listened to. Many of the taken-for-granted requirements and ways of presenting classroom tasks are more inaccessible to some pupils than others. Martin (1976) has drawn attention to the distance between written expression and ordinary talk, and others have pointed out how important talk is to thinking (for example, Barnes *et al.*, 1969; Driver, 1983).

Sybil Marshall's (1963) classic essay on primary education demonstrated the importance of talk in learning. Classroom writing tasks that can be accomplished to the satisfaction of the teacher in language that is close to the pupils' present speech are more likely to engage the pupils' co-operation. Martin believes that written tasks of this sort 'would free the writer to think in writing and to learn through using written language in the same way that he already uses talk'. Some teachers may find this inappropriate because of the gulf between the pupils' spoken language and the requirements of the topic. In such cases this draws attention to the need for particular types of expression to be taught; it is an error to assume that its lack is an indicator of missing ability. Some pupils will already have had access to elaborated literary styles of presentation; others need them to be made explicit.

Some of the disaffection experienced in classrooms is caused partly by pupils having differential access to attention and understanding. Keddie

(1971) believed that her small-scale study, carried out in a secondary school humanities department, showed that teachers preferred middle-class conformity to working-class independence of mind. Attempts by working-class pupils to relate the curriculum to their own experience of life was graded as only 'C' ability. It must certainly be the case that some teachers are so immersed in their material, or so unfamiliar with it, that they are unwilling to be diverted from their lesson plan – or the textbook. This can hinder learning in both open, discovery-learning environments and formal recitation.

A similar study in a craft department (Tickle, in Hammersley and Woods, 1984) showed that some craft teachers' implicit criteria prevented some pupils from engaging in high-level work. Those pupils who were believed to be less able actually got more teacher time but their tasks were more closely directed and they were presented with less challenging assignments and problems. Tickle suggests that, despite teacher claims to value creativity, they acted as if a facility in basic craft skills were a condition precedent to it. Some pupils in such situations must necessarily feel frustrated and undervalued. Some studies have shown that apparently free, open, discovery work is more closely constrained than teachers claim. Atkinson and Delamont (1977) describe an example from secondary school science and make an interesting comparison with the training of doctors on hospital wards. The suggestion is that this phenomenon helps teachers resolve a dilemma: the need to communicate knowledge and the ideological belief that pupils must direct their own learning if it is to be of significance.

Many teachers have been introduced during their training to the views of Rogers (1961), who asserts that significant learning cannot be taught but only facilitated. Sharp and Green (1975) show that, in a progressive primary school, pupil choice can lead to some pupils receiving less teacher interaction than others: specifically, working-class children were said to remain known to teachers only as types (contemporaries), but middle-class children became teacher consociates – known to them as well as if they were family members. Hargreaves (1978) provides a theoretical analysis of classroom-coping strategies as learned responses to material, ideological and societal constraints upon teachers. To be aware of these influences and their possibly hidden effects upon pupils is a partial aid to avoiding boredom, disengagement and disruption.

One of the most widely applied studies of teacher behaviour in orderly classrooms was carried out by Kounin (1970). A particularly valuable skill, which he termed 'withitness', consisted in giving the pupils the impression that the teacher had 'eyes in the back of her head'. Some years earlier, Dreikurs, whose work is used in Chapter 4, wrote: 'One requirement of all good group leaders – including teachers – is the ability to see everything that goes on in the group at any given time' (1957: 50).

Brophy and Evertson (1976) use the term 'monitoring'; Marland (1975) calls it the 'lighthouse effect'. Successful teachers, with respect to classroom order, frequently scan the class and regularly make remarks, which Kounin said must be timely and accurate, to show that they are missing nothing, even when they do not otherwise intervene in inattentive behaviour.

Specifically, teachers watch the behaviour of groups in order to keep the momentum of activities moving. It is necessary to remain vigilant when the pupils have been set a piece of deskwork; in some classes, distracted pupils may look up to find the teacher apparently counting them. Regular marking and giving feedback have the same effect. Copeland had some success with a computer system designed to stimulate the attentiveness and overlapping demands of the classroom. The trainee was required to 'conduct a question–answer session ... while monitoring the order of turn talking, the accuracy of answers, and another student who is supposed to be engaged in a seatwork task' (quoted in Wittrock, 1986: 425). Teachers need to maintain this classroom awareness when dealing with one individual or a group. This may be done by speaking to one pupil while looking at another or by helping an individual using a 'public' voice if the help or directions are appropriate. An expert class manager can question, explain, organize, mark, discipline and listen all at the same time – and while attending to a note from the headteacher. A teacher's day may be short in hours but long in minutes.

Kounin indicated other teacher skills to which he gave idiosyncratic terms. 'Thrusts and dangles' contributed to classroom disorder: teachers should not interrupt pupil work precipitously and neither should they leave issues incomplete and unresolved. Teachers who stayed on one issue long after they had lost pupil attention were 'overdwelling'. Those whose foresight was so hazy as to produce confusion in the pupils were sometimes engaging in 'flip-flops'. This involved starting a new activity and then returning without warning to the one just abandoned: for example, 'maths books away, take out your readers, how many people got number fifteen right?'. All these sorts of teacher behaviour interrupted the smooth flow of the lesson; the resulting loss of momentum contributed to a disorderly atmosphere.

Physical location in the classroom is part of the teacher's non-verbal communication with the class and may also influence attention and behaviour. If possible, pupil desks should be arranged across the narrow length: a closer relationship is created, with fewer opportunities for disengagement to develop, out of range and out of sight, into distraction (Grunsell, 1985). Studies have shown that pupils behave better and complete more work when seated in rows – though this may be because discussion and mutual help are defined as misbehaviour rather than work. Further, pupils seated in the front and centre of the room are said to be more attentive, although to some extent this could be where attentive pupils choose to sit. However, some experimental evidence suggests that, in general, it is helpful to insist on potentially inattentive pupils occupying a central position (see Wittrock, 1986: 402). Standing in front of the teacher's desk, rather than behind it, indicates a potential mobility and possible territory invasion that helps to keep pupils' eyes upon the teacher. Evertson and Emmer (1982) noted that some of their less effective teachers 'did not circulate among the students during seatwork and thus diminished their ability to observe accurately'. Ironically, less effective teachers were observed to be more likely to leave the classroom (Wittrock, 1986: 410).

## Responding to trouble

The first response to incipient disturbance need not be a verbal rebuke or comment. A stare, averting eyes sideways (not submissively down) if the stare is returned in an uncomfortable or defiant manner by the pupil, can sometimes prevent an escalation of the unwanted activity. Adopting an authoritative stance, for example folding one's arms, or moving closer to a disruptive pupil, invading his or her territory, are other possible ways of regaining control without attracting public attention. Sometimes an invitation to respond to a question serves a similar, low-key purpose and, with younger pupils, a touch on the shoulder perhaps. For the same reason (avoiding too public a profile early in a potential conflict), it is best to make corrective statements short: nagging, threats, interrogation and recitation of past misdemeanours should be avoided.

It is easy to underestimate the need to make requirements explicit and to target remarks by using names, specifying both the unwanted behaviour and the desired activity. Social class styles of adult–pupil interaction may sometimes be a factor here. King (1978), in extensive observations in infant schools, noted examples of a middle-class, 'oblique' mode of disciplining pupils: 'someone's being silly'. This may not be correctly decoded by some errant pupils. Reasons given for telling pupils to desist may be more readily accepted if they refer to the needs of the activity, and their congruence with precedent and routine, rather than personal preference. Torode, in Stubbs and Delamont (1976), reports on the speech used by a Mr Cramond in enforcing his rules. He refers to 'the order of events', thus confirming a shared system of rules and expectations. This protected the teacher from challenge by relieving him of responsibility for rules which he referred to as if they had a reality independent of personal preference. An extension of this technique is to focus on correcting the behaviour rather than criticizing the individual. This allows all parties to maintain a degree of objectivity and coolness towards the interaction, avoiding attacks on pupils' personal esteem. Caspari (1976) notes how difficult it is, even in marking work, to prevent some pupils from taking correction as personal criticism. Separating one's view of a person from one's view of their behaviour is much more difficult. It is similarly inappropriate to compare pupils to siblings as this, too, personalizes the unwanted activity when it is best distanced and discarded.

Kounin's research did not show clearly whether a ripple effect, his term for pupils falling into line after one of their number had been corrected, always occurred. Probably only the successful correction of pupils who have status in the pupils' eyes has this wider effect. Comparisons are similarly unlikely to be effective where a low-status pupil is the comparison: Walter is a poor model for Denis the Menace. Fontana (1985) suggests drawing attention to suitable models rather than making comparisons. Pupils may sometimes object that an individual is receiving unfairly indulgent treatment when a teacher decides to ignore rather than challenge an unstable pupil. If this differential tolerance is acknowledged, and a suitable reason given, most pupils will accept the situation: adolescents are particularly aware of their individuality and will accept unequal treatment when the reasonable circumstances are explained. Doyle (in Wittrock, 1986: 412) notes that some teachers take account of pupils' responses in deciding which rules to enforce strictly and which to apply more flexibly. In some circumstances, informality can give the teacher considerable discretion and 'power as a rule arbiter'. At the other extreme, few pupils will accept that mass punishment of a whole class or group is reasonable.

Allowing the natural consequences of misbehaviour to take their course is usually the easiest and most agreeable method of punishment. For example, homework preparation is not done so the lesson is missed, walls are defaced so they must be washed after school. Evertson and Emmer (1982) say there is no need for 'praise machines'. Co-operation in class results in positive consequences: for example, completing tasks and being allowed to answer. Punishment is probably more effective where it is supervised by a person who knows the pupil well and is respected by the pupil. Where the teacher knows that a pupil is unamenable, and intervention will result in aggravation of the situation, it is still necessary to show in a neutral way that the behaviour has been noticed and is unwanted. From time to time, overseers must overlook. Laslett and Smith (1984) make a useful distinction between 'planned ignoring' and 'just hoping the nuisance will go away'. To correct only the pupils on the fringes of disruption, pretending not to have noticed the central character, will not normally enhance the teacher's classroom status. Doyle (in Wittrock, 1986) reports that good classroom managers 'tended to push the curriculum and talk about work rather than misbehaviour'. The less successful focused on misbehaviour to the extent that work ceased, while their more effective colleagues found the working atmosphere carried the burden of control. One unsuccessful teacher, who managed to keep pupils on task for only a quarter of the time, rebuked pupils nearly a thousand times in one day.

Loud public rebukes can be effective when they are rare and unexpected; but they communicate weakness where they are a regular feature of a teacher's classroom. Soft and private reprimands, preferably in the absence of an audience, are more likely to be effective: 'a soft answer turneth away wrath'. Numerous public rebukes can disturb the class to the extent that the teacher increases the disruption that he or she seeks to diminish. An effective intervention is 'abrupt, short and does not invite further comment or discussion from the student' (Wittrock, 1986: 421). A relaxed posture, a voice pitched low, an absence of gesticulation or poking help to keep confrontational situations calm. A teacher in a unit for excluded pupils, who happened to be addicted to chocolate, sometimes contrived to unwrap and eat a bar when faced with particularly violent and dangerous situations. As eating is something we do when feeling unstressed, this helped define the situation as unthreatening and helped to soothe troubled feelings. An unwanted confrontation can sometimes be halted simply by stating the conditions under which co-operative relations can be resumed: explicitly state the peace terms and withdraw from the interaction. Where a pupil has to be removed from the room, it helps persuade the pupil that the teacher is rejecting the behaviour and not the person if the pupil is led to the door rather than ordered out. At the same time, some simple condition that must be satisfied for re-entry can be emphasized repeatedly. The rejoining of the group, on what may be privileged terms, is thus uppermost in the exchange; rejection, and the reason for it, is minimized. This style of control helps maintain a cool demeanour and avoids alarming and exciting other pupils, whose continued need for attention must not be neglected. If, in the course of dealing with an incident, the teacher falsely accuses the pupil, a generous or even extravagant apology can be both calming and evidence of the teacher's invulnerability and confidence.

## Clearing up and exit

The completion stages of a lesson or individual learning session sometimes require planning and preparation in their own right. Often the most difficult pupils are the first to finish work (to their own satisfaction) and this should be planned for. With disaffected groups, an orderly and coherent end to a lesson can leave a general impression of having achieved something worth while. This feeling is not confined to the pupils. More effective schools in Rutter *et al.* (1979) tended not to have lessons finishing too early. Laslett and Smith (1984) note that 'hard-won control is most frequently lost and learning wasted at the end of lessons'. In so far as one lesson's end is another lesson's start, professional responsibility and staffroom harmony depend upon good management in the concluding phase. As the end of a lesson approaches and release for both parties is at hand, the teacher may find less difficulty in gaining attention. It is unwise to use this period for a recitation of the errors of the past session, perhaps mixed with demands for silence, backed by threats of instant detention. The opportunity is best used to summarize and draw together the themes of the lesson's work and perhaps relate them to the intended programme for the next meeting. Review what has been achieved as if all had achieved it; experience shows that even in the most disorderly and chaotic classes a majority of the pupils are engaged on task for most of the time. It does not depart so far from reality, therefore, for the teacher to take a positive view and to define the situation as a success. An orderly dismissal, with a relaxed and smiling teacher, helps to minimize problems and is a better prelude to the next meeting than an atmosphere of recrimination and threats. Particularly unco-operative pupils may be held back for a brief word as the class leaves.

Sockett, discussing a possible professional code for teachers in Gordon (1983), lists seven items relating to classroom practice. He suggests that teachers should always be properly prepared before classes begin; they should ensure that pupils are always productively engaged; they should not frequently discipline any particular individual during teaching; they should concentrate on their pupils' successes and praise them generously; they should set and mark work regularly and speedily; they should have high expectations of their pupils and manifest them constantly; and they should be punctual. These are, as Sockett himself says, conventional and common-sense prescriptions. As with much classroom management advice, some of this may seem to be too trivial to require specifying and as likely to lower the status of teaching as to raise it. One does not suppose the BMA includes punctuality in the professional code of doctors – perhaps it is as well, for they seldom are. The impression of simplicity and triviality is a false one. Rules and prescriptions vary in their significance according to the context. For example, punctuality does have a juvenile and trivial aspect in everyday life, perhaps reviving childhood memories of reluctant compliance. In teaching, however, it is part of a professional relationship with colleagues as well as with pupils. This context makes imperatives of many seeming trivialities. The summary at the end of this chapter, which is in the form of fifty tips, should be read with this caution in mind.

Research on classroom management yields much information helpful to experienced teachers who wish to work with less effective colleagues. Those intending to use it in this way should note Laslett and Smith's (1984) advice on helping colleagues. One should listen with empathy, keep confidences, try to offer practical advice, reassure the teacher that asking for help does not imply incompetence, and avoid punishing a request for advice by involving the teacher in extra labours. Research is also not without value to those who already feel confident of their classroom competence. Doyle (in Wideen and Andrews, 1987) suggests that such data should not be used uncritically as a list of rules to be applied. Experienced teachers use research as activators or modifiers of their existing planning, filtering it through existing schemas and integrating it into their practice. A further suggestion of Doyle's is to use research to identify more encompassing instructional functions.

This takes us back to the problem raised earlier: much of the advice is appropriate only in some contexts, and much of it seems obvious and trivial. Some of the skills identified are clearly of a more general level than others. For example, using names, making eye contact, standing in a central position and issuing authoritative statements are all lower-level activities that might be encompassed in the higher-level skill of gaining pupils' attention. Gaining pupils' attention is a more general teacher skill necessary in all teaching contexts, whereas the skills encompassed by it may be merely contingent: there are many ways of gaining attention. This goes some way towards explaining the disagreements among teachers about what skills betoken an effective teacher. If the skills identified are low level there will be much disagreement, just as there is in moral debates about low-level rules. For example, there can never be agreement about whether it is wrong to tell lies or not. Faced with a murderer asking after one's friend, we have to defer to precepts of more general application. Doyle suggests three candidates for the role of instructional functions: coverage, as measured by such things as the opportunity to learn, pacing, and the match between class activity and curriculum documents; explicitness, which must be neither too little nor too much for the task; and accountability, which includes the monitoring activities by which many students are motivated. Activity 3.3 is an opportunity to begin what Doyle terms 'practical reasoning' with respect to classroom management skills.

## SECURING LEARNING

In Chapter 2 we made use of data from school inspectors' reports on schools to examine the association between elements of school provision and exclusion. These reports have for a long time been an unpublished and therefore neglected source of information on the features of good-quality teaching. Prior to the privatization of the inspection service, HMI was the sole source of reports on schools, and its expertise and knowledge drew on more than a century of work in schools. The criteria it used in judging lessons were not made explicit. Indeed, in DES (1990: 8) it was even denied that there were any:

Nor are inspectors' observations and judgements of what is going on decided by predetermined criteria. Inspectors, over a long period of inspection, decide what they think of what they have seen, work out criteria and, where appropriate, apply them.

This cannot be correct. Even before the advent of Ofsted and the publication of criteria, HMI reports mention the percentage of work seen that was good, satisfactory or poor. Good work is sometimes subdivided into 'good' and 'very good' or 'outstanding'; inadequate work sometimes includes upper and lower sections labelled 'poor' or 'very poor' and 'less than satisfactory' or 'with some weaknesses'. Some random quotations from different reports illustrate the usage: '84 per cent of lessons were satisfactory or good, with 7 per cent being very good'; '30 per cent of lessons were poor with 3 per cent of these being very poor'.

Unremarkably, the best lessons are described as having a lucid introductory exposition, 'a clear sense of purpose, well-structured use of time and a variety of activities'. Objectives are 'made clear and set in the context of earlier work ... apt in the context of the course'. More surprisingly, at least for many teachers, is the expectation across the curriculum that teaching will include frequent opportunities for pupils to work independently in small groups. Approving references are often made to lessons where there is 'a considerable amount of oral work ... discussion in pairs, in small groups and in the whole class ... a high level of pupil participation'.

I have found that when teachers are given extracts from reports to study, they are struck by the frequency with which reference is made to active pupil involvement and talk. This is not to say that HMI was happy to see teachers take a back seat: 'While it is good for pupils to take responsibility for their learning ... teachers must accept their responsibility to ensure an acceptable rate of working.'

Pupil participation in lessons does not imply lack of challenge and progression. Teachers should 'clarify points and draw attention to issues in an unobtrusive way'. Talk is good not in itself but only if properly managed, as these extracts from reports show: 'while talk is plentiful in lessons it is under-exploited as a means of teaching and learning'; 'only infrequently do pupils make longer, more complex statements or pursue an argument'; 'there were few examples of pupils asking questions or initiating discussion'; 'pupils are not encouraged to draw on evidence to support their conclusions, to be critical of expressed opinions or to explore alternative hypotheses'; 'not enough importance was attached to the spoken word and the need for pupils to have a range of opportunities to develop their ideas through talk with their teachers and with their peers'.

In the light of this, HMI comments on poor work can be predicted. Weak lessons are described as tending to follow a common pattern, 'in which classes work as a whole at the same task ... the work is inappropriate for some pupils and the pace is slow'. An over-didactic teaching style leaves some pupils uncomprehending and asks too little of others: 'teacher-dominated activities lead to lessons which lack pace'. One response to the breadth of ability in all classrooms – irrespective of whether the breadth has been marginally reduced by streaming – is to prepare individual worksheets. This, too, comes in for critical scrutiny: there can be 'too much reliance on the delivery of information by means of worksheets'.

These reports and other research evidence support the view that insufficient regard is paid to the range of ability and attainment in classrooms. This is not to lend support to the simplistic view that teachers should adopt pupil-centred teaching styles. To concentrate on what the teacher only is doing is to ignore the goal to which teaching is merely the means – pupil learning. As the evidence shows, neither didactic exposition nor experiential activity necessarily reaches all parts of the classroom. Involving people in their own learning through active experience is the notion that has always underpinned apprenticeships and is now one justification for the policy of placing teacher training more firmly in schools. A straw poll of any group of teachers will result in the majority agreeing that they learned their art through practice rather than lectures. The cynical view that teachers begin their training as infants in schools and end it on retirement, with a gap of three or four years while they undergo formal training, has a little truth in it.

Experience is a rich source of learning, apprehended as it is by all the senses, but more importantly because, when responsibility is included, it forces us to think. In real situations, real consequences follow from our decisions and we are therefore compelled to reflect on our actions. Without the need to think about our experience, it is left in a state of mere awareness, and such learning as does occur may be evanescent. Some pupils may resist responsibility and it is possible that traditional, teacher-dominated classrooms are the optimum environment for the introverted – or the neurotic. Those who need more active challenges may fail in such a system, only to succeed in later life as enterprising industrialists and entrepreneurs or, regrettably, inventive criminals. One of the great puzzles of the 1990s must be how school failures as young as 11 years can, without a key, open and drive away fast cars. Perhaps some of these tragedies could be avoided if more active opportunities to learn were available.

We all have experience, as parents or teachers, of the futility of assuming that telling is the same as teaching, and teaching is the same as learning: 'I've told them a thousand times, I just can't get it into their heads.' The commonly used metaphor of delivery could not be less apt. Delivering knowledge is in no way similar to delivering a commodity –

any more than delivering piles of bricks is the same as building a house. The seminal work of Barnes (for example 1969, 1976) has brilliantly shown up this error. Learning and understanding are part of a spiral process, in which the structure and meaning of our knowledge are continually evolving and becoming more differentiated and refined. What is learned from new encounters depends upon what has been learned in the past, and the new can change our understanding of the old. A pupil will understand air pressure all the better for having inflated bicycle tyres; younger children will more readily grasp the nature of pneumatic tyres through having blown up balloons; earlier still, in making sense of balloons, children will draw on their experience of blowing candles out on a birthday cake. To the ignorant, these earlier experiences will seem just so much useless play, to be dismissed in favour of sitting children in front of a chalk-board and telling them things.

The misunderstandings of the very young tell us about their state of knowledge and perhaps its sources. For example, a nursery teacher planned, when the ageing class guinea pig died, to let the children see it. They would be upset, but it would be an opportunity to extend their understanding of life and death, and they would go together and bury it in the grounds. All these fine sentiments were momentarily arrested when the actual day came. Informed that Percy was dead, the children wanted to know who had shot him. Researching the teaching of science, Driver (1983) uncovered an example of how experience without the opportunity to talk things through could handicap learning. Some very young children, having grown pea plants in a damp jar, had not appreciated the role of moisture and light as had been intended. They interpreted what had happened in terms of their existing schema. Young children's lives are controlled and managed by adults – people clear up after them and get things ready for them. In the light of this, some thought that the change in the pea was due to their teacher's interference after they had gone home. Time spent in focused talk would have cleared away these confusions.

To be effective, learning must engage all the faculties. Pupils must be emotionally receptive and attentive; they must be cognitively awakened through teaching which is clear, thought-provoking and compelling. Active engagement must be secured through structured tasks or open-ended activities. These might require pupils, in pairs, to explain concepts to each other, to work through a problem, or to evaluate a decision. Cognitive, affective and active involvement in learning are preconditions for success: the journey from ignorance to knowledge cannot be accomplished without travelling.

There is a certain irony in arguing for active learning through the pages of a book, though the end-of-chapter activities are designed to overcome some of the shortcomings of passive reading. An experiment at this point will serve to convince those sceptical of the argument I have been advancing. The past couple of pages have exposed readers systematically to a definition of effective learning. Please lay the book aside and take thirty seconds (no more) to write down a few words or phrases that would form the elements of a definition of effective learning.

Your reading so far has been a close equivalent of listening to a lecture, although if you have paid for the book you may have been interacting with the material by making critical notes or underlining parts of the text. If you have been reading only, you are quite likely not to have done as I have asked. The first thing this experiment might have shown you is that even in child-centred, discovery-orientated classrooms it is important that the teacher remains in control. Adopting a tone I have so often used in my school teaching career, let me invite you once again to formulate a definition of effective learning before reading on.

Using this exercise with groups of teachers, I have found that, when asked to compare notes, no more than a third find that their definition matches that of their neighbour. Worse still, no more than a third find that their definition matches the one that I think I have been explaining. I think I have been arguing that effective learning is an active process that combines experience and reflection, engages thoughts and feelings, and requires talk and activity as well as watching and listening. Your notes may not agree, but that does not mean blame should be apportioned to you or to me. Solitary learning – or reading – needs to be put to use or subjected to discussion to be made secure. Some people can readily hold such analytical discussions with themselves, but for many of us it is easy to slip into an unreflective, passive mode. As it says in the Code of Jewish Law, 'One should not learn alone but with a partner'. Learning alone, one Rabbi said, makes one foolish; we should open our mouths and 'let the words shine forth'. Whatever else you think of this experiment, at least we can say that it has forced you to think critically about the nature of learning, and therefore to learn.

Meeting pupils' individual needs necessitates the provision of a variety of opportunities to learn in different ways, whatever their skills, attainments, attitudes, interests or dispositions. Teacher exposition is more accessible when it incorporates a judicious question or one-minute exercise at critical points. For example, invite the pupils to write down the key points so far, or to explain a concept to each other; put three or four statements on the board and ask the pupils to decide if they are true or false; make them write the answers to a few questions. There is no need to check individual answers, as the purpose is to let the pupils check their learning and thereby secure it. Teachers already use such quick checks but often as a disciplinary measure and without appreciating the significance and potential for learning: 'What did I just say Jonathan?' We know he does not know and he knows that too, if nothing else. Some other child – perhaps one of those introverted, passive learners – will give us the answer, and we will proceed with our lesson, steered by the attentive pupil but unaware of the extent of ignorance in the class. Later, perhaps sensing that we are not getting the material across, we might ask for questions but get none. Admitting ignorance is not an activity likely to enhance a pupil's standing with the group, or his or her personal esteem. It is much better to make it safe to admit to difficulty by stating that you are sure people have questions, telling them to check one problem each with a partner, and then put unresolved questions to the class.

Attempts at group work sometimes founder because the pupils sit in a group but do not work as one. Perhaps one or two members engage in the task and the others become distracting or disruptive passengers. To avoid this, and ensure that all members of the group are in a position to contribute to its work, pupils should have a few moments' solitary work to do before beginning the joint activity. This can be making notes or just thinking for a minute or two. If they are then put into small groups of two or three, and begin by sharing ideas, then even the most reluctant and least able should be able to contribute.

Pupils inexperienced in co-operative activity benefit from tasks being structured and carefully timed. Roles can be allocated in much the same way as they are in co-operative projects in the world of work. For example, in television productions there will be editors, researchers, people responsible for graphics, and so on. A useful piece of homework or preparatory work is to ask the pupils to note the roles listed at the ends of the programmes they watch. Some roles need adapting to classroom work but others can be adopted without change. The role of editor, for example, should ensure that the pupils review and redraft their work – a task that, even with the advent of word processors, it is still difficult to get many children to do. When the task is completed, television-style credits can be added. In difficult cases, even more structure may be needed: for example, no one speaks twice until everyone has spoken once; or a model microphone can be passed round to allow everyone an opportunity to contribute to the vital process of talking things through.

Co-operative classroom work should not stay at this restricted level and teachers should try to develop pupils' capacity to work independently in groups, initiating discussion and activity, posing their own questions and developing their own procedures and rules of discourse. Highly structured groupwork is no more than a starting point, but it is an important one for inexperienced or unco-operative pupils. I have developed a series of texts covering personal, social, work and health issues for troublesome teenagers (McManus 1990/1). These grew out of work with pupils in exclusion units and special placements, and they are highly structured and prescriptive. They do, however, aim to reproduce as far as possible the characteristics of accessible exposition, with a focus on pupils themselves engaging in learning activities and talk. Themes are introduced through picture-stories, repeated in simple prose with a reading age of around 10 years, and developed through guided discussion and written work. Some of the themes are directly relevant to the lives of troubled youngsters and examples are included in the activities for Chapter 6.

## TEACHING SKILLS FOR TRADITIONAL CLASSROOM MANAGEMENT

### Early encounters

1 Get there first, introduce yourself, supervise entry.
2 Occupy centre stage, make directive statements, plenty of eye contact.
3 Give impressions as well as instructions: voice tone and pitch, facial expression, posture, use of space, proximity – relaxed and confident.
4 Scan class to get attention, mid-sentence stop and wait, stare.
5 Demeanour brisk, hard, resist queries, keep mystery.
6 Part or whole of first lesson: content simple, undramatic, not too exciting, perhaps on rules, safety, management.
7 State rules or draw them out in 'discussion' – work, property, talking, movement. Use consensual 'we'.
8 Discover and use names.

### The main part of the lesson

9 Give the lesson a clear form and state it.
10 Make a businesslike start: leave last lesson's leftovers or inquisitions on missing work till later.
11 Starting with a little deskwork helps to settle restless classes and organizes books and equipment.
12 A fresh and vigorous approach engages pupil attention; personal study or observing a colleague may revive a jaded topic.
13 Preparation should include time and materials as well as the content of the topic.
14 Organize and plan movements (who, what, why, where, when), give warnings of changes in activities, remind pupils of any changes in rules.
15 Show how content is related to pupils' present concerns or future interests and connect it with their existing knowledge and attainments.
16 Vary the activities and learning styles: watching, listening, writing, making and question-and-answer sessions, as well as working in pairs and groups.
17 Beware of unequally distributing your attention, questions, evaluations: be flexible enough to value unexpected contributions.

18 Some groups need explicit instructions for relatively unstructured or pupil-directed tasks: specific questions, lists and set times for each component.
19 Keep a roving eye: show that everything is noticed, even if intervention is avoided.
20 Do not let an individual or group monopolize your attention: mark, explain, organize, discipline, read and listen all at once.
21 Keep the momentum: vary the pace without confusing halts.
22 Do not stay on one issue too long: use telepathy.
23 Regularly mark, praise, encourage, give feedback or evidence of careful monitoring.
24 Do not interrupt the flow of a lesson unnecessarily: keep till later things suddenly remembered or noticed.
25 Do not leave an activity and then return to it abruptly after starting another.
26 Be aware of your use of space: at front, across narrow length, potentially mobile for exposition; at rear or moving for pupil work.

**Responding to disruption**

27 Try to nip trouble in the bud using eyes, gesture, proximity, territory invasion, touch or an invitation to contribute to the lesson.
28 Use pupil's name, specify unwanted behaviour and the target activity.
29 Give task-related reasons for disapproval rather than stating personal preference.
30 Make corrective statements short: avoid nagging, threats and interrogation.
31 Do not recite past misdemeanours.
32 Do not make unfavourable comparisons with siblings and use only models that the pupil respects.
33 Correct the action not the actor: infer approval of the individual while correcting the behaviour.
34 Try to let natural consequences be the punishment and have a respected person responsible for their supervision.
35 Avoid mass punishment of a class or group.
36 Do not be an inflexible ruler: pupils usually understand the need for exceptions if reasons are given.
37 Where a child is unamenable to your control, show in a cool, dispassionate way that you are aware and disapprove.
38 A hard stare, averting eyes sideways if necessary, can be more effective than a verbal rebuke.
39 Focus on the principal in any disturbance: do not pick on supporters – they will fall into line if the chief agent of the disorder is controlled.

40 In a confrontation, keep voice low, arms still, posture relaxed and avoid poking.
41 Soft and private reprimands are sometimes more effective than loud public rebukes ('A soft answer turneth away wrath', Proverbs 15: 1).
42 Break off arguments with peace terms clearly and simply specified.
43 Where a child must be ejected, lead out while repeating some concrete and achievable conditions for re-entry.
44 Do not neglect the rest of the class while dealing with a difficult pupil.
45 Give generous apologies for mistakes: imply your authority is invulnerable to error.

### Clearing up and exit

46 Prepare and organize the ending of a lesson: it may not happen naturally – plan and leave time for it.
47 Be prepared for the most difficult pupils to finish their work ahead of the class.
48 Review what has been achieved and relate it to future plans.
49 The departure of the class allows an opportunity for a brief word with those who have not co-operated.
50 An orderly dismissal, with a relaxed and smiling teacher, minimizes problems and is a good prelude to the next meeting.

## ACTIVITY 3.1: BASIC TRIALS

The group should divide into pairs or threes for this exercise, each taking one or more examples for discussion. Ten minutes is usually ample time for small group discussions before sharing ideas with the whole group. In reality, of course, decisions are usually required in a considerably shorter time than this. For each incident, decide what action should be taken and what further information you would like or other factors you would take into account. The principal task, however, is to decide on the appropriate action and to be able to justify it by reference to experience, reason or other evidence. There are no certain answers but there are some things to avoid and some strategies likely to be more successful than others. Some comments on this exercise are offered and these are based on my own experience of using the task with teachers and students.

1 In a busy corridor at change of lesson time a pupil has apparently just kicked an orange along the corridor. You have told her to pick it up but she does not move or speak.
2 On duty at break time you see a crowd gathering. Two sturdy boys are facing each other and a fight seems imminent.
3 As the class enters your room, one of the pupils says in a loud voice

that she is doing no work for such a boring teacher as yourself. She slumps in her seat with folded arms.

4 During your exposition in the early part of the lesson there is a sudden outburst of laughter from a group. Other pupils turn in its direction and look at you as the laughter spreads.

5 Although you and the class are waiting to begin the lesson, two pupils continue their conversation as if oblivious to your presence. They continue chatting, ignoring your call for attention.

6 You enter a classroom to find the whole class in turmoil and completely out of control. You consider calling one out to the front but fear it will be (accurately) described as victimization.

## Comments on the 'basic trials' exercise

In general, the more varied the experience of the group, and the higher its level of expertise, the more its members' decisions will have provisos and reservations attached. Such groups are also more likely to feel further information is necessary before a decision can be taken. When these cases are presented to inexperienced student-teachers there is a greater readiness to offer a general solution, often described as if no alternative were possible in principle. This indicates both that experienced teachers do have a professional knowledge that is not merely common sense and that thoughtful reflection is a factor in professional expertise. This difference between the experts and the beginners is reflected in studies reported by Berliner in his chapter in Calderhead (1987). When shown films or slides of classroom scenes, teachers saw complex activities where beginners saw only surface features. Suggestions from teachers and, for comparison, students are given below.

1 'Try to deal with it when the audience has gone – if it's change of lesson time, that should be possible.'

'Pick it up yourself and say something like: "that's a bit of luck, I don't fancy school lunch today".'

'It would depend on who had done the kicking and whether I was sure – I would be able to estimate their intentions and know what to do. It would probably be too trivial to get into a row about defiance over.'

A popular solution from the inexperienced: order the pupil to go to the head, and if they refuse take their arm and lead them or go and fetch the head yourself.

2 'I think you would have to intervene at once, but in a light way. I'd ask who was paying them; no sensible person gets themselves bashed for free – I might get rid of the crowd by pretending to take a collection.'

'You have to be careful not to rush up with a blue light flashing – if there's a weaker one he might take the opportunity to get a quick one in as rescue is at hand, and so you might actually cause a fight to start that might have been avoided.'

'I might hurry slowly if they were equally matched and it wasn't too serious – let them have a brief punch – I find they're easier to separate then because honour's satisfied and they are both a bit hurt.'

'It would depend on the pupils and when it was – I usually find a sharp shout stops them.'

'If it was something silly I'd shout: "give 'em room". If it was more dangerous I would get there as fast as possible.'

Inexperienced students usually see no alternative to instant reaction to what is always assumed to be a very serious situation.

3 'No one's going to admit they have this, but when it happens I say: "fine, school's supposed to be boring; I spent last night working to get this lesson as boring as this dear; I take my job very seriously".'

'I would say: "okay, join in when you like". I might not take any notice at all – I'd make some brisk remark and leave it at that.'

'It would depend which class it was. I usually say: "look, you think it's boring but I've been doing this lesson for twenty-five years – just think how bored I am with it".'

'I would avoid feeling challenged and probably ignore it in most cases – secondary pupils are always bored whatever you do.'

Most students assume that the pupil's remark is intended as a serious comment: they would explain the importance of their subject.

4 'This is usually because you've said something that means something rude to the pupils. Just shut them up and carry on.'

'With little ones it's usually that someone's made a noise – best to ignore it.'

'It reminds me of the music hall comedians' rule: unexpected bursts of laughter – check flies.'

The inexperienced would make the pupils come out and tell the joke to the class in order to silence them.

5 'It depends whether it is deliberate or not – some kids do get involved and don't notice. I might say to the class: "shush, these two are talking and I can't hear".'

'I would probably pull a chair up if it was some kids I know and say, "do go on, how interesting".'

Students are generally at a loss in this particularly tricky situation, sometimes referred to in the literature as 'thirdpartying'. One of the most inappropriate suggestions made was to threaten that, for every minute they continued talking, the whole class would be kept in for five minutes at the end of the lesson. This idea did not come from a mathematician.

6 'I wouldn't bother about being called unfair – I'd just say I always pick on someone with some sense when I want a job done.'

'I would apologize, in a very loud voice, for keeping them waiting – that usually causes enough puzzlement to produce enough quiet to make a start.'

'You can just go in and shout any name, tell them to come out to the front. They all want to know what's going on, so they go quiet and you've got them.'

Beginners would usually shout until they got silence. The most interesting suggestion ever offered was from a student who would 'just speak to the quiet ones'.

## ACTIVITY 3.2: PERSONAL QUALITIES

Think of a good teacher whom you know: it could a colleague or someone who taught you – it could even be yourself. Write down three or four words or phrases that you might use to describe the teacher and say why he or she is a good teacher. If you are working in a group you will find that you have many words and phrases in common. Compile a list of about twelve characteristics and then try to allocate those with common features to general groups – which you should be able to name. If you are working alone, extend your list to about a dozen words before carrying out this part of the activity.

Comments on this activity (which should not be looked at yet) are placed in the final section of Chapter 5.

## ACTIVITY 3.3: DISCOVERING GENERAL TEACHING FUNCTIONS

This is a ground-breaking activity, in that little work has been done in this area and original insights are therefore possible. The purpose is to clarify the relevance and application of classroom management skills to your own circumstances; discovering which general principles are important will clarify the role of particulars and help prevent disagreement about items which are functionally equivalent. This exercise will help you think more systematically about the familiar classroom scene, alert you to the ambiguities of classroom-management rules, and give you insights into and confidence in your classroom practice. The fifty tips presented as a summary of this chapter are distributed for convenience into the lesson-phases identified by Hargreaves *et al.* (1975). You are asked to redistribute them, adding any you think are missing, by grouping them into clusters which can be encompassed in more general teaching functions. There are many ways of using the list of teacher skills; the one outlined here is probably a good way of sorting out ideas and clearing up disagreements.

The first thing to do is to clarify two meanings of the term 'general'. General can mean that something is prevalent or generally applicable. For example, teachers generally spend their first lessons explaining their classroom rules. General can also mean something abstract, high-level or inclusive. For example, a general teacher skill is to get attention. Note that general (prevalent) skills can be quite low level and specific; general (inclusive) skills are, by definition, higher level – and probably prevalent, too.

Groups of three or four should spend about thirty minutes on this activity. Begin by deciding which skills are prevalent in your particular school; in many cases it will be easier to list those that are not applicable to your circumstances. Keep a note of disagreements. The next step is to try to group the skills into generally inclusive groups. You could begin with those skills that are not applicable to your school, or those on which there was disagreement. The three categories proposed as starters by Doyle (Doyle and Carter, 1986a) (coverage, explicitness and accountability) may be helpful, but there must be others. You should find that disagreements disappear when low-level skills are grouped into higher, inclusive categories. For example, a teacher who begins lessons by calling for order is not in contention with one who begins by waiting silently: both are using forms of attention-getting. Your group work is complete when you have resolved, or at least understood, disagreements and decided on some general inclusive categories into which specific skills fall. If a category you believe to be a generally inclusive one seems to include nothing but itself, then it is probably low level and applicable only to limited contexts; if a category seems to include everything, it is too inclusive and should be divided. (Two absurd examples would be, respectively, distributing pencils and surviving.) Beware of taking the generally applicable nature of a skill for granted. For example, in the Evertson and Emmer (1982) research, eye-contact was found to be less important in maths than in English; and Japanese pupils are said to remain attentive without lifting their gaze from their desks (Martin Monk, *TES*, 17.6.88: 20).

# Chapter 4

# Pupil perspectives, motives and strategies

It is pithily said: 'Give a dog an ill name and hang him'; and it may be added, 'if you give a man or race of men an ill name, they are very likely to do something that deserves hanging'.

(Sir Walter Scott, *Guy Mannering*, 1815)

Cooper (1993) studied a group of exceptional pupils in a residential school for difficult pupils. Their views on their teachers and on schools in general are remarkably consistent with those of more conventionally behaved youngsters. They welcomed the opportunity for individual attention that helped them to learn, to cope with domestic trauma and develop their confidence: 'Since coming here I can talk to my mum better. We get on now. I think I'm ready to go back' (Cooper, 1993: 55). They respected teachers who were not too formal or humourless and who were interested in pupils' personal welfare: 'Here they're flexible ... more friendly. Staff will give you more time if you want to talk to them.' The picture that emerges is of pupils valuing their teachers' understanding, and one pupil contrasts this with his previous experience: 'They was trying to make out I was worse than I was.' This seems to contradict any view that such pupils were merely seeking escape from school, and reveals them to have more in common with the mainstream of young people than might be expected. A similar conclusion can be drawn about some of the excluded pupils discussed in Chapter 2 who, in their new setting, valued strict teachers who enforced reasonable rules and made them get on with their work.

Much research on pupils has attempted to uncover their views and opinions rather than treating them as objects whose attributes can be measured. Finlayson and Loughran (1975) found that top-stream boys perceived their teachers to be less authoritarian in their behaviour towards them than was the case with the perceptions of lower-stream boys. In comparisons between schools, teachers in low-delinquency schools were perceived to be less hostile in their behaviour towards pupils than their colleagues in high-delinquency schools. If pupils think teachers are hostile towards them this would clearly influence pupil co-operation. Even if the pupils are mistaken, there are implications in these findings for how teachers present their discipline requirements. If the connection between disruption and domestic upheaval is accepted, then it is important for teachers to avoid confirming the pupils in their antagonism towards others. Some pupils will be working off their ill-feelings towards adults in the relatively safe surroundings of the school. Not surprisingly, they may engender teacher hostility by their behaviour. Whatever the case, it is arguably our professional responsibility to understand what may be happening and take the first steps towards breaking out of the cycle.

Many studies find pupils of all ages and dispositions to be in general agreement about how teachers should behave. Teachers must keep order, explain things clearly, have interesting lessons, treat pupils with respect, be fair and friendly and have a sense of humour. Teachers who have favourites or who show pupils up in front of their peers are strongly disapproved of. A summary of several enquiries is included in Docking (1980: 108–9).

I have found pupils excluded from school to have similarly conventional views, and they often blame the weakness or unfairness of their teachers for their own predicament. This may be pupils seeking to come to terms with their behaviour by blaming others, or it may be simply a clash of views: what some pupils call 'having a laugh' is what some teachers call unacceptable insolence. Others, whose reasons for their behaviour are related to their domestic troubles or obligations, may cover these shaming facts by blaming teachers. Tattum (1982) refers to the neutralizing effect of pupils' explanations in helping them account for their misbehaviour. Teachers who had not interested them and who had picked on them unfairly deserved to be treated with disrespect.

Werthman (1963) took delinquents' justifications of their behaviour at face value and Marsh et al. (1978) found pupils judged and repaid teachers who transgressed their standards by not knowing pupils' names or being too soft and not teaching anything. Woods (1980a) is a useful collection of papers on pupils' strategies, the dynamics of friendship groups and pupils' attempts to negotiate space for themselves amid the competing pressures upon them. In most respects, pupils appear to be relatively conservative, particularly in their expectations of teachers. Davies (1984), in a study of difficult girls, suggests that they had more rigid moral standards than average and were less tolerant of teachers who deviated from their requirements. They were said to be annoyed by teachers who set a poor example, were rude, arrogant or who insulted the girls' 'reputation'. Schostak (1986) quotes Empson's remark that the criminal is 'the judge of the society that judges him'. Davies' girls, in close agreement with pupils in other studies, expected their teachers to have knowledge, to teach it and to be able to keep control without over-reacting 'when there was no need'.

Taking pupils' perspectives seriously is itself an important development, irrespective of the utility of the information gathered. It requires teachers to understand that on the public stage of the classroom, private intentions are vulnerable to interpretations not intended (Schostak, 1986). The work in this chapter, particularly the analyses of Dreikurs (1957) and Balson (1982), depends upon accepting pupils' perspectives and motives and seeking to satisfy the legitimate concerns that they expose. Studies seem to find that pupils have a rational basis for their behaviour. This is partly a consequence of researchers setting out to find one, but the evidence seems to be that pupils are capable of trying to be objective and rational when given the opportunity. To accept this as fact is to move a long way from the once popular view that difficult pupils had something wrong with them and that to be cured of it they needed to be removed for specialist treatment. Pring (1976), describing his difficulties with a group of inattentive and disorderly fourth-formers, asked himself not what was wrong with them, but what was it to educate these pupils who, in spite of their behaviour, had 'minds that questioned, puzzled, doubted, drew conclusions'. He continues: 'They were already engaged in some form of mental life (even Deborah) and it was that that made them educable.'

This argument is taken a stage further by Cronk (1987), who attempted to achieve understanding and co-operation with a chronically disorderly class. She argues that pupils can be trusted to be concerned with teachers' interests and that misunderstanding is at the root of antagonism in schools. She attempted, with some success, to banish it from her classroom. This involved both accepting the pupils' point of view and getting them to accept her own position in the school, bounded as it was by colleagues' expectations and other constraints. The solution to the problem of conflict is to convince pupils, through an accepting relationship, that they are people of value. Both teachers and pupils need to acknowledge each other as people and not seek refuge in the categories of (authoritarian) teacher or (intransigent) pupil. This may seem to be a circuitous route to getting pupils to comply with the traditional teacher role that pupils seem to expect. And it still leaves the problem encountered by Herbert Kohl (1986): is it essential to establish control first and become flexible later? Or can friendly negotiations be conducted from the outset? And how honest have they been if the outcome is always compliance on the teacher's terms? The process of reaching this result is not unimportant. It may be impossible to be fully and genuinely democratic in the class-room, but we do not avoid trying to be. Accepting pupils' points of view, revealing one's own feelings and dilemmas, sharing concerns and aspirations all imply genuine efforts at openness, communication and understanding: not a bad basis for classroom co-operation.

Pupils' classroom behaviour can be taken under two major headings: discovering and testing teachers' rules, resolution and ability to maintain order; and displaying, developing and defending personal identity. Most pupils also wish to establish and maintain a place in their chosen friendship or peer group which may or may not be one that is approved of by their teachers.

## TESTING TEACHERS AND DISCOVERING RULES

From time to time pupils, like any other workers, seek a little light relief from the inescapable tedium and tension of daily life: they like to 'have a laugh' and they prefer their teachers to have a sense of humour too. The particularly difficult motives of pupils who may be in an extreme state of distress and confusion will be discussed separately. Motives may be in conflict. For example, a pupil may wish to develop and display a personal identity as a bright pupil, pleasing to adults. He or she may also wish to retain an acceptable status in a classroom group where over-zealous, compliant pupils are rejected as 'swots and creeps'. Apparently incomprehensible behaviour may thus be witnessed from time to time. A successful and academically ambitious pupil may be caught in a piece of extravagant misbehaviour by which he or she intends to demonstrate to classmates an enjoyment of, and affinity with, their irreverence for schooling. For example, a bright primary school girl put a drawing pin on her teacher's chair, explaining that she feared that other pupils thought of her as a 'goody-goody', which of course she was. For an example of this in a prestigious grammar school, see Lacey's (1970) discussion of Sherman, a top pupil who balanced his achievements with mischief.

How pupils perform under each of these headings will depend upon their beliefs, expectations and attitudes. Their accumulated experience of dealings with adults, and in particular their parents or guardians, will to a large extent set the context for their first encounters with teachers. For some pupils, classroom disruption is no more than a temporary strategy adopted to break the tedium of a boring lesson or to punish an incompetent or humiliating teacher. Their misbehaviour is transient, of no wider or deeper significance, readily abandoned and easily controlled. Other pupils perceive the classroom as an extension of a harsh, unjust, unpredictable and unforgiving world: a world of stress, poverty, indifference or cruelty that most of us are fortunate enough never to have encountered. For such pupils, school offers a relatively safe environment for the exploration of their distrust, apprehensions, anger and insecurity. Their classroom disruption and disaffection may appear even in the most exciting and well-conducted lessons. It is difficult to bear and apparently impossible to eradicate whatever the level of care and encouragement given. Its significance and source of energy are largely from without the classroom.

This is not to say that such behaviour is a straightforward, determined effect of domestic environment: this behaviour is part of an active strategy. It is not determined in a mechanistic sense, and it is this that allows the teacher some purchase upon it. Pupils of all ages want to know what rules are in operation in any given situation. The less specific and convincing the teacher, the more the pupils will explore the boundaries of what they suspect to be permissible. As we saw in Chapter 3, it is not enough to state rules and expectations verbally: tone of voice, expression and demeanour are among the non-verbal types of communication by which pupils assess whether teacher means it and whether he or she has the determination and ability to control their wayward experiments. Pupils, like adults, form expectations of others in the light of their appearance and perhaps their reputation. They may be pleased to discover that they were correct in their prediction or disappointed and troublesome if the teacher turns out to be unexpectedly permissive or unaccountably strict. A pupil interviewed in a unit for disruptive teenagers blamed his present placement on the fact that he had not had 'big enough teachers'. The boy was of small build and physically unprepossessing, so we may assume he was speaking metaphorically.

Teacher testing is particularly prevalent at the start of the school year. And equally prevalent at the same time are teachers' attempts to make rules and expectations clear and to make them stick. For a long time this particular teacher activity remained invisible to university researchers and writers, partly because higher education takes a longer summer break than schools do and partly because teachers are reluctant to be observed 'licking the pupils into shape'. This has had unfortunate consequences for the training of teachers.

One of the studies reported by Wragg (1984) is of a trainee science teacher who had observed the regular class teacher conducting orderly lessons while lounging on the desk, making quips and flirting with the girls. The student attempted a similarly relaxed performance when his turn came, only to find it received with outraged indiscipline. The student had not observed, and had not been informed about, the extensive rule setting that this relaxed teacher had engaged in earlier in the term. The majority of secondary school science teachers choose rules and safety procedures for the first lesson of the year. The implicit message is here congruent with the explicit one: the teacher decides what is allowed and what is not; the pupil is expected to comply.

To recognize these skirmishes as merely teacher tests is usually all that is necessary to prevent them escalating into hostility. Teachers who perceive them as personal attacks on their authority and competence, or who explicitly identify them as stupidity, risk prolonging and aggravating the behaviour. From one point of view, pupils are not so much challenging the teacher's authority as trying to discover its form and extent in each particular case: they rebel in order to find out to what rules they must conform. McDermott claims that some low-ability pupils used misbehaviour in order to 'draw the teacher back to their group so that reading instruction could continue' (Wittrock, 1986: 420). Forms of misbehaviour which are often taken as tests of the teacher's authority may also have a beneficial function. For example, Delamont and Galton (1986) note that for some pupils fighting is an essential part of sorting out peer-group relationships. It may be that in more liberal schools pupils' increased area of discretion requires more of these sorting activities. 'Rough-housing' may help to produce an orderly school. Whether this is so or not, there is no doubt that to accept these testing encounters as part of the ordinary routine is to cut away their power to offend: pupils find not an opponent but an understanding and indestructible adult with whom they are content.

Teacher testing takes many forms. A powerful negotiating counter on the pupils' side is the level of noise in the classroom – a matter over which they have considerable control. The closed classrooms so prevalent in primary schools, and to a greater extent in secondary schools, are an organizational feature largely responsible for creating the noise weapon. Noise is one of the few features of classrooms that can be detected from without: above a minimal level it betokens indiscipline and disorder. As Nash (1973) noted, keeping pupils quiet is part of the teacher's job. It is no help to cite evidence that pupil talk is essential to learning in a wide range of subjects, including science, where practical activity might be thought a suitable substitute for talk (for example, Barnes, 1969 and Driver, 1983). The significance of noise in classrooms is extensively treated in Denscombe (1985) and in his chapter of the book edited by Woods (1980b).

Not all pupils need to be actively engaged in testing behaviour, and many members of a class may gain much valuable information from the active service of a few. Ball (1981) noted that the fate of those explorative pupils who elected to test the boundaries influenced the behaviour of others in the class. A noisy dispute between two pupils may be serving as a test. Teachers who seek to pacify and mediate in such public arguments may unintentionally and implicitly display their ignorance of pupils' more subtle forms of warfare. The appropriate tactic is to silence the parties briskly, perhaps with an offer to settle the dispute for them in their own time after the lesson. Teachers who did not lose their tempers, did not ignore the tests and did not show confusion were more effective in establishing control (Ball, 1981).

Verbal disputes may take a stylized and alarming form as in 'sounding or woofing' imported from American youth culture, though Doyle says it is not widespread (Wittrock, 1986: 418). Beynon (1985) observed this type of misbehaviour and noted that a smiling 'victim' indicated that a teacher-testing tactic was in progress. Verbal tests include requests for readily available information or the offer of counterfeit or absurd answers. Non-verbal tests often take the form of outdoor clothing and hats if the encounter takes place indoors. Other strategies include an over-literal response to instructions, a walk that is too fast or too slow, an inappropriately relaxed or stiff posture and extravagant yawns and displays of tiredness. Werthman (1963) provides an interesting early description of some of these tactics employed by American teenagers. The wise teacher will expect to be tested by pupils in early encounters and he or she will therefore be neither disappointed nor dismayed. It is important not to identify testing behaviour wrongly: it is not so trivial that it can be ignored but it is not so serious that it merits excessively vigorous suppression. Pupil mythology contains stories of teachers who were easily baited and driven into rages in which they sometimes injured themselves. The best tactic is to appear unsurprised and to react in a calm, clear and unconfused manner. Early encounters between secondary school teachers and their classes have been illuminatively researched by Beynon (1985). The topic is also treated by Ball in his chapter of the book edited by Woods (1980a). Pupils expect teachers to keep order and to make curricular demands upon them. They expect teachers to be worthy of their attention and respect and to be able to withstand their probing and provocation.

## DISPLAYING, DEVELOPING AND DEFENDING PERSONAL IDENTITY

Becoming an autonomous person involves rejecting some characteristics and adopting others. Parents, teachers, brothers, sisters and friends may all be rejected and new affiliations experimented with as adolescents attempt to carve out what they are and what they are not. The eager compliance that many young children display gradually – and sometimes not so gradually – gives way to the stubborn independence, reluctance and defiance of the teenage years. This is seldom a straightforward progression. Caspari (1976: 22) notes that 'at one time they want to be looked after like very young children, at other times they oppose whatever those in authority say'. Reconciling the need to choose an individual path with the limitations imposed by family, school and society is not an easy task. Few accomplish it without trauma. It is necessary to accept that deviant behaviour is a normal part of growing up and a part of becoming a person in one's own right. A population of compulsive rule-followers is an unwanted, appalling and sinister alternative. Adolescent pupils are known particularly to resent rules about and criticism of personal features such as dress and hairstyles, and teachers are wise to be flexible in these matters (Werthman, 1963; Reynolds and Sullivan, in Gillham, 1981). The growth of individuality involves sensitivity to perceived attacks on personal morals and dignity as well as a wish to have some autonomy (Marsh *et al.*, 1978; Corrigan, 1979; Davies, 1984). An interesting difference in the possibly differing approaches of boys and girls to impending adulthood is mentioned by Stott (1982). He quotes a survey which showed that whereas boys who ran away from home tended to involve themselves in petty crime, girls did not. The suggestion is that boys run away in order to accomplish illegal purposes but girls run away in order to resolve personal problems. Girls seem to face the fact that they must one day separate from their parents, perhaps to create a new family, earlier than boys. Unable to cope with the uncertainty in respect of time, and the need to prepare for a break from parents to whom they still need close attachment, some choose to make a break immediately. For them, the certainty of instant separation is preferable to the continuation of what they come to perceive as a jeopardized relationship. When young people go beyond acceptable limits it is therefore important to show that although the behaviour is disapproved of the teacher still values the individual. The inappropriate act must be corrected without rejecting or attacking the pupil's self-image. Some confused and troublesome pupils complain that teachers do not recognize them as the sort of person that they really are, deep down below the surface hostility.

It is part of Cronk's (1987) philosophical argument that conflict between people, and specifically between secondary school pupils and teachers, is a consequence of misunderstanding: that is, a failure to communicate with each other and to understand intentions and feelings as well as the constraints under which each is acting. On a related theme, Sharp and Green (1975) quote the distinction between knowing someone as a contemporary and as a consociate. Put simply, this is the difference between recognizing someone as a member of a category of people and knowing someone as if they were a member of one's own family: the difference between noticing a black child, a middle-class child or a disruptive child and meeting Peter or Jane. Where the category is feared or distrusted by the teacher, or simply mysterious to them, there is little hope of understanding and every possibility that ignorance will grow into hostility. Familiarity is more likely to breed understanding than contempt; hence the phenomenon of 'going native' and coming to share and reinterpret the world from the perspective that was originally the object of dispassionate study. The plain conclusion to be drawn is that there needs to be space and time in schools for teachers and pupils to meet and get to know one another. This may be through regular timetabled contact at times which allow informal communication; it may be through a whole week shared on a field trip or holiday. Timed arrangements may not be essential. Where teachers have responsibility for, and discretion over, the treatment of their pupils, both parties will see the benefit of understanding one another. If the school provides the purpose and incentive, the time may look after itself. It may be objected that teachers cannot take account of individual pupil needs but are constrained to treat all equally regardless of individual development: accusations of unfairness have to be avoided. At least with adolescents, this objection is not difficult to counter. Teenagers who are trying to become independent can be persuaded that different treatment is appropriate from time to time.

## CONCERNING EXCEPTIONAL CHILDREN

Some pupils have a limited number of inflexible strategies in their interactions with others. They may comply, ignore or fight, and assume that other people's behaviour always fits one of these categories (Horney, quoted in Laslett, 1977). Experience of adults has led them to adopt rigid and restricted views of adult behaviour; they may be reluctant to accept that anyone can be genuinely concerned about them. This attitude is sometimes a strong compound of two elements: that other people are heartless, ruthless and untrustworthy; and that they themselves are defective and worthless individuals. Adult attempts at making a friendly relationship and showing kindness may be construed as weakness, want of intellect or deception. Sometimes such children give evidence of their perspective in gross misunderstandings: a smile may be interpreted as a challenge to fight or as a sign of someone's contempt. Teachers who work with difficult children are not unaccustomed to having their normal, relaxed facial expressions misconstrued. They may be greeted first thing on a frosty, winter morning with: 'What's up with you? You're in a bad mood aren't you?'. This hypothesis can sometimes be self-fulfilling. Stott (1982) believes hostility to adults is usually an extension of hostility to parents. This does not necessarily betoken parental fecklessness or cruelty. Hostility is often a reaction to a fear of being abandoned or removed; such fears can be engendered through circumstances under no one's control. In some cases the child's fears result from misperception due to a physical or intellectual impairment. Parental perfection is unattainable and parents may fail to live up to their children's expectations through illness, poverty or other misfortune.

Stott (1982) stresses that children need a secure attachment to a loyal, dependable, caring parent figure. Deprived of a permanent, secure attachment, a child seems to prefer the certainty of abandonment to the uncertainty of unpredictable adults: like a jilted lover who seeks revenge upon, or destruction of, the lost one. Generalizing from experience, some pupils may hypothesize that all adults are similarly unreliable and seek to avoid any kind of attachment. One consequence of this is that those teachers who feel and show most concern may receive the most hostility, though it be interspersed with trust. Stott describes examples of family situations conducive to the development of behaviour likely to be described as maladjusted. First, the preferred parent may be lost through divorce or death and the remaining parent may prove an inadequate replacement: a father may die and the mother take to drink, for example. Second, the preferred parent may be undependable through tiredness, lack of interest or weariness induced by a tiresome baby. Those infants who wake at dawn and do not require sleep again until late evening, and then only fitfully, try the patience of even the most comfortable and well-disposed parents. Third, there are situations of potential loss where a parent threatens to have a child put into care or sent to live with a relative. Often this threat has massive credibility, for some family circumstances lead occasionally and unpredictably to such separations. The fourth situation is again one of potential loss: this may be through a parental illness requiring periodic hospital treatment; it may be through occasional imprisonment or flight from creditors; it may be because parental rows persuade a child that family break-up is imminent.

Hostility, then, may be viewed optimistically as the aggressive search for that which is lost. Laslett (1977) discusses the distinction between deprivation and privation. Those who have suffered privation have never known a warm, human relationship, either through sensory disability or the lack of appropriate parenting. They may become withdrawn, for they cannot seek that which they do not know they have lost. Deprived children, on the other hand, have experienced the loss of a valued relationship and aggressively search for a replacement. Interestingly, teachers often unwittingly identify this motive in accusing troublesome pupils of behaving as if the world owes them something: from one point of view this behaviour, exasperating though it is, can be seen as a sign of potential progress. Hostile children may be expressing disappointment at finding adults to be less than they wish them to be. From a practical point of view, it matters not at all if such an estimation is incorrect. To believe that improvement is possible is to act towards the pupil in an encouraging way and to help to bring improvement about. A possibility defined as real may turn out to be real in its outcome.

Some pupils seek refuge from reminders of wretched memories in extreme behaviour. They may have periods of complete frenzy, climb dangerous scaffolding, or wander fairgrounds or city centres in search of distraction. Stott (1982) terms this wild, excitement-seeking behaviour 'avoidance compulsion' – its purpose, however dimly appreciated by the child, is to blot out present reminders of past traumas. To avoid reminders of experiences that have wounded in the past is a form of self-defence in a literal sense. It may be the prospect of meeting a teacher who is particularly valued by the pupil, and who therefore revives fears associated with past relationships which became painful or were destroyed. Even the architectural features of a particular room may trigger turbulent feelings associated with a past trauma. A milder but more disruptive way of distracting oneself is to hum, whistle or make repetitive groaning noises in the classroom. Such behaviour is less intensely annoying if it is interpreted as a desperate attempt to remove discomfort.

Balson (1982) does not refer to this pupil strategy but it is possible to use one's own feelings, as he suggests, to help identify it. For example, in Chapter 2, I described a teacher whose response to a pupil's name elicited avoidance-compulsion behaviour from the pupil. This pupil had a fear of new people and situations which he disguised as insolent disobedience. On trips to museums, for instance, he would defiantly and abusively refuse to get out of my car. He tried to get himself sent home from my unit by inciting other boys, and nearly succeeded when he bribed one to stand on a wall exposing himself to passing traffic. When this failed, he began arriving earlier than me, pulling the door handle off, and blocking the lock with putty. This continued until we agreed a truce one morning, just before 7 a.m. He was the only surviving baby born to a tragic couple; perhaps obsessive sheltering had something to do with his fears. In ordinary school, and a school for the maladjusted, he created mayhem, was suspected of arson, and was impossible to communicate with. He was not, as many thought, a delinquent but might have been transformed into one by being put in custody. Now in his twenties, he has never taken a job, has somehow found a wife, and is an unexceptional parent. Not a success story, but better than might have been expected. An ordinary school would have needed two things in order to cope with him: sufficient and suitable teachers and the courage to give at least some discretion in dealing with him. In other words, schools need staff with the skills and understanding, but flexibility and liberty are required in the organization.

Children who have grown up accustomed to being let down by adults may repeatedly and severely test teachers who seek to help them. Periods of peace and progress may be broken by violent and distressing confrontations. Often a recent recruit to a school's staff is the person who seems to make progress with a difficult pupil and to have caused the pupil finally to settle down. But from the pupil's point of view, the situation is by no means stable. Past experience has taught them to expect disappointment: they must test to see whether 'interest is genuine and permanent' (Stott, 1982). Confronted with a teacher who appears to be friendly, the pupil may be confused. He or she may suspect deception. He or she may be prone to loss of control and may wonder whether the new ally on the teaching staff can withstand such a crisis. The pupil may seek relief ·from uncertainty by staging a scene or relapsing into disruptive behaviour. It is at this point, when the teacher's reserves of patience and optimism are stretched, that continued patience and optimism are vital to the disturbing pupil's progress.

It is well to remember that only the apparently genuine merits testing and to take the crisis as an unskilled and socially inept method of indicating provisional approval. It may not feel like one, but to be the subject of such a test is a compliment to the teacher's ability to shake the pupil's misanthropic convictions. A teacher who is willing to invest in such an unpromising relationship must accept the possibility of loss and be determined enough to begin again. A pupil may steal money from the teacher as well as trust. In one case a girl confronted a teacher who had expended much effort upon her, including taking her home and taking her out with her own daughters of the same age. The girl climbed on to a table and dived to the floor at the teacher's feet, injuring her head. In these circumstances it is not easy to see any purpose in continuing evidently wasted efforts. This is what the pupil expects but may not hope for. To be able to carry on after such incidents, to prove to the pupil that whatever happens they will still be accepted, is to be able to take control and exercise influence at a time when the circumstances are most opportune for change. The pupil least expects to be accepted after such crises. A teacher who is still welcoming, and possibly still smiling, may make a dramatic impact on a disturbed pupil's shell of fear and hostility.

Pupils who carry burdens of past troubles often find difficulty communicating feelings of regret in a way that is easily recognized. It is important that their self-initiated attempts at restitution are not thwarted. Wills (1945) thought that punishment removed the pupil's need to learn how to repair damaged relationships. They may try to make amends for actions they regret in ways that may create a fresh offence. This camouflaged reparation may take the form of attacking another pupil whom they judge to have offended the teacher; they may insist on finishing a piece of work, previously praised by the teacher, at an inconvenient time; or they may choose to strip the bookshelves in order to tidy them and in the process prevent the rest of the class from using the books or carrying on with their work. In circumstances where the pupil's activity must be stopped, a positive form of words indicating recognition and acceptance together with postponement is advisable. The most dramatic example I have encountered was on a visit to the elegant gardens of a stately mansion. A pupil who had behaved outrageously on the bus journey chose to make amends by ripping plants from the carefully classified arrays and presenting a bouquet to her teacher. The flowers said one thing to the teacher, another to the gardener.

Pupils may sometimes be the agent of their parents' motives. Some parents may believe that their interests are served by having a problem child at school. Certainly those who were humiliated or failed by their own schooling may take satisfaction in having a child who illustrates their conviction that teachers are ineffectual. Those seeking vicarious revenge range through the social class spectrum – from straightforward criminal to 'militant muesli'. In other, more tragic, cases, a parent may hope to hold together a crumbling relationship or marriage by magnifying and encouraging problem behaviour in a child – perhaps to convince the errant partner that their child needs both of them. Related to this are those cases where a child is not permitted to think well of a parent who has deserted, the remaining parent's bitterness being a source of confusion in a school environment where loving two parents is implied in activities, talk and reading.

Delamont and Galton (1986) remarked on how the idealized, stereotypical family with defined roles penetrates and permeates school life. There are those children whose parent is unable to come to terms with the death of a partner. We must minimize the hazards for a pupil unable to think well of both parents, as others do (Hanko, 1985). Many pupils in these situations are unable or do not know how to express their confusion in school; and their frequently abstracted attitude may lead to their being typed unhelpfully. Hanko (1985) contains casework examples and Schostak (1986) speaks eloquently for such pupils: 'There is an aspect to being alive that is non-transferable, unutterable, opaque and alone. Pain cannot be shared – self licks its own wounds.'

By the time serious behavioural problems have developed – for example, where a child substitutes a coping strategy of withdrawal for one of aggression – the original event may be long past. The past can live on in the present through its effects and its memory. Teachers may find that they are presented with emotions and feelings that rightfully belong to another person, another time, another place. Dyke (1987) suggests that to recognize that one is acting as a focus for projections 'can enormously assist the teacher in resisting being overwhelmed by these feelings'. The attitude of mistrust or hostility has to be viewed as the pupil's problem not the teacher's. How they choose to react, however, can help or handicap its solution; receiving hostility becomes a professional duty not a personal failing. In many cases of domestic disorder, poverty is the most obvious handicapping factor. Poverty acts upon children through their parents and some parents are more resilient than others. Teachers sometimes feel powerless when faced with situations that seem remediable only through massive injections of skilfully managed cash; but it is always possible to help a family to cope by helping a pupil to learn self-control. Domestic problems cannot be solved, but teachers 'can go a long way towards alleviating them if they recognise they exist' (Chandler, quoted in Hanko, 1985: 62).

Sometimes there are no features in children's lives or domestic circumstances that seem relevant to their testing strategies or disturbing behaviour. In such cases the only possible conclusion seems to be that there is some biological or psychological pathology in need of chemistry, not education. Sometimes this diagnosis is accompanied by the claim, only partly humorous, that the wrong child was brought home from the hospital: he or she does not even look like the others in the family and they have no behavioural problems. The pessimistic acceptance of a pathological cause is unwarranted. Children have to win attention in their families as elsewhere. For example, a child may be unable to gain parents' attention and rewards as a quiet and studious person if that role is already occupied by a sibling. The busier the parents, the harder the offspring must battle for a scarce commodity: some children learn to use tantrums, some extreme greediness or selfishness, others use sickness and pains. They may find that merely being noisier or less sociable is effective. Some develop food fads, which change if they are ineffective attention winners. Stott (1982) claims that institutional children do not use this strategy for this reason. He gives examples of pupils who used learning failure to win the attention of parents: dyslexia, like knowledge, can be power. Those children who try a succession of such strategies only confirm the adult's opinion that they are truly maladjusted.

It is not suggested that any information schools may have on domestic circumstances and history is for intervention or remedy by teachers. Caspari, for example, points to the unreliability of domestic information and says that it is, in any case, 'only of limited use in the day-to-day relationship between teacher and children in the classroom' (Caspari, 1976: 2). She then goes on to say that such information 'will of course increase [the teacher's] understanding of the child's behaviour and will influence his reaction towards the child'. This is not a slight benefit, however. There is value in understanding how a pupil's behaviour in school is related to an inextricably tangled network of interactions, past, present and possible. Knowledge helps to prevent unintentionally reproducing the domestic traumas in school. All teachers recognize, for example, that care must be taken when pupils are bereaved.

There are many other situations that can be unintentionally evoked: for example, the accidental re-enactment of rejection, abandonment or restriction that is the domestic cause of a pupil's distress (Hanko, 1985). It is also not the case that the families of troublesome pupils are necessarily feckless: for example, some children lack a relationship with a dependable adult not because the adult is not there, but because unsuspected deafness has interfered with communication. The effort to understand how children have experienced and responded to their home lives should also counter the pessimistic determinism that often accompanies discussion of pupils' homes. Home conditions are not a determinant irrelevant to teachers' concerns. The assumptions, expectations and attitudes that pupils carry into school are rooted in their experience and influence the strategies they adopt in encounters with teachers. Recognizing this, we may feel inspired to disappoint the pupil's pessimism and remain open and friendly – willing to accept the pupil's feelings. It is part of our professional role to receive and cope with emotions and confusions.

This includes those that belong to past relationships or to troubles elsewhere.

Children's behaviour is usefully viewed as an active response to their experiences, not an unconscious causal result. As Bastide (1972) notes, problems from another time or place can affect the present only by being retrieved in the present: traumas are not single but double. If children's behaviour is to be changed it is necessary to avoid reproducing or re-enacting the domestic stresses and attitudes that have contributed to their present difficulties. Resisting the automatic combat response that some pupil behaviour evokes is the first step in changing one's own behaviour and thereby improving pupil experience. The teacher's tactic must be to be patient and determined that the pupil will find his or her fears to be groundless. Understanding must be strong enough to withstand whatever havoc the pupil can create. The teacher must provide security and predict ability: a splint in which a damaged self can heal. Banishment and reproach must be avoided, and even kind words may be unacceptable, but acceptance can be communicated without words. Before troublesome pupils will risk facing up to themselves they have to be sure they have found a teacher in whose company it is safe to fail.

## ATTENTION, POWER AND REVENGE

> In dealing with cunning persons, we must ever consider their ends to interpret their speeches; and it is good to say little to them, and that which they least look for. In all negotiations of difficulty, a man may not look to sow and reap at once; but must prepare business, and so ripen it by degrees.
>
> (Francis Bacon, *Of Negotiating*, 1625)

A useful approach to troublesome children is to be found in Dreikurs (1957), whose ideas are developed in Balson (1982). This involves trying to identify and analyse pupils' motives and use this information to guide teacher responses and strategies. Far from concerning itself with surface behaviour, this method recognizes that the same observed activity may signify radically different motives. For example, what appears to be attention-seeking behaviour may in reality be a struggle to defeat or have revenge upon the teacher. The correct identification of the pupil's motive is a condition precedent to effective action. Balson (1982) suggests that we should ask ourselves what the pupils' purposes are in their behaviour and not simply seek answers to the question 'Why?'. This is not merely a semantic distinction. To ask why a person acts in a particular manner often brings an answer in terms of causes external to that person. We often speak of pupils' home backgrounds as if they were inaccessible causes whose effects lie beyond our control. By asking what purposes the pupils have, we leave responsibility for action and the possibility of remedy with the pupils. Passive, deterministic pessimism is replaced by optimistic effort.

Dreikurs (1957) proposes four goals of disturbing behaviour which he relates to the child's experience in the family. Balson (1982: 92) says: 'All maladjustment has its origin in a basic loss of confidence.' Attention seeking results where young children have done badly in the competition with siblings for parental attention: 'Children prefer being beaten to being ignored' (Balson, 1982: 13). Efforts to control the child result in struggles for power in which there can be no final victory, for to win is to teach that power struggles are valuable and worth while. This struggle can develop, where parents are bent on victory at any price, into mutual revenge. A fourth goal, the display of inferiority, will not be considered in this book.

Dreikurs goes on to suggest that in pursuing these goals a child may be active or passive and may use constructive or destructive methods. For example, there are four ways in which a pupil can be an attention-seeker in the classroom: an active and constructive way would be to be a 'teacher's pet', always attentive, willing and helpful; an active and destructive way would be to take the role of 'class clown'. A passive form of attention seeking could be to become very pleasant but helpless, in need of constant attention, kindly given; a passive and destructive form could be stubbornness.

The type of behaviour that causes teachers most concern is of the active-destructive type, and Dreikurs suggests that a pupil may progress from being a nuisance to a rebel and, finally, vicious. Improvement does not involve retracing these steps, for a pupil 'can become adequately adjusted if he can be convinced that he is liked and can be useful' (Dreikurs, 1957: 16). However, Stott (1982) warns that in a hostile pupil's route to improvement there may be a period of heavy attention demanding: a vicious rebel might become a nuisance before abandoning disturbing behaviour altogether. The analysis is detailed but succinct, and interested readers are recommended to go to the original text, which is rich in examples and cases.

Dreikurs points out that the same behaviour can serve different motives and each child may have different purposes from time to time. For example, being lazy can be an attention-seeking strategy; it can be a struggle for power with a teacher; it can be revenge upon an ambitious parent. The same child might seek revenge upon over-judgemental parents by being disruptive at school and disappointing them; he or she might try to get sympathetic attention at home by being passive, quiet and withdrawn. The inevitable clash of views between home and school on his or her behaviour would satisfy the child's wish for power. Two clues are available to us in identifying the pupil's motive and knowing how to respond. The first is observing one's own feelings: if irritated, attention seeking; if challenged, power; if outraged, revenge. The teacher's 'automatic reaction is generally in line with what the child wants her to do' (Dreikurs, 1957: 34). The second is observing the child's reaction to correction: if the behaviour stops momentarily, attention; if it continues, power; if it gets much worse, revenge.

Much difficult behaviour in classrooms is described as attention seeking. If the child is using an unacceptable repertoire only to gain attention, then it is likely that the teacher will feel no more than mildly irritated. Balson suggests that the child is saying, 'I'm special, attend to me'. Such behaviour is likely to stop when attention is given and resume as soon as the teacher turns to others in the class. The strategy most likely to succeed here is to be watchful and exploit opportunities to give attention to the attention-seeker when he or she is engaged on the proper tasks. As far as is possible, the unwanted behaviour should be ignored or only partially attended to. For example, the child may be instructed to resume the proper seat and wait, but the teacher avoids eye-contact, giving only the minimal attention necessary to the delivery of the instruction. Dreikurs suggests giving attention, but in unexpected ways: for example, instead of telling off someone who repeatedly falls off their chair, invite the class to stop work and watch. He suggests disclosing the pupil's motives to him or her in a non-accusatory style ('Could it be that you want to keep me busy?') and agreeing a fixed number of times for special attention ('Ten times enough? Okay, that's one'). Explicit rules are not possible, of course, and Dreikurs notes that 'each teacher must experiment . . . and establish her own technique' (Dreikurs, 1957: 53).

What appears to be, and is typed as, attention seeking may in fact stem from different motives and produce stronger and more distressing feelings in the teacher. If the teacher feels the pupil's behaviour is a threat to his or her authority, and feels angrily impelled to force the child into line, then the pupil's motive is power. Both pupil and teacher are likely to be feeling that they must show the other that they cannot be dominated. Balson advises that the impulse to fight is best resisted, thus depriving the pupil of an opponent and reducing the likelihood of such an unsuccessful pupil strategy being repeated. Dreikurs suggests encouraging a power-seeker to exercise it in legitimate ways: for example, help and protection for others, but discreetly supervised. Openly admitting that the teacher ultimately has no real power can also disarm the pupil.

To resist habitual impulses is not easy and extinguishing unwanted power-seeking behaviour in this way may take some considerable time. Any discomfort or uncertainty shown by the teacher rewards the pupil's efforts and gives the pleasure of victory without a struggle. Other pupils are unlikely to remain unaffected by these phenomena. To be convincing the teacher must genuinely feel unchallenged, so that without the need of speech he or she communicates imperturbability. This is easier to achieve if we recognize the discouraged and 'frightened child behind all the manifestations of grandeur' (Dreikurs, 1957: 56). Dreikurs points out that children rarely understand 'the predicament in which the teacher finds herself as a result of her exposure to so many pressures' and advises giving the pupil a sense of significance by showing the pupil that he or she has the power to help. This is essentially the same argument that Cronk (1987) develops and illustrates.

A further escalation in motivational intensity is evidenced when the teacher feels more deeply hurt and unjustly treated. In such cases the child may be seeking revenge for some real or imagined hurt in the present or in a past situation. The child is seeking to even the score and the offended teacher may feel urged to do likewise. This impulse must be resisted if the child is even to consider abandoning this strategy. Dreikurs observes that the support of other pupils, all that the teacher wins in struggles with revenge-seekers, can serve to isolate the individual further. 'It takes a great deal of stamina to convince the revengeful child . . . that he can be liked. Here the group can be an extraordinary help but it can also be a dangerous accomplice' (Dreikurs, 1957: 57). Balson (1982) says: 'All misbehaviour reflects children's decisions about how they can most effectively belong to the group.' To continue work with pupils exhibiting such extreme behaviour requires a self-assurance and conviction well beyond the norm. To understand and perceive behaviour in the ways described by Balson and Dreikurs is a powerful support to the teacher's will. To become convinced that one understands the pupil's real feelings is to gain the power to produce real consequences for the pupil.

Each of these three motives – attention, power and revenge – may be evidenced by similar pieces of behaviour; lies, nagging, bullying, stubbornness or destruction of equipment are not in themselves evidence of one motive or another. It is necessary to examine one's feelings and to observe the effect of one's response in order to discover the pupil's motive. For example, suppose a primary school child refuses to join a line of pupils preparing to cross a dangerous road. If the teacher feels irritated and on taking the pupil's hand has no difficulty persuading him or her to comply, then the pupil's motive was to seek attention and no more than that. If the teacher feels challenged and on taking the pupil's hand has to use force to drag the pupil into line, then the motive was power. If the pupil is seeking revenge the teacher will approach with gloom and foreboding. On taking the pupil's hand, the pupil will not only resist but also kick and struggle.

The action taken may in each case be identical – and in matters of safety or possible harm to others instant intervention is essential. This does not mean that the pupil will perceive all intervening teachers' actions as the same. The teacher who appreciates and empathizes with the pupil's perspective will inevitably communicate through tone of voice, facial expression and general demeanour that the pupil's distress, bitterness or confusion are understood and accepted, even though the behaviour must be prevented. It is not the case that understanding and accepting a person's rational and reasonable basis for action necessitates permitting those actions.

When confronted by behaviour of this sort, which may or may not turn out to be attention seeking, it is helpful to have a four-point strategy in mind. First, the feelings and emotional reaction produced in the teacher by the pupil's behaviour are probably intentionally so produced. Second, the automatic impulse to respond in a habitual fashion, perhaps in kind, is a signal to pause and reflect on the pupil's motives and intentions. Third, the teacher's own feelings and impulses are a clue to the pupil's state of mind and may be a mirror image of them. Fourth, in order to deprive the pupil of success in his or her attempt at manipulating the teacher's reaction, the teacher must take control; this involves rejecting the normal impulse and dodging the pupil's snare, however painful the necessary agility. Such a strategy takes seconds to describe but will normally operate in a fraction of that time. It is not suggested that teachers who are responsible for pupils should respond to crises with passivity and a caricature of thought. Crises are to be accepted as inevitable increments of progress. The term does indicate a turning point and, knowledgeably and carefully handled, a crisis becomes a turning point from which progress follows (Hanko, 1985).

As with adolescents, the behaviour of young children is orientated towards others, but although it is clear that infant and pre-school children depend upon adults it is sometimes not noticed that they depend upon their peers, too. Aggressiveness in pre-school children is common and often results from attempts to join games that others are playing. Many young children have difficulty expressing their wishes to their peers. Those whose verbal skills are less developed, or whose experience of playing with others is limited, may push others or throw things in an attempt to attract attention and join the game. During a period of observation in a playgroup I watched a boy lying along a slide and preventing three other children from using it. The three had been following each other up the ladder and down the slide with a good deal of merriment and noise. A member of staff told him to move, and when he did not she told him not to be naughty and took him away. The trio resumed their game, but before long were again blocked by the troublesome boy. This time they called out and a different adult came. She took the boy's hand and helped him up the ladder and down the slide; the other three joined in and the game became four children chasing up the ladder and down the slide. It is not difficult to imagine the boy's development if he always had his behaviour defined as naughty; and it is easy to see how much more helpful it is for the teacher to assume the best motive and respond to that. As children grow into the primary age range, some find that to be accepted as a friend they have to show that they can find their own friends elsewhere (Caspari, 1976: 17). Occasional rejection becomes part of the relationship (Davies, in Woods, 1980a). To know this is to know how to respond to pupil disputes and also how to help them cope with them.

Manning and Herrman (in Cohen and Cohen, 1987) have identified some characteristic strategies of young children who have more than the average number of behavioural problems. The games of poorly adjusted children appear to have fewer roles in them than those of well-adjusted children. For example, children playing in the house might include visitors in the game as relatives or tradespeople; the troublesome child may refuse to allow anyone else in and restrict the game to only two. Difficult children are more rigid in their application of the rules of the game, less willing to accept ideas from other people or to suggest roles for anyone other than themselves. Problem children spend more time in the group than alone. Perhaps having few interests to occupy them when there is no room in a chosen game contributes to their stressed behaviour. In sharing, they risk losing control of any game they have gained entry to or started. These characteristics of very young children are similar to some of the school features associated with difficult behaviour in later years: easily broken rules and a restricted range of topics and ways of learning.

I have argued that pupils' disruptive behaviour may result from understandable perceptions, beliefs and intentions; and that understanding and accepting this insulates the teacher from personal hurt, permits the possibility of communication and gains, however slowly, the pupils' attention and respect. Cronk (1987) argues powerfully for the view that pupils can be trusted to respect the interests of others and that disruption and disorder result from misunderstanding each other's intentions and personhood. She proposes open discussions, where teachers and pupils can get to know one another as people, accepting and respecting each other's intentions and the constraints under which each operates. Her argument is philosophically complex but was tested in her attempt to teach, and get to know, a disorderly class. Her path to success with 3Y was littered with difficulties but mutual respect, understanding and calm were eventually achieved: a familiar result to teachers who choose to spend their working lives with disaffected children. In large schools, opportunities for personal interaction of an honest and open kind may not occur automatically, but Cronk's experience shows that time can be allocated without disrupting or threatening organizational efficiency.

Focusing on the mental and emotional state of pupils does not lead to easily listed techniques or explicit guides to action. Caspari (1976: 3) cautions against expecting to acquire perfect understanding and points out that 'the wish to understand our children and ourselves in relationship to them has a profound effect on this relationship and on our ability to deal with troublesome children'. This approach, however, does benefit both pupil and teacher. It necessitates considering the pupil seriously as another thinking person and reflecting upon the pupil's point of view. To adopt this approach is to communicate to the pupil, not necessarily in words, that he or she is seen as significant, important and deserving of time and effort to be understood. Pupils learn that their surface behaviour, over which some fear they do not have complete control, will not be taken as a complete reflection of their personal qualities and feelings.

Dreikurs (1957: 20) says that up to the age of 10, a child will show the characteristic 'recognition reflex' when informed about his or her goals, and give up the behaviour. Older people, who have 'an increasing power to rationalise and put up a front', will take longer to abandon their goals – though they too will recognize them. Dyke (1987) points out that there are times when to present an interpretation may not relieve the child: '. . . it may feel to him like someone prodding him on his sorest spot'.

Sometimes the correct identification of deep motives and intentions, or merely the attempt so to do by the teacher, can defuse a threatening situation and cause the pupil to abandon mutually unwanted behaviour. For example, in one incident in my unit: 'You can't come in here with that knife, you will frighten the pupils, and you frighten me.' Satisfied that he was not powerless, as he feared, the knife was redundant and surrendered. Pupils also learn that teachers' expectations of them are high. No doubt their spirits are lifted by this optimistic declaration of faith, which may appear all the more genuine for being implicitly and non-verbally communicated. Pupils learn, perhaps for the first time, that they are worthy of consideration, in both senses of the word.

A policy of understanding pupils has benefits for teachers but it also extends their professional responsibilities. Learning to analyse pupils' mental and emotional dispositions is necessarily learning to adopt a dispassionate and objective perspective. On learning of a pupil's fears we come to see behaviour in a different light (Hanko, 1985). Understanding provides partial insulation from personal involvement of a painful and overwhelming kind. Teachers can understand why they are the focus of pupils' confused and misdirected feelings and not perceive such feelings as personal attacks. They can sidestep antagonism, focusing their concern instead on pupils' deeper motives. They may also understand why some sorts of behaviour and attitude distress them more than others, for no one is wholly exempt from inner conflicts and uncertainty. It becomes easier to see difficult behaviour as part of ordinary life and, for many pupils, a necessary manifestation of their present concerns.

Coping with conflict is seen, not as grit in a machine that would otherwise work smoothly, but as one part of teachers' professional responsibilities: an aspect of the job, not an impediment to it. So resolved, it becomes as irrelevant to wish it away as it would be for dentists to complain of patients' tooth decay or police to blame their failure to catch burglars on the number of traffic offences to which they have to attend (naturally, teachers are not the only professionals tempted to limit their responsibilities). This takes us back to the concept of the deviance-insulative teacher (Hargreaves, 1975) and the disarming strategies discussed in Chapter 2. The ideal teacher tries to be optimistic, defends, understands and allows for difficult pupils, avoids confrontation, respects pupils' dignity, and engages them informally in a sympathetic and sharing climate.

## ACTIVITY 4.1: IDENTIFYING MOTIVES

The task here is twofold: to identify the pupil's motives and to determine what action would be appropriate. Although there can never be certain answers, some reactions are usually avoided by teachers experienced in the management of difficult pupils. In some of the cases it is possible to identify speculatively a commendable motive; in others it is only understandable. It should be remembered that similar actions or interventions may be experienced in importantly different ways by the pupil. The teacher's feelings may be non-verbally communicated to the pupil: being restrained by someone who sympathizes with and accepts your perspective is not the same as being restrained by someone who believes you are simply evil. Some comments follow at the end.

1 In a nursery or reception class a pupil repeatedly pushes a dolls' pram into a wall of plastic blocks that two others are trying to construct. The builders protest but the pram-pusher looks set to continue the demolition work.
2 In a primary school playground at break time, you see a boy of nine chasing some pupils round the yard with a large pointed wooden sword. Some seem frightened and the sword looks dangerous.
3 A secondary school pupil comes to your registration group wearing wholly unsuitable clothing which clearly contravenes the school's uniform regulations. These rules are generously drawn, as the school serves an area of extreme poverty. The outfit is clearly newly purchased and looks as though its designer intended it to be worn on the beach.
4 A pupil in the class is a constant irritant. She falls off her chair, drops things and is regularly at your desk asking for help or repetition of instructions already given.
5 One of your pupils is often late without reason. If challenged, a confident or arrogantly stated excuse is given and there is invariably a refusal to comply with instructions or follow the lesson.

6 A regularly attending but nevertheless completely unco-operative pupil seems to spare no effort in being as unpleasant as possible to both pupils and staff. He is sometimes found pretending to be asleep on top of cupboards or on chairs placed for visitors near the school entrance. He responds violently when checked by staff or challenged by pupils by stealing or spoiling other people's property.

## Comments on the activity

1 The common-sense, unsubtle and untutored response is to see this behaviour as naughtiness and even to confine the child to what is known in some nurseries as the 'naughty chair'. A more refined perspective chooses to see the demolition as merely an inexpert and socially inept attempt at interaction: a clumsy way of asking to play by a child who wants to join the game. The appropriate action is therefore to encourage all three children to co-operate in the project – and to stay to see that this happens – perhaps suggesting a purpose for the building that includes the pram.

It may be that the demolition expert is in fact driven by a baser motive, and the strategy may need to be revised – for example, the teacher may have to occupy the child constructively upon some other activity. To begin by assuming the former motive avoids the possibility of wrongly labelling the pupil and perhaps assisting the development of a disruptive self-image. Alternatively, a pupil intent on disruption may revise the strategy on being unexpectedly pleasantly treated. Even if the child has to be removed, the teacher can take care not to begin a cycle of scolding and response by saying something like: 'I know you want to play with the bricks, but there are too many children there at the moment.'

2 This case illustrates how important it is not to assume that consideration of pupils' motives necessitates inaction. In a situation of danger, instant intervention is the first and most essential action. The common-sense response would be to summon the pupil and confiscate the sword. The optimistically disposed teacher would similarly call the pupil but might accept the pupil's pride in his possession, one perhaps made in the school's workshop, and understand his wish to demonstrate its effectiveness: the weapon would be admired and shown to others. In such an atmosphere, the pupil may well accept the dangers and willingly surrender the sword for safe keeping. Nothing is lost by beginning with this assumption and the end result, with respect to safety, is the same; but in the hands of a thoughtful teacher a high-spirited pupil may escape receiving a negative evaluation. If the assumption is mistaken, and the pupil is intent on harm or revenge, then his reaction will be hostile and the sword will not be surrendered without a struggle. In these

circumstances the teacher would have to remain controlled and cool, using only the minimum force necessary, while giving a calm and firm explanation. As far as possible, the urge to become embattled must be rejected if the analysis and advice of Balson (1982) is accepted.

3 In this situation the habitual response is along the lines of: the school has regulations; they have been breached; there is a referral procedure; it will be invoked and the pupil sent home to change. A more sensitive response, and having regard to the poverty in the locality, would again be to accept that the pupil wishes to demonstrate personal pride in new possessions. He or she wishes to show them off to friends. The pupil may also wish to show teachers a newly acquired adult taste in clothes. (The industrial and commercial interests that schools are encouraged to serve are here caught red-handed.) With this understanding, the outfit may be favourably commented on, with the proviso that it is not entirely suitable for school and must be replaced on the following day. The pupil's attempt at identity construction will not have been damaged. In many such cases some remnant of the inappropriate clothing may reappear on the following day: for example, many pupils attend state schools in their only pair of shoes and it is unlikely that they will all put the school's requirements before teenage fashion when making a purchase.

4 This case, and the two following, are of the type often described as 'attention seeking' but which Balson (1982) suggests may sometimes be more complex. If the restless behaviour makes the teacher feel irritated, and if it stops momentarily when attended to, then the child is most likely to be seeking attention only. The behaviour is the equivalent of saying: 'Look at me, give me some recognition.' The teacher typically feels wearily exasperated: 'Not you again.' As far as possible the behaviour should be ignored, or partially ignored. The pupil may be told to stop, or resume her seat, but in a detached way, eyes averted and denied full interaction with the teacher. The next step is to ensure that the pupil receives attention, and rewarding interaction, while properly engaged in the lesson at her desk. This is very difficult to achieve: when a time-consuming pupil is quietly engaged, teachers automatically turn their attention to the other pupils whose rights have been neglected. However, this is the most crucial time for an attention-seeking pupil, and effort expended by the teacher at this point will usually be rewarded. Some teachers find that an occasional, humorous role-reversal can help: they suggest pestering the pupil at her desk, peppering her with questions and enquiries. Punishment, which in these cases often functions as a reward for the unwanted behaviour, is usually ineffective and is, in any event, unhelpful to the youngster's personal development.

5 A clue to the pupil's intentions is invariably found by examining one's own feelings. Most teachers on reading this case feel challenged and impelled to exert their authority. Sometimes this is possible, through threats or cajolery, but if the pupil is motivated to demonstrate personal power, then a struggle may ensue and serious confrontation becomes unavoidable. One way of avoiding this is to reject the impulse to become tangled in a battle of wills and not allow oneself to be manipulated into a confrontation. Appear unconcerned about the challenge, while conveying disapproval of obviously inappropriate behaviour. Try to feel impassive, nonchalant, detached: this is what we are doing, take it or leave it.

Where the lateness is persistent it cannot always be ignored merely because it is taken to be an instrument of a power struggle that we are seeking to sidestep. Lateness with older and more determined individuals is difficult to eradicate, and often springs from domestic responsibilities or upheaval. If punished by detention, lateness may become absence. Remember that there is a very high correlation between absenteeism and poverty. The most profitable approach may be for the pupil's personal or group tutor to negotiate an agreement and have the pupil regularly report to him or her.

6 This is an extreme case and few ordinary schools encounter individuals as distressing and distressed as this. The behaviour could simply be an extravagant example of attention seeking, were it not for the violent responses elicited by pupils and teachers. Since the reaction goes further than a struggle for power, space and time it probably falls into the category Balson describes as 'revenge seeking'. The pupil is seeking redress for a real or imagined hurt, perhaps an event in the past or a continuing unfavourable circumstance. This may not have included the school and its population at the outset; they may have had feelings belonging to some other situation deposited upon them and, in consequence of an understandable reaction, have become part of the pupil's pool of adversity. Teachers who expend time and patience on such pupils often find the hostility hurtful.

One possible strategy, for a school that wishes to retain and make progress with such a pupil, is to reject the impulse to repay injustice; recrimination and counter-attack only prolong the cycle of hostility and malevolence. Convince yourself that other people's hostile attitude to you is not your problem but theirs. The proper response to this distress that they feel is sympathy – perhaps even pity. To respond to hostility with hostility produces a sort of defamatory badminton. If the resentful exchange is to stop, one party has to lay down the racquet and withdraw. The responsibility falls on the teacher as the dispassionate, cool and controlled professional. At every opportunity, try to indicate that you understand the pupil's confusion and believe the surface hostility to be unrepresentative of them as they really are, deep down. One teacher in a unit for troublesome pupils told such disturbing individuals that they were an ocean: on the surface, choppy waves and tumbling water but deep down all was still and cool and peaceful, but occasionally a big ugly fish would pop out and try to take your arm off. This sort of overdrawn imagery, an unexpected response in a conflict, can allow laughter to displace violence. As in all difficult cases, much progress depends upon the school making it possible for at least one teacher to get to know such a pupil thoroughly.

## ACTIVITY 4.2: ATTENTION, POWER, REVENGE

What appears to be a similar sort of misbehaviour can in different pupils or different circumstances betoken different motives. In these examples, the task is, first, to identify the motive; second, to forecast the likely reaction of the pupil to a teacher's attempt to correct them; and, third, to suggest a strategy for avoiding an escalation of the trouble.

A pupil is constantly scraping his chair during the lesson, which is otherwise going well and in which the class is fully engaged and interested.

1 The teacher feels irritated and annoyed and finds herself thinking: 'Not you again.'
2 The teacher feels challenged and finds herself thinking: 'I'm not having that in my lesson.'
3 The teacher feels a sense of foreboding and finds herself hesitating and thinking: 'Why do you want to cause harm now?'

### Comments

Briefly, in the three cases we have the severity of the motive escalating from attention seeking through power seeking to revenge.

In the first case we might expect the scraping to stop when the pupil is corrected – only to resume later. The appropriate longer-term strategy would be to ensure that the pupil gets attention for good work along the lines described in this chapter.

In the second case we might expect the scraping to persist or be immediately replaced by some new disruption which has a similar effect. The appropriate strategy would be to avoid sounding challenged and challenging in stating the facts of the case to the pupil. One possibility might be: 'Your chair is better than my voice at reaching all parts of this room. I wonder if you could let me have a few minutes to finish explaining the work to everybody?' Longer term, try to find opportunities for the pupil to exercise legitimate power and responsibility in the daily life and routines of the school. As with the attention-seeker it is necessary to ensure that good classroom work is encouraged, noticed and rewarded.

In the third case we might expect an escalation of the noise and possibly some abusive response or threat of violence: the chair might be picked up and used threateningly. It is very difficult to say what a teacher should do, because when pupils have reached such an advanced stage of disturbance they are obviously almost intractable in most situations. The first thing that can be done is to recognize the pupil's motive and thereby remove some of its power to hurt us and disturb our equilibrium and judgement. We can try to contain the pupil's hostility and hope that this will help us contain them too. (See Emanuel, 1990, for a discussion of this concept.) It might be appropriate to disclose to the pupil the effects of his action in a tentative way. Perhaps something along the lines of: 'I'm sorry you don't feel like being quiet today.' If this does not work, and the disruption continues to deprive the other pupils of their rights to your time, then more direct disciplinary action will be required, irrespective of the consequences. In the longer term, we would seek to act towards this pupil as in the two earlier cases and try to convince them that they can be members of the community on terms other than as an enemy.

## ACTIVITY 4.3: FOCUS ON ONE PUPIL

The purpose of this exercise is to apply the method of analysing pupils' goals to a particular individual. You should have particular regard to the work of Dreikurs and Balson described in this chapter and outlined in the questions below. It is helpful to spend some time alone considering a troublesome pupil before discussing your thoughts in small groups.

1 What are your feelings about the pupil's behaviour – irritated, challenged, wounded?
2 How does the pupil respond to correction – momentarily stops, persists, gets much worse?
3 What motives therefore do you believe the pupil has – attention-seeking, power, revenge?
4 Following this, and from your knowledge of the pupil, do you now see his or her behaviour in a different light?
5 What new policies, or understandings, could be tried?

## ACTIVITY 4.4: TEACHING PUPILS ABOUT THEMSELVES

The two pages reproduced here in Figure 4.1 are from a textbook for lower-attaining secondary pupils (Chapter 14 of *Home, Health and Family*, McManus, 1991). Teachers with access to secondary pupils who might benefit from reflecting on this story might try it and review its effectiveness. Chapter 10 of the same book contains a piece that would also be suitable for primary pupils.

# 14. Melanie's a problem

### *Personal troubles?*

*Figure 4.1* 'Melanie's a problem'
Source: *Home, Family and Health*, McManus, 1991.
Reproduced by permission of Hodder & Stoughton Ltd

It can be hard bringing up young children on your own. You might be tempted to take risks that sensible parents would not take. For example, Melanie's father left the children alone while he went to the phone.

Melanie is only eight years old, with a six-year-old sister and two-year-old brother. When young children lose a parent, they sometimes think that they are to blame in some way. It may affect their behaviour at home and at school. They often cannot understand why they have lost the parent, or explain how they feel about it.

They may be used to being told off by a tired and unhappy parent. They may expect to meet the same sort of treatment in school. They may be used to having to do without treats and holidays. They will know that other children get them. They might keep very quiet or become very naughty, like Melanie, just to get more attention.

Nowadays, many young children lose a parent through divorce – it happens to one child in every five before they are old enough to leave school. Lots of young children have to get used to having only one parent, simply due to the fact that their parents will no longer share a home. It has to become the normal way of life for many children.

1  Can you explain why Melanie behaves as she does at school?
2  Can you explain why her father behaved as he did in this story?
3  What would you expect the social worker to say to Melanie's father?
4  The social worker would probably wish to visit the school and talk to Melanie's teacher. Make notes on the items you think he/she should discuss.

5  Imagine that one year after this story there is a meeting to discuss how things are going. Those attending are the social worker, the teacher, Melanie's father and Melanie. It is up to you to decide whether things have worked out well or not. Write out a statement for each of the four people of what has happened over the last year.

# Chapter 5

# Controlling stress and confrontations

Our remedies oft in ourselves do lie,
Which we ascribe to heaven: the fated sky
Gives us free scope; only doth backward pull
Our slow designs when we ourselves are dull.
(William Shakespeare, *All's Well That Ends Well*, I. i. 212)

## SOURCES OF STRESS

In this chapter we will look at two aspects of responding to and preventing stress and confrontations. First, I shall describe ways of coping with troubles and confrontations, including problems that can arise between colleagues – directly or indirectly as a result of pupil behaviour. This part of the chapter will largely focus on skills and techniques. Second, I will take the discussion further by considering the moral and personal aspect of teaching that we have touched on already in Chapter 3. The activities for this chapter are extensive and include opportunities to work on examples of stressful or confrontational cases and to formulate strategies for dealing with potential areas of conflict. There is also an invitation to reflect upon the place of the personal and moral dimensions of teachers' work, and the contribution of such reflections to coping with difficult pupils. In focusing directly on day-to-day experiences, this chapter is in some respects a test of the argument and hypotheses of this book; and, in using activities more extensively than text, it practises the claim I have made in Chapter 3, that we learn more through active engagement than passive reading.

The stress of managing large groups of pupils with all their demands and difficulties is sometimes compounded by uncertainties and unrealistic expectations. Confronted by troublesome behaviour, teachers can never be sure how much they themselves have contributed to the problem; and most teachers probably suspect that the gap between perfection and what they manage to achieve most days could be filled with extra effort on their part. Other professions, which work with far less intractable material than teachers do, are able to accept that failure is an inevitable part of ordinary life. For example, general practitioners fail to diagnose half the asthmatic children who come to them correctly (research reported in *TES*, 5.8.88: 6). Naturally, when dealing with children, this sort of thing is to be expected; but it is easy to imagine what the politicians and the papers would say if teachers explained a 50 per cent failure rate in this way. The common finding by HMI that one lesson in five is less than satisfactory is regarded as a disgrace requiring tough action. Yet there can be few professions or industries able to claim an 80 per cent satisfaction rate; and none that faces the complex and competing pressures that are the daily routine of schools. The first task in coming to terms with reality is to understand that perfection is unattainable. Of course, we all try to be perfect, we do not deliberately try to fail, but to fret over not achieving that which cannot be achieved is to make failure ever more likely.

The inevitability of structural conflicts in teaching is implicit in the sociological work on teachers' general coping strategies. Andy Hargreaves (in Hammersley and Woods, 1984b) describes the constraints that teachers must accommodate: such ideological conflicts as the contradiction between fostering individual development and preparing pupils to fit into an existing, and in some respects uncongenial, society; and material considerations such as pupil behaviour in crowded classrooms and the scarcity of resources. Woods (in Hammersley and Woods, 1984a) has described some strategies teachers use to manage perceived constraints. These include compromise and co-operation with pupils (negotiation and fraternization); keeping self and pupils occupied in predictable and manageable activities (ritual and routine, occupational therapy); and indifference, absenteeism and staffroom cynicism (absence and removal, morale boosting). These accommodations made by teachers enable the school system to survive; even those that seem to defeat educational purposes may have a longer-term function. For example, in a time of high unemployment with resulting pupil disaffection, business, routine and compromise may prevent serious rebellion and organizational collapse. Bird *et al.* (1981) noted that the strategies of pupils, too, 'are usually those which enable a quiet life rather than a profitable and purposeful educational experience'. These writers demonstrate how an inefficient system could survive through the accommodations made by those who suffer under it: coping strategies are kisses of life from victims.

The principal causes of stress in teaching are generally found to be poor staff communication, disruptive and noisy pupil behaviour, poor working conditions, lack of time and too much work, and trying to uphold standards (Kyriacou and Sutcliffe, 1977, 1979; Galloway, 1985; Woodhouse *et al.*, 1985). There is a superficial congruence between some stressors arising from pupil behaviour and some of those involving colleagues. In the survey by Woodhouse *et al.* (1985), disruption of lessons was matched with administrative disruption; aggression appeared among both pupils and staff; truancy was matched by absenteeism; and inappropriate classroom talk was said to be the equivalent of communication breakdown in staff meetings. Teachers claimed, in response to a questionnaire, that their main coping strategies included trying to be consistent and honest, establishing a routine that kept the pupils occupied, and trying to get things into perspective (Dewe, 1985). However, when Woodhouse *et al.* (1985: 121) asked teachers to keep diaries, punishment appeared in 74 per cent of incidents with pupils and in 33 per cent of incidents with staff. The authors comment that this automatic response, an attempt to regain control, is inefficient whatever its immediate benefits: 'The legacy of the punishing approach for the person using it was listed as damaged interpersonal relations, alienation, anxiety and personal suffering.' This takes us back to the arguments discussed in Chapter 1. The complexity of causes and meanings associated with stress in teachers, and the dependence on self-disclosure, make research findings no more than suggestive. For example, although there is said to be a correlation between low job satisfaction and high stress, one survey found that the more effective teachers reported higher levels of stress, possibly because they had the confidence to be honest (Kyriacou and Sutcliffe, 1979; Woodhouse *et al.*, 1985). This suggests an interesting conversation to have with oneself when feeling stressed: teachers who feel stressed are probably superior teachers; being so informed, they no longer feel stressed; not feeling stressed, they are not superior, but if not superior, they feel stressed, which suggests they are superior after all. And so on.

Caspari (1976: 41, 57) suggests that the teachers' fear that troublesome behaviour is partly their own responsibility can delay discussion and action until a dramatic and public crisis has been reached. Teachers delayed drawing attention to problems 'if they were afraid that the behaviour of the child might be a reaction to the behaviour of the teacher'.

Hargreaves (1982) has commented on the non-supportive relationships among many teachers, leaving each to solve problems alone. To offer help is to 'suggest incompetence' and 'violate professional autonomy': 'Teachers bear their stress in painful isolation. It attacks the heart of the teacher, both physically and metaphorically.' Stress in teachers is known to lead to physical illness, which itself becomes an additional burden (Kyriacou and Sutcliffe, 1977). Effects of this sort are clear evidence that a taboo prevents real problems being shared and tackled. It is as though personal difficulties cannot be taken seriously until they have become transformed into physical afflictions.

Bastide (1972) suggests that psychosomatic disorders represent the triumph of natural medicine: only disorders in the soma – ulcers, heart disease, cancer – command attention. For some teachers, difficulties in personal relationships, felt as personal guilt, are hidden away and re-presented as physiological trauma. The symptoms then come to be seen as the substantive problem; personal pathology protects organizational inefficiency, administrative injustice and collegiate indifference. Troubles in the classroom are contributed to by all the participants, including the teacher, but this is no reason to cover up. It is in the nature of things that some pupils and some teachers will find each other difficult to bear. Specifically, teachers vary in the range and intensity of feelings they can cope with – between themselves and within themselves – from day to day. As explained in Chapter 4, teachers should not always blame themselves if they are the target of a pupil's problems: to be selected to carry a troubled pupil's burdens is in many respects a compliment.

Learning to perceive school troubles in the ways suggested in this book is one way of reducing their intensity and power to hurt, and it makes possible the sharing of problems with colleagues, in consultation not competition. Stressed teachers cannot think objectively or effectively. A task's complexity can affect a person to the extent that the worry survives the original problem and the task itself becomes lost in a fog of anger and misery. Misperception transforms tasks into problems, which become more inclusive and refractory. For example, after a bad time with a disorderly class, teachers may begin to see it as symptomatic of 'what things are coming to', as well as their own hopeless entrapment in a job in which they no longer have faith. Instead of thinking about the specific, difficult lesson, they brood over what is now seen as personal failure, a wasted life, a hopeless future. Definitions of stress, like definitions of misbehaviour, recognize this combination of real-world problems and the personal perceptions of them. Some teachers see some matters in a more serious light than others do. As Mahoney (quoted in Hughes, 1988: 5) says, 'an individual responds – not to some real environment – but to a perceived environment'. In the productive decade of curricular inno-vation, the 1960s, some teachers in trial schools found the experience stressful; others welcomed the freedom brought about by what Jenkins termed 'institutionalized chaos' (OU course E283); and, to the despair of innovators, some teachers took no notice at all.

Comprehensive definitions of stress include both halves of the equation; these are sometimes termed the engineering model and the psychological model. Briefly, stress is an unwanted and overwhelming feeling resulting from a person's perception of the demands of their situation. Stress results at the point where a person's perceptions, understandings and attitudes conflict with what they see as the demands and deprivations with which they have to work. Stress has been defined in an aphorism as anger turned inwards; for a full discussion and definition see Kyriacou and Sutcliffe (1978). Gray and Freeman (1988), dealing with stress in teaching, distinguish the personal dimension from the organizational. Where physical and organizational circumstances are beyond our control, all that may be left to us is the modification of our perceptions and the readjustment of our expectations. This is no small thing. From one point of view, our perceptions can often be the only source of stress: in normal circumstances, whatever situations we find stressful someone else will find enjoyable or will be indifferent to them. Although it can be as difficult to alter our attitudes as it is to alter the external stressors, those that are our own are at least potentially under our control. This assumption underpins much of Chapter 4.

Writers on stress distinguish two personality types: type A people, who are said to be ambitious, perfectionist, pressurized autocrats; type B people, who are relaxed, detached, easy-going and phlegmatic. Type A people are more stressed than type B and the suggestion is that, to avoid being over-stressed, we should try to be like type B (see, for example, Gray and Freeman, 1988: 55). These types are in many respects similar to the insulative and provocative teacher types discussed in Chapter 2. The difficulty with this model is not that it oversimplifies – constructing ideal types for comparative purposes has had a long history in social science; its major flaw is the assumption that people behave according to the same personality type in all situations. Indeed, when we encounter examples of people with varied lifestyles, this fact alone is often taken as evidence of mental instability: for example, philandering clergy and shop-lifting magistrates. A teacher may be perfectionist and[3] autocratic in a drama class but relaxed and easy-going in written composition; and calm and unruffled with a disruptive pupil but snappy and intolerant with his or her own children. The concept of personality is not very helpful here; fixed personality traits are, by definition, relatively stable and resistant to change, for good or ill. The danger in discarding the concept of fixed personality traits is that people are then seen as enslaved in the situation: individuals turn themselves 'into the kind of person the situation demands' (Lacey, 1977, commenting on Becker). For this reason it is important to realize that a situation's nature is to a considerable extent decided by us. In Chapter 2, related problems were discussed with respect to teacher types. The concept of strategy, a way of achieving a particular goal in a particular situation, is more useful than type. Where common elements are present in a person's strategies it may be possible to identify them as one of several personality types. In helping people cope with stressful situations, however, the emphasis needs to be on strategy: personality type is felt as a given, fixed, objective entity; strategies are limited, local and changeable.

## RESPONDING TO STRESS

In any situation, take the first feelings of stress, powerlessness or despair as a signal that action is needed. It may help to see a cue, like a studio light, indicating the need to prepare oneself. Pausing in this way involves rejecting the unwanted feelings or the urge to become embattled in a confrontation. Teachers in general are said to have a tendency to over-react with pupils and under-react with colleagues. In either case, if the habitual response leads to stress it must first be rejected to clear the way for a more helpful strategy. Pausing and rejecting put the threatened person in control. Realizing that one has taken responsibility for one's actions is an encouraging indication that the control of stress is within one's power; it is not the same as feeling that responsibility is thrust upon us by external constraints. This feeling of power over oneself while under stress reverses the pressure. We feel less overwhelmed and more able to make the decisions: whether to react; in what way to react; how energeti-cally to react. The urge to retreat or fly from the situation should diminish: knowing we have control over our impulses removes the need to escape. As Miller puts it: 'If I can stop the roller coaster, I don't want to get off' (quoted in Woodhouse *et al.*, 1985). Much of the procedure described so far is no more than old-fashioned self-control, but like many traditional remedies it can be effective. For example, Hughes (1988) describes how talking oneself through problems (or 'engaging in self-statements') has been helpful in controlling a range of unwanted impulses: smoking, obes-ity, phobias, learning and behavioural difficulties. In some studies a 'turtle response' is advised, which involves withdrawing, psychologically at least, and relaxing. This technique is not always possible in teaching situations.

Action can be of two broad types, and elements of both are needed in most circumstances. We can pay attention to and seek to change those external stressors that displease us; or we can look inwards to our own particular attitudes. Those who are successful in taking control and accept-ing responsibility should be able to use it in their relations with others. Woodhouse *et al.* (1985) reported some success in encouraging teachers to take control of their own behaviour and change their behaviour at work. Stress resulting from the organizational arrangements of a school, or the actions or omissions of colleagues, may be countered by asserting oneself. Hall *et al.* (1984), in evaluating an in-service course, found that teachers saw assertiveness training as 'a potent learning opportunity'. Assertiveness requires essential issues to be identified and stripped of their extraneous personality factors: communication must be open, honest and direct with specific, clear statements. Assume an upright posture and, whether standing or sitting, use full eye-contact. It may help to clasp your hands or fold your arms. Clearly state the facts and your feelings: for example: 'This class is too large; I do not wish to take it until it is halved.' Gray and Freeman (1988) advise identifying that part of the problem that is yours and concentrating on that. This means not being sidetracked into discussing other people's difficulties. For example, when told that there are not enough rooms or teachers to split the oversized class, do not suggest possibilities. These will invariably be rejected and you will swiftly find yourself drawn into discussing administrative problems over which you have no control. Of course, if you know there is an easy solution that has been overlooked then point it out. But if it is rejected, withdraw and stick to your own part of the problem. Repeat the facts and state your feelings and demands.

Beware of being drawn into discussing your reasons, and if you do give them do not let them obscure the main issue. Gray and Freeman (1988) suggest offering to discuss reasons at some later time, and simply repeating your objection like a broken record if necessary. Criticisms and general statements are best questioned rather than replied to. For example: 'When you say unprofessional . . .?' This may lead to their being abandoned and the focus returning to your problem. If it does not, return to the principal issue by reiterating your opening statement. Another red herring to watch for is the irrelevant reply to a demand. For example, having complained about the oversize class, the person in charge of the timetable might say: 'There are lots of oversize classes, and other teachers are not complaining.' This is, of course, an implied criticism of you, but do not respond with a catalogue of your contributions to the school. Make your original statement again but preface it with: 'I appreciate that but . . .' If you feel it is appropriate to adopt a more authoritative stance, use a stronger preface instead: 'I am not asking you that. This class is . . .' This latter opening might be inappropriate and hazardous when there is a large status gap. The general procedure therefore is to accept all responses, not to respond to them, and to continue repeating your problem. In stressful encounters it may be easier to keep your mind on the strategy if you determine to include the word 'no' in every statement you make. Then, even if you are sidetracked, introducing the 'no' reminds you to make your simple, direct demand.

It is not uncommon to prepare for these assertive encounters only to be met with instant capitulation. Perhaps the added assurance is non-verbally communicated, and the adversary sees at once that resistance is useless. On the other hand, there may be a flat refusal to talk, the phone may ring and be gratefully seized, you may have a class waiting, or your target may be practising the same assertion techniques. In these circumstances, state that you will return later and withdraw. This prospect may produce the action you want or some concession, and, if it does not, take up the issue again. Remember that even if you lose on one issue it is not a total loss: if you are in the right, you can be sure that other unjust burdens are now less likely to be put upon you. Finally, if you are reluctant to try assertion, or particularly timid, you can increase your determination to face up to a person by resolving to tackle a number of problems, perhaps in different spheres and with different people, over the coming months, and planning this before you begin. Garfinkel (1967) found, in an experiment to encourage students to haggle over prices in shops, that those given several to do were less likely to back out at the last moment. They were surprisingly successful, too.

The second type of action is personal and is appropriate to situations where there is no particular external factor that can be changed. For example, you may be depressed about teaching in general, your inability to interest pupils in a subject you value, the gap between your moral and social attitudes and those of your classes. In so far as these feelings result from exceptional personal standards, and not ineffectiveness as a teacher, this situation calls for a reorganization of priorities. Goals must be altered and ambitions which have become unrealistic must be abandoned. Some teachers hold an image of an ideal teacher which they believe they should attain. Perfection eludes all of us, of course, and recognizing this fact may remove one source of stress. Some teachers believe that only they have problems and meet each one with continuing dismay, as if they hoped that after surviving their last problem there would be no more. This, too, is an unrealistic perception of life. It is necessary to recognize that problems are part of everyone's daily routine. They should not be greeted with surprise but accepted; like the others, they will pass in time, solved or not.

Some personally orientated strategies are sometimes dismissively termed palliatives. These include having a moan in the staffroom or at home, sleeping on the problem, having a drink, or developing a time-consuming interest that occupies the thoughts through the day. This last can take the form of religious or political action: one person's palliative is another person's salvation – or election. Staffroom humour or cynicism seems to be widespread in secondary but not primary schools (Delamont and Galton, 1986; Woods, 1980b). Palliatives are said to outnumber direct actions in the ratio of two to one (Dewe, 1985). However, the distinction between direct action (problem solving) and palliative (regulation of emotions) is not a certain one. Among the palliatives listed are many items that are arguably problem solving, such as talking to more experienced colleagues; indulging in self-analysis to sort out the problem; building up self-confidence. On the list of problem solving, direct actions are such things as taking shortcuts on things you don't like; disciplining the children; keeping the children occupied. Dewe's conclusion, that organizational structures limit direct action, seems unsupported by his evidence. Nevertheless, palliatives may be the only appropriate strategy where more direct intervention proves futile or could jeopardize a teacher's career. The historical, literary and artistic world offers some consolations, if not feasible possibilities. It is well known that many important historical characters, writers and humorists were driven to their achievements partly by personal unhappiness or domestic disorder. Transforming one's problems into heroism or literature may be unrealistic, but it is possible to delight in the efforts of others. For example, the author of a weekly column in the defunct humorous magazine *Punch*, usually Michael Bywater, worked off a quantity of personal stress through the colourful description of those who had wounded him: nail-faced managers, thick-legged, horse-faced racquet-bashers and hateful, speechless oafs who shout and reek.

In severe cases of tense depression, a straightforward relaxation exercise may help (Iwanicki, referred to in Woodhouse *et al.*, 1985). A simple one is as follows: take deep breaths for two minutes or so, breathing in deeply while slowly counting to five, or more if you can; exhale slowly, counting again, and press the air right out of the lungs; tense the muscles, while imagining you are very cold, then relax and feel yourself becoming warm. In this state of relative calm it may help to imagine yourself managing the depressing or stressful situations more successfully. This is a form of talking oneself into coping: work reviewed in Hughes (1988: 8–10) suggests that it may help sufferers to change their behaviour. The sceptical and observant may have noted that deep breathing, relaxation and daydreaming are very much the benefits associated with a brisk walk followed by a doze.

The acronym SCRAPP summarizes the coping strategies described so far. The first feelings of Stress are a Cue for action; the first step is to Reject the urge to become embattled, the anger, the depression or the feeling of powerlessness; then Accept responsibility for your own behaviour, take control of yourself and decide whether and how energetically to react; finally, consider Physical, direct action, such as asserting yourself, or Personal, self-orientated action, such as discarding unrealistic ambitions, developing other interests and trying relaxation exercises.

## CONFRONTATIONS

> For whosoever exalteth himself shall be abased; and he that humbleth himself shall be exalted.
>
> (Luke 14:11)

Coping in situations of confrontation and severe conflict is an extension of the earlier discussions on understanding pupil motives and controlling teacher reactions. This section concerns confrontations that the teacher has not provoked and does not wish for. It is assumed that everyone understands that unwanted confrontations can result from pupils being subjected to humiliation or sarcasm, and therefore such a style is best avoided. From time to time it may be judged desirable to confront a pupil and risk, or even hope for, a crisis. Where a teacher has shown patience and tolerance over a considerable period, presenting a pupil with some harsh truths can provoke the sort of crisis that becomes a turning point in the pupil's efforts to reform. Laslett and Smith (1984: 87) suggest that occasional confrontations of this sort can benefit the pupil, the class and the teacher's management. This kind of confrontation is controlled and most effectively managed by a teacher who knows the pupil well and for whom the pupil has respect. The points that follow apply to situations where conflict is unlooked for and in danger of being uncontrolled.

### Avoid being manipulated

The first sign of approaching trouble is the cue to be on guard against slipping into an habitual or automatic response. It is necessary for the teacher to accept responsibility for his or her actions and to accept that they are in control and able to avoid knee-jerk reactions: the serene, dispassionate professional, not a puppet of the pupil's capricious emotions. The warning signs include a feeling of personal hurt resulting from both one's positional authority as a teacher being attacked and one's attempt at reasonableness – there has invariably been one (Pik, in Cohen and Cohen, 1987). In the first stages of a conflict, both the office and person are rejected: two blows which are often sufficient to preclude the possibility of the teacher retaining equanimity or recovering control.

Confrontations always take place with at least one of three possible audiences in attendance, whose effect on the actors is to heighten tension and drive judgement off the stage. There is invariably an audience of pupils present. The teacher therefore feels constrained not to lose face and often feels that, for the sake of the others, there is no alternative but to stand firm, irrespective of consequences. From the pupil's point of view, the presence of others hinders any inclination or opportunity to back down from a public act of defiance. If the audience can be removed, or the teacher is able to remove the pupil or allow a retreat, serious conflict is less likely. The two other possible audiences are often absent but are none the less influential. The teacher may feel constrained to stand his or her ground on principle, perhaps having in the past declared such principles to colleagues and friends. These people constitute a shadow audience, constraining the teacher's actions. Wagner, in a chapter of Calderhead (1987), terms the conflicts resulting from 'self-imperated cognitions' as 'knots'. The suggested remedy for the problems that arise from refusing to see things as they are but only as they should be is: stop being ruled by 'musts' and determine to accept responsibility for choosing anew in each situation. There is an apparent contradiction in advising that one must not be ruled by musts, but a rule about rules has a different logical status to a rule about things. The pupil may have a parallel audience, who similarly give him or her 'no other choice'. The third possible audience consists of those persons who will inevitably appear on the scene if the conflict does not evaporate. For the teacher, this audience consists of colleagues and superiors; for the pupil, parents, and friends from other groups.

All three audiences contribute to the fear, embarrassment and tension and put accurate perception and balanced judgement at risk. Pik (in Cohen and Cohen, 1987) includes the sadness teachers often feel in such unlooked-for conflicts as another factor confusing wise judgement. To be aware of the effect of these audiences is the first step in understanding and controlling one's reactions. If the audience of pupils is to be encouraged to accept the reintegration of the pupil into the community, care must be taken to define the crisis in a way that makes this possible. For example, saying 'Helen is not herself today' is preferable to 'Helen will not be able to stay in this school if she does not improve'. The words and actions of a teacher who is highly regarded by pupils will influence the troubled pupil's view of self and the class's view of him or her, too. Future harmony depends on words being carefully chosen.

## Identify the pupil's point of view

Unlikely as it may seem, a time of acute stress is a time to try to step into the pupil's shoes and understand and possibly accept the reasonableness of their behaviour from their point of view. Another way of looking at the situation is to see the confrontation as the pupil's particular distress, not the teacher's. As Hanko (1985: 80) puts it, what others think about us is their problem; our reaction to this is ours. Wills (1967) tells a story about a Quaker who was the victim of a murderous hold-up on a lonely road. With a gun at his head there was good reason to be alarmed but his distress was directed elsewhere, for he said to the robber: 'Dear fellow, what has brought you to this?' It may be that the teacher has carelessly or unintentionally provoked an outburst, and most teachers are able to accept this and restore calm with a placatory or apologetic statement. The attempt to grasp what is driving the pupil's action helps to distance the teacher from the feelings of personal hurt and professional incompetence. The pupil's feelings may be a mirror image of the teacher's and the latter may often be used to discover the former. The teacher may also reflect on the influence the pupil's audiences are having upon his or her behaviour and the possible reasons for the pupil investing so much in what may have begun as a trivial exchange or minor offence. Often, the open discussion of these audience effects can stop a confrontation situation developing. For some teachers, who habitually show patience and have good relations with a pupil, a sudden aggressive confrontation can be exceptionally distressing and undermine the teacher's confidence in his or her understanding. A distressed pupil may finally lose control when faced with a teacher who is, from the pupil's point of view, unusually kind. This contradiction, perhaps added to several lessons of failure and frustration, can be the trigger that causes the pupil to relinquish self-control. To be selected in this way may be seen as a confirmation of one's importance in the pupil's eyes. To worry about it is inappropriate, just as it would be for a specialist surgeon to worry because all the most hopeless cases were pushing at the door.

## Avoid ratchet statements

Ratchets turn only one way and any threat or remark that cannot be abandoned or withdrawn inevitably carries the dispute forward and raises its temperature. Threats of force or removal are particularly effective in bringing a crisis to a violent climax. There should always be some physical or interactional escape route for both pupil and teacher. Assaults upon teachers sometimes result from physical attempts to block doorways to escaping pupils. The feeling, and subsequent claim, that 'there was no alternative' is an example of the tyranny of 'musts' discussed by Wagner (1987). There is always an alternative to every imperative – except this present one. Confrontations are times when hurtful things are said. Laslett and Smith (1984: 104) describe a case in which the teacher shouts insults and threats. These are difficult to withdraw and there is greater than normal danger that a pupil may store and live up to any deviant labels that have been applied. Some pupils even have difficulty separating corrections of their work from personal criticisms of themselves. Caspari (1976) gives examples of this. It is much more difficult to separate comments on one's behaviour from attacks upon oneself. The primary offence must be prevented from becoming the focus of later, secondary action as the pupil seeks to live up to the deviant designation (see Lemert, quoted in Hargreaves *et al.*, 1975: 5).

## Accept or divert an attack

It sometimes costs nothing in terms of esteem or control simply to accept an insult or act of defiance. This is to apply one of the principles of judo to verbal contests: go with the opponent's force rather than resisting it, and use it to unbalance him or her if possible. One teacher in a school for maladjusted pupils recalled how a pupil noticed the wedding ring on her finger and said: 'I don't know how you ever got a fella, with a face like yours.' She admitted that such remarks can be hurtful but she was not wounded by it, for as she said: 'I had long ago come to much the same conclusion myself, and I told the pupil so.' Kohl (1986) suggests diverting attention from the threat by giving misused objects a name. For example, as a chair is lifted ready to be thrown, 'Don't do that to Boris, he cannot stand heights.' Another example given in Robertson (1981) concerned a teacher who entered a classroom to find a pupil about to hit another with an iron bar taken from the gym: 'Right, pokers away, books out.' These examples are not merely evidence for the common belief that a sense of humour helps in a crisis: humorous judo is more than a facility for easy jokes. Turning the other cheek is a strategy with a long pedigree.

## Try procrastination

A straightforward technique is simply to refuse to become embroiled at the particular moment chosen by the pupil. The dispute is postponed without surrendering any other issue. Kohl (1986) advises putting the burden of choice on the pupil: withdrawing from the struggle and leaving the pupil to decide when he or she is ready to resume co-operation. In this case, the teacher specifies what the pupil must do to mend the breach and then withdraws. There is no need to specify a time limit and the importance of the conflict may rapidly diminish; with luck, postponement becomes cancellation. Inflammatory or ratchet statements can sometimes be withdrawn in a graceful and humorous way by being put off till later. For example, teachers sometimes say: 'I shall ask you once more and then . . .' A threat follows. To be sure, the teacher will have to ask once more and no doubt the prospect of having to carry out an impossible threat, or abandon it, increases the tension by another notch. One way out is to add, having paused, an absurd date and time in the future when the pupil will be 'asked once more'.

## Repair the relationship

Where a confrontation has occurred and does not end in a satisfactory way, the pupil should be seen alone before the next timetabled meeting takes place with its attentive audience waiting breathlessly to be entertained. A private, face-to-face talk can be disarming – particularly if it begins with conciliatory remarks from the teacher. A closeness and openness is possible face to face that is often unachievable in classrooms: 'in the face-to-face situation, the other's subjectivity is available to me through the maximum of symptoms . . . no other form of social relating can reproduce the plenitude of symptoms of subjectivity present in the face-to-face situation' (Berger and Luckmann, 1971: 43). More succinctly: 'If thy brother shall trespass against thee, go tell him his fault between thee and him alone' (Matthew, 18:15).

People who are unsure of themselves find apologies embarrassing and shaming; those who have authority can sometimes use apologies to confirm and enhance it. It is therefore important for teachers to feel confident in their expertise and to understand that 'it is not demeaning to make an apology' (Laslett and Smith, 1984: 102). Some schools, determined to succeed with disturbing pupils, ensure that such meetings follow conflict and may emphasize their importance by setting aside the headteacher's room for them. In rare cases the pupil will decline to co-operate, but it is still possible for the teacher to indicate that the matter is closed by a light comment. One teacher suggested that it was always possible to offer a brief apology for an offensive remark if she had made one, or a self-deprecatory gesture and a wink and a smile in passing.

### Confirming continued co-operation

Despite protestations to the contrary, and in the face of all the evidence, most confrontational pupils do not want to be rejected. Some may even be using confrontations to test, in a socially inept way, the reliability and sincerity of their teachers. They must therefore be assured that, despite what may have been said during the conflict, and irrespective of future behaviour, they are expected to continue following the same timetable at the same school with the same teachers. For many pupils this will be unexpected, for they may frequently have been threatened with banishment from both home and school. It also reassures them that perhaps they have found someone they can trust to forgive them and with whom they are sure of a welcome even if they fail: till death us do part, if necessary.

## STRESS CONTROL AS A PROFESSIONAL VIRTUE

If a teacher teaches and the pupils do not understand, he should not become angry with them but should repeat and be prepared to teach his lesson 400 times. A short-tempered person should not become a teacher.

(Maimonides, twelfth-century Jewish philosopher)

Activity 3.2 in Chapter 3 asked you to consider what the characteristics of good teachers were. Using this exercise with several hundred teachers – primary, secondary, state, independent and in higher education – I have found a remarkable consistency in responses. The most common offerings are approachable, enthusiastic, understanding, patient, flexible, sense of humour. These might be grouped together as personal qualities. The next most common words are alert, attentive, precise, unambiguous, well organized, strict. These are arguably all skills, although some teachers challenge this category and suggest that many of these, too, are fundamentally personal qualities. The final category is usually represented by one word and is sometimes not offered at all. The word is 'knowledge-able'. It is almost always offered last and sometimes after prompting. Naturally, some teachers object that it is too obvious a word to offer, since knowledge is essential for teachers. The same might be said of patience and understanding, but when we think of a good teacher most of us think of personal qualities first.

In one school, a selective independent where one might have expected knowledge to come first, the person who eventually offered knowledge-able qualified it: she did not mean subject knowledge but 'all the odd and idiosyncratic bits and pieces that make a subject come to life, the quirky things about a subject'. Examples offered included speculating on what might have been on Nelson's mind, in the light of his marital problems, impending retirement and the foolishness of his exhibitionist mistress, when he made himself such an easy target, pacing the deck of the Victory; and an elderly British athlete's recollection of the look of fear on Hitler's face at the 1936 Berlin Olympics when he realized that Jesse Owens was approaching to shake his hand. So back we are carried to enthusiasm, warmth, humour – the personal characteristics and charisma that secure pupils' attention and co-operation in classroom management.

In the light of these features it is not surprising that those who reject our efforts to teach them are able to cause us so much distress, for if our qualities as a teacher are so much bound up with our qualities as a person, it is not surprising that we feel rejection of our teaching as rejection of ourselves. Teaching is a vocation in a way that perhaps few other professions are, and its accomplishment is more akin to success in personal relationships than success in a technical craft. Interestingly, there is a suggestion of this in the profession of medicine too, where the common-sense view would be that success is a matter of the appropriate application of technical skills. Brody (1994) suggests that doctors' success is related not just to their skills but to their social prestige and personal charisma. As it is rare for any society to hold teachers in high regard, the contribution that social prestige could make to educational success must remain unknown. Tantalizingly, the Jewish community seems to be a notable exception, and ample support for the reverence to be accorded teachers can be found in Jewish literature (Angyalfi, 1994). For example, Jacob, on hearing that his lost son Joseph was alive in Egypt, sent Judah ahead to found a school; cities that did not maintain schools might be destroyed; teachers are described as stars upon the firmament of mankind and the true guardians of the city; neighbours were even forbidden to protest about the noise of a school.

Perhaps the moral and personal aspect of their role is one reason why teachers seem to resist the implementation of cold, behavioural tech-niques with difficult youngsters – and why, despite some initial success, such impersonal methods do not fulfil their promise. Young people them-selves usually know very well that poor behaviour, unlike poor reading and writing, is morally poor and not simply a gap in their technical, interactional skills. Youngsters in exclusion units are often defensive about their behaviour and ready to blame others for it – but they do not deny that they have done wrong; they are defensive because they know in their hearts that they are not merely innocent victims of provocative teachers, inept parents and callous government. Attempting to make the education of troublesome youngsters a technical activity that is value-neutral is an attempt to treat them as less than human. It devalues the pupils and it devalues the teachers.

Trends in British education over the past decade seem to many people to have all but eliminated the human and humane aspect of teaching, but this is a mistaken view. Although the National Curriculum might appear to be a teacher- and pupil-proof impersonal catalogue that could be programmed into a computer, there is plenty of evidence that those who contributed to it never saw it that way. The National Curriculum Council (NCC, 1989) commented, in relation to pupils with special needs, that 'some pupils meet attitudes and practices in schools which do not actively encourage full participation' and that there was a need for 'positive attitudes from school staff who are determined to ensure their fullest participation'. Guidance on English even goes so far as to warn of an over-emphasis on behaviour management 'without attempts to understand the child's feelings'

In a DfE-commissioned contribution to school discipline (Gillborn *et al.*, 1993), we find teachers who have been successful in trying circumstances emphasizing the importance of relationships in their work. Says one of those interviewed: 'All other things come later.' Those responsible for the training of new teachers have to have regard for what appears to be an impersonal list of competences (DfE, 1992). I have no doubt, however, that they cannot be attained by trainee teachers unless they satisfy the twin requirements of being good teachers: that is, they must be good in the sense of being effective in terms of the competences required, but also good in the sense of being morally good and possessing the virtues of prudence, temperance, justice and fortitude. I will illustrate this startling assertion by reference to two of the more routine competences that new teachers must attain. Section 2.5 of DfE (1992) specifies, among other things, that teachers must be able to 'assess and record systematically the progress of individual pupils ... and use such assessment in their teaching'. At first sight, nothing could be more straightforward and mechanical. Some (futile) approaches to assessment in the National Curriculum have treated assessment as if it were a clerical task, ticking boxes on forms and piling up boxes of evidence. To be carried out objectively, assessment in terms of the DfE's apparently simple competences requires virtues: prudence, in being concerned for and careful of the consequences of decisions, and appropriately cautious and circumspect; justice, in being impartial and treating all with equity, honesty and fairness; temperance, in maintaining calmness and moderation, and

resisting any temptation to make hasty decisions or form excessive conclusions; fortitude, in having the strength of will to act upon the results
assessment in ways that might require us to modify our own practice, and
the resolution, moral courage and firmness of mind to carry the effort
through. All this for just two items in a list of 27.

This chapter has detailed many techniques for coping with stress and
fleetingly raised the issue of the wider personal and moral dimensions of
teaching. I will conclude with what is still for me a painful story, but one
which emphasizes the importance of not relying too heavily on skills-
based approaches.

Three years before the first edition of this book appeared, I left my
post in a school for difficult pupils to take up a secondment to research
and write on behavioural problems. I had worked in the school for five
years and although a hard place to work, I had long passed the stage
where I was troubled by the pupils or even found myself challenged. If I
had reflected on this I would probably have put it down to my experience,
expertise and understanding. The secondment came to an end but the
book based on my researches and experience was in production and I
returned to my school full of ideas and confidence. I found I could not
control my classes. All my skills and understanding had no effect. None
of the pupils I had previously taught was still in the school and I found
myself being tested and tried out like any other new teacher. I had led
courses for teachers on coping with conflict and written a book about it
but now I couldn't survive myself; the shock was so great that I came
close to giving up teaching.

What had happened? In taking a detached approach to troublesome
pupils I had begun to treat all aspects of the matter as if they were
merely technical – even, in a bizarre sense, those that stressed the personal
qualities. I *knew* all about the need for resilience, patience, optimism and
indestructibility. I had even wanted to title the book *Shatterproof Teaching*
but the publishers would not let me. Somehow, in adopting an academic
approach I lost the ability to apply what I knew. Establishing trust with
difficult pupils takes time: they are used to rejection and turmoil in their
domestic and school lives. After a turbulent term, things improved slightly
and by the end of the school year I was more or less back on the
relatively stable footing that I had enjoyed before I had left the school
for the secondment. It was not as if I did not know all this. I had often
comforted distressed teachers in exactly the same trouble as I was myself,
and what to do was all set out in my own book – as those who have read
this far will know. It should not disappoint readers to learn of the abyss
that can open between knowledge and practice. To be interested in
developing techniques and skills and enhancing professional expertise is
just the sort of personal quality essential in those who work with troublesome children. Those who seek have found.

## ACTIVITY 5.1: THREE STRESS CASES

In each of these cases, discuss your feelings, how you would cope and what action, if any, you would take. Note any recommendations that would need to be considered on a school-wide basis. There are no comments following these cases; participants need to consider how the advice in this chapter would apply if these incidents occurred in their own particular circumstances.

1 After persistent difficulties with an aggressive and difficult pupil in a largely co-operative class you order him out of the room. He refuses to leave so you go and fetch the deputy head, who takes him away. After a few minutes he returns unabashed and resumes his seat. Shortly before the lesson ends the deputy enters and proceeds to tell off the entire class for their 'continual bad behaviour' in your lessons. Unspecified action is threatened if any more is heard from you about them. The deputy, clearly satisfied that this action has given you support in a forthright and helpful way, leaves the room. You have another class to go to.

2 You are behind with the end-of-term reports and have been pressed by the head for completion. You have the last period of the day free and intend working on them then and staying in school until you finish. Just before your free begins, a pupil brings a message from the deputy asking you to retain your present class until school ends as their next teacher has gone home with a sudden headache. The class is a tough and difficult one and you are exasperated after barely surviving a double period with them. You could bring up the whole matter of frees and absenteeism at the next staff meeting, though you know from experience that the missing teacher, who is often absent, will not be there.

3 On a November morning, a cold, wintry rain is sweeping the playground. Only the staff are in school, as it is a training day, but two pupils, poorly clad against the weather, are sheltering in the doorway. They did not remember or were absent and never received the instruction to stay at home, have travelled several miles, are wet through, and it is well known that neither will find anyone in at home. A senior teacher tells the pupils to go, and that it is their responsibility if they are locked out. They protest but are pushed out and the door is locked. Both pupils are in your special group and you can hear their incoherent protests above the noise of the wind and the rain.

## ACTIVITY 5.2: THINKING ABOUT STRESS

The purpose of this exercise is to compare perceptions of the sources of stress in your situation and to identify areas producing general problems.

There are many ways of doing this. For example, Grunsell (1985) suggests filling in equations of this sort: stress = x + y − z. Below are some points which should guide thinking, and they themselves have benefited from anger management techniques described in Hughes (1988).

1 Exactly describe one cause of stress to you. Briefly but specifically note exactly what happens.
2 Identify any organizational features or other forces that create or maintain the unwanted situation.
3 Write down your goals or ambitions in this situation. Could they be altered, and if so in what way?
4 You should now be able to identify those aspects of the problem directly under your control and those that are external stressors. Using a popular analogy, you should be able to separate that part of the problem that is an excessive load on the bridge and that part caused by weakness in the bridge.
5 Be clear about those parts of the problem that are yours and that will form the basis of any self-assertion strategy. List some alternative actions that you could try in your stressful situation. Note the preparation and self-statements you would need. Consider what might happen with each alternative.

In groups, compare your problems, share solutions, and try to analyse and suggest remedies for each other. You will certainly find that there are different hierarchies of stressful situations. You may even discover that one person's stressor is regarded favourably or with indifference by others. This illustrates the role of perception in stress. The plenary session may identify school-wide problems which require continued staff co-operation and management.

## ACTIVITY 5.3: CONFRONTATION WITH MALCOLM

For this exercise the group should divide into pairs or threes to permit full contributions from all participants. The purpose of the exercise is to identify examples of the points discussed above, and to identify points at which the teacher could have taken alternative action and, in particular, any examples of inappropriate action. One way of learning from this case is to begin with one teacher empathizing with Malcolm and another with the teacher. If groups are in threes, the remaining member may try to consider the situation from the viewpoint of a colleague or one of the other pupils.

There cannot, of course, be a model solution to this or any other example. The value lies in practising confrontation management techniques. The paragraphs are numbered to facilitate reference in discussion.

The course leader should read the comments on the exercise before the plenary session.

**Incident report from a teacher**

1 The trouble began when I set them to do the exercise. Malcolm said: 'It's boring!' and shut his book with a loud snap. I told him he would have to do the work like everyone else and if he didn't do it now I would see he did it later. His reply to that was a lot of very foul language. He said: 'Just try and make me', or some challenge like that.

2 I went straight up to him and opened his book at the page and I tried to make him be sensible – I spoke to him very quietly and reasonably – but he just threw the book down on the floor and rocked back on his chair. I just couldn't let him get away with that. I knew there was no point in ordering him to pick the book up, so I did and put it on his desk again.

3 As I attended to another pupil I heard him rip the book in half. I didn't turn round straight away – I was telling some others to get on with their work – they were watching his performance. They were looking to see what was going to happen next. Then I saw the book fly across the room.

4 I explained to him how patient I was being and how I had defended him against other teachers' complaints on more than one occasion. His response was more swearing.

5 I told him not to be silly and went back to my desk, but he then took other pupils' work and threw it on the floor. It was just out of control and he was obviously heading for a showdown.

6 I warned him that if he didn't grow up I would bring the deputy but he just laughed and said 'Go on and fetch her'. Those are not the actual words he used. I ordered him out but he defied me again.

7 The class went very quiet; he was standing up in an aggressive style. I turned to go for the deputy and he then came up behind me and punched me hard in the back. When I came back he was in his place and the deputy took him away. He had calmed down by then. It was a good thing the lesson was nearly over as the kids were really high.

**Comments on the exercise**

Too much should not be read into the actual wording or the form of this report. Although it is based on a real report, extra information has been added to give a full enough picture for analysis.

1 Malcolm's action should have caused an alarm bell to ring in the teacher's mind: here is a typical cue to avoid unconsidered responses

and get control of self. Here the teacher's positional authority as a teacher is rejected. Note the suggestion that the work must be done at any price, the threat that 'I would see' that it was, and the feeling of being challenged. The teacher is personally involved from the outset. Accepting the comment on boring work may have avoided further activity.

2 A juxtaposition of a challenging response (opening the book) and conciliation (speaking quietly and reasonably). The teacher's personal reasonableness joins the professional authority on the floor. The teacher is driven by imperatives: 'couldn't let him get away with that'. You could let him get away with it and others might accept this exception being made: perhaps a comment like: 'Malcolm's not himself today.'

3 Here we see recognition of the role played by the audience. The pupil's further provocation suggests that it is affecting his behaviour too.

4 Personal reasonableness takes another blow. The feeling of hurt expressed here suggests that this pupil is seeking revenge: the teacher is receiving punishment belonging to some other person in some other relationship.

5 Apparent evidence that the pupil is determined to continue irrespective of teacher's response, and the teacher's feeling of inevitability confirms this. Accepting the inevitability of events hastens and does not hinder their progress.

6 In the light of (5), ordering the pupil out seems unwise. It might have been appropriate, even at this late stage, to specify some simple achievable behaviour and withdraw. 'Grow up' is both imprecise and insulting – although it cannot be denied it is deserved.

7 This conclusion is doubly distressing for the teacher: having been assaulted, the teacher brings help to what appears to be a situation of no threat, easily managed. Staff support groups and discussions would be helpful here, as will be explained in Chapter 7.

## ACTIVITY 5.4: INCIDENT IN AN EXCLUSION UNIT

Five teenage boys sit with their teacher at one end of a long, drab and chilly room. The room forms part of an old prefabricated hut and it was once used as a science laboratory. Now it is a unit for pupils excluded from school. The boys sit at desks near the door, their heads bent in silence over their work. All are struggling with work in the basic skills of mathematics and English, and their attainment levels are between two and four years behind their actual age. The teacher is absorbed in the books and papers on his desk. Piled untidily at the other end of the room are benches, chairs, boxes of bottles and discarded scientific equipment.

On one of these benches sits a sixth youth. He is silent like the others but his expression is hostile and he does not work. In each hand he holds a long glass tube that he has found among boxes of junk. He taps them together rhythmically and gently but with slowly increasing force, as if testing the strength of the glass and stopping as close as possible to the breaking point. The noise is impossible to ignore, although the teacher appears to do so, fixing the pupils with an authoritative stare when they look up or twist round at the source of the distraction. Just as it seems the next tap will break the tubes, the tapping ceases and then begins again softly: a series of tantalizing crescendos.

When the crash of broken glass eventually comes, it brings two of the boys to their feet. What is the teacher going to do about it? He tells them to sit down. The begetter of the disturbance strolls to the door, whistling with conspicuous nonchalance. The teacher calls a cheery 'Goodbye', telling him to return as soon as he feels like working properly. The door slams but opens again immediately. The youth returns, demands a cigarette from another boy, lights it and is gone in an instant. After some protests, the class returns to work. The teacher takes out a folder and begins to write.

**Points to consider**

This incident took place in a small unit for pupils excluded from secondary schools. Over a period of seven weeks there were ten examples of indiscipline serious enough to warrant formal recording: this was one of them. All of the pupils were permanently excluded from schools. In the light of this low level of indiscipline in the unit, you might formulate some issues deserving enquiry in the excluding schools and in the policy and practice of the unit. Prepare a list of questions for the school, the unit teacher and the pupils. These should cover the schools' efforts to meet the pupils' needs, the rationale for the unit teacher's actions, and the motives of the disruptive pupil. What are the costs and benefits associated with the unit's policy? Consider how other teachers – including you – might have reacted to this incident. Devise a policy for maintaining order in the unit which also meets the social and educational needs of this difficult group.

**ACTIVITY 5.5: THE MORAL DIMENSIONS OF TEACHING**

In this chapter we saw how assessment of pupils required the virtues of prudence, fortitude, temperance and justice. It is sometimes asserted that learning requires experience plus reflection on that experience: only what the mind processes remains as learning. Consider what virtues are required if a teacher is to be able to learn from experience – or perhaps to learn at all. Use your findings to refine your view of what characterizes good teachers and good teaching.

**Comments on the activity**

Many teachers are unhappy about calling someone a good teacher merely because they are effective in causing something to be learned. The means used and the aims in view seem to be essential components of teaching: it has to be an intrinsically worthwhile or ethically good activity. The reading and activities of Chapter 3 should have cleared away any superficial view that teaching can be usefully classified into didactic or experiential, or pupil-centred or subject-centred. You might find it helpful to consider some examples of famous or notorious people who fit these categories. For example, Charles Dickens' character Fagin was an advocate of experiential learning and, in the main, a successful practitioner. Could he be described as a good teacher? Consider a didactic performer like Joseph Goebbels, alas not fictional but effective and (to make matters more complicated) a man of sincere spiritual beliefs. He conducted moving funeral services and, at the very end, even as Soviet shells were falling on the bunker, took the news of Roosevelt's death as proof that God would still intervene to save the Nazis. Can a definition of a good teacher be formulated that excludes him? Returning to the equation (experience plus reflection equals learning), my colleague Paul Martin has pointed out that *Mein Kampf* is unquestionably a reflection on experience, but what did its author actually learn? Hegel said: 'What experience and history teach us is this – that people and governments never have learnt anything from history, or acted on principles deduced from it.' Perhaps we do not learn, if we do not, because we are not virtuous enough.

## ACTIVITY 5.6: DIFFICULTIES WITH PARENTS

If there is at least a thread of rationality accompanying even the most bizarre behaviour of the most troublesome pupil, the same applies also to the most hostile and antagonistic parent. Consider this case presented by a teacher on an in-service course.

A pupil came to school in very expensive, so-called designer, trainers. The school had expressly forbidden such items, and most parents had been very happy to co-operate with a rule against what they regarded as a commercial swindle. During the course of the morning the trainers were stolen. The pupil went home and returned before the end of the lunch break with a kitchen knife. He wandered about the grounds looking for another boy who was alleged to be the thief. He was apprehended by a teacher who (with no difficulty, she said) confiscated the knife. The pupil ran home again.

Father then appeared, without his son, but in a great rage and demanding the knife, the trainers and the alleged thief (who turned out to be one of his children by a former marriage). He was told by the head that he could not have any of these things. He stood in the foyer of the school shouting abuse, threatening violence and refusing to leave. The police were called.

What possible strategies could have been tried to avoid this unpleasant confrontation? Think about instant reactions as well as longer-term policies.

## Comments on the activity

This distressed parent's behaviour could be analysed in the same way as a pupil's, using the Dreikurs typology of attention, power and revenge. Attention and power are involved here, certainly. In such confrontations we might also be on the look-out for displays of defensiveness and denial ('He's no trouble at home'), triumph ('You teachers can't handle him'), or indifference and helplessness ('I can't do anything with him'). Instant reactions might include sympathy ('We're sorry about the trainers'), acceptance of the parent's anger as justified ('You're right to be angry'), restatement of the school's policy ('We cannot allow knives in school'), with an offer to listen to the grievance ('You must come into my room and give me all the details').

Once away from the audience there is a better chance of rational discussion. Start with the positive ('I'm glad that we have this opportunity to meet') and reiterate your acceptance of his feelings ('You're right to be angry about such expensive things going missing'). Try to shift the discussion into an exploratory frame ('I wonder if...?' 'Is it possible that...?'). You have a genuine interest in getting a solution and it should show. How can you and the parent lighten the load that has come upon you both? Stick to neutral statements of fact; reflect back the parent's feelings to clarify issues. It can help if the room you use allows you both to sit together, rather than across a desk, and at similar heights, so that non-challenging eye-contact can be maintained. You will usually find that in such a genuinely helpful atmosphere the parent will become calm and rational. In this particular case you might expect such statements as: 'I wish I'd never bought them', 'I've told him about knives', 'I can't do anything with him'. Longer-term policies would ensure that all staff were familiar with suitable reactive strategies and that, in cases where the parents of troublesome pupils refuse to attend the school, relationships with parents were well developed through home visits.

# Chapter 6

# Individuals in context

If you want drunkenness and facility for being intimidated – impulsive, unreflecting and violent people, do you go to the top [of society] or the bottom?

(Robert Lowe, parliamentary debate, 1866 [quoted in Speck, 1993])

Lowe is remembered as the author of the Revised Code, a nineteenth-century attempt to raise the standards attained in state education by relating payment to schools' results. The contempt implied in this rhetorical question of his is congruent with the neglect that, with occasional exceptions, has characterized social policy ever since. Even Gladstone's witty riposte ('Lancashire') does not look so funny from 'the bottom'. Although this chapter focuses on the classroom and school contexts – the places where pupils' behaviour may be operated upon – it is essential to keep pupils' domestic circumstances in mind. Pupils' perception and interpretations of their school experiences, the schema they bring with them, are rooted in their domestic lives. In the same way, our understanding and interpretations are rooted in ours, and few of us have had the misfortune to sample life at the bottom. The belief that many of us entertain, that life has improved for everyone, is just not supported by the facts. In Britain, relative poverty has actually increased since 1980, with the poorest half of the population seeing its share of the national income shrink. This decline in standards was felt disproportionately by children, with the proportion living in poverty doubling over the period from 1980 to 1987. In the hackneyed but depressingly accurate phrase, 'The rich got richer and the poor got poorer' (Ian Gilmour, former Conservative minister, quoted in Ward, 1994).

Consider, for example, what this anecdote from a nursery teacher tells us about some children's home life.

Amy, aged four, is having trouble with the baby. It won't go to bed. We can hear it crying from the home corner and we can hear Amy, who has learned from home how to put a baby to bed, getting cross with it. The doll is thrust under the cover and thumped repeatedly: 'Lie there you bastard.'

It might be a scene from a John Cleese production, but it's a vignette from a nursery on a deprived, post-war council estate. Amy is one of the lucky ones. There are estates and inner-city zones with higher rates of unemployment, more lone parents, worse housing, fewer amenities and no nurseries. HMI (in HMSO, 1993), reporting on urban education, assembled a quantity of statistics to describe the areas it studied and provided some first-hand accounts: 'Litter, graffiti and the effects of vandalism are readily apparent in these dismal environments.'

According to HMI, attending a nursery makes a recognizable improvement in children's ability to settle into school, and therefore to settle into and help to form an orderly society; so from an accountant's point of view (never mind the moral issue), action to relieve deprivation makes sense. Natural justice demands action from those who are capable. The technological revolution that was going to leave so little work to do that we could share it and worry about what to do with our leisure seems to have left the poor very much as they were. It is a comfort to the better-off, but no comfort to the poor, to say that in absolute terms conditions are actually better than they were a century ago. People have to live in the present and react to the environment they perceive, which includes the expectations engendered by the display of wealth and success that surrounds us in Western societies.

Schools can help, of course, but, says HMI, 'beyond the school gate are underlying issues of poverty, unemployment, poor housing, inadequate health care and the frequent break-up of families'. The inspectors conclude that most schools lack the capacity to carry out sustained programmes of renewal unaided.

We know that some schools can do more for their pupils. In secondaries and primaries HMI found that standards varied from class to class and subject to subject, suggesting that where some can achieve, others could follow. This evidence, gathered in 1992/3, supports the findings of the 1988/9 HMI survey of provision for special needs in ordinary schools: the quality of what is offered varies and the pupils' efforts and achievements vary with it. The chances of pupils in deprived areas receiving challenging and rewarding teaching throughout their educational careers are described as 'slim'. Much teaching seems to have been defective, in failing to focus on pupils' learning – on what pupils can contribute to the classroom through discussion and how they can extend their understanding by talking things through.

In line with earlier work by HMI and the findings of the Elton committee, behaviour was found to be generally good with a 'good-natured atmosphere' in most classrooms. HMI thinks the cost of this benefit has been a too-comfortable pace and insufficiently challenging work. This conclusion is supported by the evidence of inspection but there's more to it than that. The sense of community responsibility that has died out (if it ever existed), the ghost of which lives on in political rhetoric, is alive in our schools. Many teachers feel that their good-natured, unchallenging relationships are worth keeping when the future holds so little for their pupils. As HMI says itself, it's not a case of expecting schools just to try harder; long-term, co-ordinated efforts are needed.

With these caveats in mind, we will first look at the classroom itself and describe a method of analysing and altering behaviour. Second, we will consider the influence of the organization and climate of the school. We are principally concerned here with troublesome pupils and not implying that all pupils, or even a majority, will necessarily be adversely affected by the contexts discussed, nor that all can be influenced by the manipulation of them. Pupils, like any other people, are not infinitely malleable. As Eisner (1985) puts it: 'Children have an enormous capacity to learn how to cope with treatments that they wish to manage for their own purposes.'

## THE CLASSROOM

Schostak (1986) quotes Bain's assertion of a century ago that 'for the single pupil, individuality may be studied and appealed to, for the class, individualities are not considered'. Caspari (1976) describes some aspects of behaviour in groups which indicate some of the behavioural features to expect in classrooms that may be missing from individual and small group interaction. These are that members are more dependent on the leader, who may be used as a target for negative feelings that are felt for others; that to gain attention in groups, forcefulness is necessary; and that it seems to be easier to be destructive than positive. It is this last point that is often made by those advocating one of the more widespread interventions in disorderly classrooms, a programme based on the principles of behaviour modification, or behaviour management as it is now more often called (typical texts are Galvin and Singleton, 1984; Cheeseman and Watts, 1985; and Wheldall and Merret, 1984). The strength of this approach lies in its ability to offer practical programmes and solutions: there is something straightforward that can actually be tried. Desired types of behaviour are rewarded, or positively reinforced, and unwanted types of behaviour are negatively reinforced and extinguished by having their reinforcers withdrawn. A pupil who rarely sat at his or her desk would receive smiles, sweets or other attention when found to be sitting, and would be ignored when leaving the desk to pester the teacher for attention. In some cases, approximations to the desired behaviour are rewarded with the long-term intention of shaping the end result by encouraging improvements towards it. A procedure known as task-analysis may be used to determine the sequence of small steps which, when rewarded, will add up to or lead towards the desired behaviour.

Punishment may take the form of withdrawal of reinforcement or removal from an interesting activity. This is called 'time out' and may involve a few minutes' exile within or outside the classroom. Behavioural programmes may be useful with dull or very young children and, significantly, the textbook examples do not usually include pupils over the age of 12. However, Porter (in Coupe and Porter, 1986: 64) notes that, even for children with severe learning difficulties, the behavioural approach 'should not be viewed as a panacea'. Older or more reflective pupils readily see that they are being manipulated and are able to thwart a simplistic tactic that does not recognize motive and action.

The limitations of behavioural programmes and their distorted view of human action are handicaps that have been recognized, not least by therapists themselves faced with outcomes that were only partially or temporarily successful. A major drawback is that they take little or no account of the constraints of classroom management. Doyle concludes that the weight of the evidence is against them: '... early recommendations for elaborate and complex systems of token economies, systematic contingency management, and ignoring undesirable behaviour while praising desired behaviour were impractical for individual classroom teachers' (Wittrock, 1986: 423). On a related issue, Evertson and Emmer (1982) note that 'instructional approaches (for example, an individual diagnostic-prescriptive method)' that do not take account of the pressures of the classroom setting are not easily or correctly implemented. The claim that it was safer and more objective for teachers to attend only to the behaviour, ignoring other factors and possibilities, is now seen to be over-optimistic. Certainly, time can be wasted in futile speculation but to ignore the social context is to limit one's vision. It is similarly limiting to ignore the subjective motives and intentions of the parties, for it is an objective fact that people are subjective. Further doubts are sometimes expressed about the wisdom of using external reinforcement, its effect upon the pupil's intrinsic motivation, and the apparent lack of attention to the nature of the learning that the pupil is being trained to accept. Attending only to what can be observed and measured can result in pupils' intentions and meanings being ignored, but it is often these motives that determine what the behaviour actually is. It is difficult to describe a human action without including or implying a motive or other state of mind. A pupil may swear at a teacher in order to win esteem from a delinquent peer group; another pupil's swearing may spring from frustration, personal failure and the prospect of future unemployment. Without attention to the pupil's meaning, intervention is likely to be ineffective or aggravating. The same difficulties apply to determining what counts as ignoring, or as a reward or punishment. The success of the behavioural approach hangs on an uncertain congruence of view between teachers and pupils in these matters.

These limitations have led to the typical product of behavioural programmes being described as the pupil who '. . . stays glued to his seat and desk all day, continuously looks at his teacher or his text . . . does not talk to or in fact look at other children . . . does not laugh or sing . . . and assuredly passes silently in the halls' (Winnet and Winkler, quoted in Hughes, 1988: 20). In reality, however, this parody has proved more an indictment of the intention than the result. Behaviourally orientated authors have expanded their repertoire in order to meet some of these difficulties. Wheldall and Merrett (1984) pay attention to environmental antecedents; Cheesman and Watts (1985) throw in a list of strategies 'tried, tested and approved by teachers' or tips, as they might be called. It still may be, as Docking (1980) suggests, that behavioural methods are appropriate only for novices or the inexpert, and even then as long as control does not become an end in its own right.

Hughes (1988) describes a more radical extension of the behavioural approach into a new specialism, termed 'cognitive behaviour therapy'. This discipline takes account of the active role of human perceptions and the extent to which we act in environments created by ourselves. The cognitive behavioural approach retains the interest of behaviourists in experimental verification of carefully defined programmes but with a new emphasis on interaction between therapist, or teacher, and pupil. More time is spent in showing the pupil what to do, taking turns to practise alongside him or her, and working together co-operatively. The pupil is no longer a passive object of therapy but is fully involved in the aims and direction of the programme and regarded as its legitimate owner. Pupils are encouraged to talk themselves through their problems and practise controlling their impulses and wayward inclinations. Teachers help by giving the pupil encouraging explanations for failure: for example, that it is a temporary setback that does not preclude future success; that it is at least partly a matter of bad luck; and that the pupil has the ability to succeed with a little more persistence and effort. Pupils are invited to consider alternative strategies, and their different consequences, that might be more appropriate in situations where they habitually resort to violence or disruption. If troublesome pupils are to have a fair chance of using the new strategies, it is often necessary to involve their classmates. Hughes (1988) warns that other pupils may react on the basis of reputation rather than current efforts and unintentionally thwart troublesome pupils' attempts to improve.

A troublesome pupil's classroom behaviour may be a partial result of his or her experience of trying to establish a role in the group. For example, an insecure or semi-literate pupil may have found that other pupils respond to his or her tumbling on to the floor with rewarding smiles and laughter; the teacher may respond by describing the pupil as naughty or as a distraction – labels the pupil may see as a suitable cover for his or her lack of achievement. The pupil, over time, may develop and elaborate an identity as a mischief-maker which may both disguise and excuse an inability to read. There is, in fact, a well-established correlation between inability to read and troublesome behaviour (Laing and Chazan, 1986), although the direction of causality is impossible to identify with certainty. One study does suggest that poor verbal skill at the age of three is associated with difficult behaviour at the age of eight (Stevenson, summarized in Cohen and Cohen, 1987). It is necessary to identify precisely the unwanted behaviour, discover any predisposing conditions and unintended rewards, and devise a strategy for change.

## Precise identification

To describe pupils as noisy, cheeky, uncontrollable or hyperactive is insufficiently accurate to focus observation and improvement. A pupil can be noisy in many ways that may be identified with more precision: sings, drums feet, whistles, shouts to pupils or teacher, scrapes chair, drops equipment. Being cheeky can be pulling faces, staring, parodying or repeating the teacher, packing books away before the proper time, as well as offering rude comments. A teacher's rules take meaning from particular contexts (Hargreaves *et al.*, 1975) and therefore it is not enough to know, for example, that a pupil 'will not stop talking'; this may mean that he or she is cheating, interrupting, being rude, disturbing others or refusing to work. The physical setting and the expectations associated with it also influence the meaning of behaviour; conversation that is appropriate in CDT may not be so in history. Pupils may regard some areas with awe and fear but see others as 'soft' (Delamont and Galton, 1986). In some specialist rooms, there is more scope to demonstrate the intrinsic worth and practical value of what is being taught (Schostak, 1983); the discipline of the subject can aid the discipline of the group.

Precision is more easily achieved with some types of behaviour than with others. For example, it is, in principle, impossible to know with certainty whether someone is paying attention or not, as we cannot think another person's thoughts. In such cases, a rough approximation has to serve, and pupils are usually regarded as paying sufficient attention if they are facing the teacher and apparently engaged on the task. It is an unnecessary use of time to go to absurd lengths in precisely describing pupil misbehaviour. An example sometimes quoted is the definition of 'out of seat' as being 'when no part of the seat part of the person is in contact with the seat part of the seat'. It is possible to use elaborate and detailed checklists for recording behaviour, and examples may be found in Galvin and Singleton (1984), Coulby and Harper (1985) and Grunsell (1985).

## Measuring the extent or frequency

If progress is to be measured, then some sort of baseline must be established; we need to know how often a particular unwanted action occurs or what proportion of a typical lesson is spent in unwanted behaviour. If the unwanted behaviour is a discrete action, for example leaving the seat and kicking another pupil, then the number of occurrences can be counted. This can be done over a single lesson, or teachers can collate figures for several lessons. If this shows wide variations in the frequency of the misbehaviour, then this in itself is a useful piece of information. Where the behaviour is not measurable in this simple way then the co-operation of a colleague may be necessary. Observations are taken at intervals – every minute or every two minutes the pupil's behaviour is recorded – which produce a measure of the frequency of the unwanted behaviour. Generally speaking, misbehaviour measured in these ways turns out to be much less prevalent than expected. It is common to find that a pupil is able to give an impression of perpetual disruption while attending the lesson, or being harmlessly disengaged, for two-thirds of the time. Congruent with this phenomenon is the observation reported in Wragg (1984) that in some classes which are apparently totally out of control, two-thirds of the pupils are in fact on task. This discovery is welcome news to the teacher and helps to get the management programme off to an optimistic start. Some pupils are sometimes able to record their own off-task activity rate, and in such cases the additional attention and teacher interaction make the pupil's aims in misbehaving redundant.

## Picking a target

There is often a whole range of behaviour exhibited by a problem pupil. It is tempting to begin work on eradicating the most serious, even if it is not the most frequent. Unfortunately, the most serious types of behaviour are often the most difficult to eradicate, and the close observation and analysis programme is therefore vulnerable to a speedy and unsuccessful end. It is wiser to focus on an easy target first, particularly if it is a high-frequency type of behaviour; relatively trivial misbehaviour is often a necessary precondition to committing more serious offences. For example, a pupil who hits others and spoils their work is also off-task and out of his or her place. The most profitable procedure, therefore, is to increase on-task activity and decrease the time the pupil spends out of seat. Choosing to reward an appropriate behaviour that is incompatible with an unwanted alternative has the added advantage of creating a more rewarding environment for a pupil accustomed to ignoring punishments.

Unwanted behaviour may need teacher co-operation for it to occur: pestering for attention is one example. It is usual to advise ignoring such behaviour but this is rarely possible in the classroom or indeed in principle: to ignore deliberately is to attend in a negative way and the pupil usually knows this. A determined pupil may then escalate the attention seeking until the teacher gives way: all the pupil has learned is to be persistent and the behaviour is therefore made worse not better. An equivalent strategy to ignoring is to attend to the pupil in a detached and distant manner – denying eye contact and moving away while speaking, for example. As soon as the pupil is observed on-task, the teacher can give full and rewarding interaction. In extreme circumstances it may be necessary to remove the pupil from the classroom and, as far as possible, from stimulating and interesting surroundings. Behavioural psychologists term this treatment 'time out'. Few schools have an appropriate spare room, or even a walk-in cupboard, that can be made available even for the few minutes that may be necessary. However, many of the features of time out and ignoring can be produced by the planned and deliberate coolness described above.

## Predisposing and confirming circumstances

There are some very simple aspects of classroom environment that influence attentiveness and distraction. Bull and Solity (1987: 137) provide a list of such things as seating, task difficulty and teacher behaviour. Chapter 3 deals with such factors. Curricular variety and relevance at the primary and secondary level have their equivalents in pre-school contexts; and evidence from nurseries can help in observation of older age-groups. Smith and Connolly's study of three- and four-year-olds (summarized in Cohen and Cohen, 1988: 139) showed that ample play equipment reduced conflict but also reduced sharing activities; reducing the quantity of toys encouraged more conflict but also more sharing, and fewer children were left out of activities; severe crowding (less than 15 square feet per child) reduced the scope for rough-and-tumble play but increased aggression. This work shows that if provision is always lavish some children will be denied opportunities to learn to share. Interestingly, Laslett (1977) suggested that although maladjusted pupils need exceptionally patient teachers, they should be exposed to less tolerant outsiders, too. Research discussed by Laing and Chazan (1986) suggests that a 'tight organizational pattern', which required young children to participate in activities in a pre-arranged rota 'whether they were interested or not', created disruption opportunities for some pupils. Organizational patterns of this sort are an inevitable feature later on.

The close recording and measurement of behaviour may reveal other previously hidden factors. For example, it may be noticed that the pupil under observation is not the only one involved in many of the incidents. Sometimes several pupils co-operate in mischief, perhaps inciting the target pupil to join in. When the teacher notices and corrects them, all but the target pupil fall into line. Hargreaves (1980) describes an example of this. It is therefore important when observing to take the whole context, which includes other pupils, into consideration. Some pupils create trouble only in some subjects, or with some teachers or at certain times of the day. These conditions are not usually easy to remedy but in serious cases a change of timetable or personnel may be considered justifiable. Sometimes, of course, teachers may need the advice in Chapter 3.

It is more common to find misbehaviour being unintentionally rewarded, so that, from the pupil's viewpoint, its utility is confirmed. With younger pupils, the reward for unwanted behaviour often consists of isolation with a kind and sympathetic teacher – for example, after throwing a spectacular scene. It is not unknown for some senior pupils to behave badly partly because suspension from school gives them freedom and the opportunity to earn money. In other cases, appropriate behaviour is insufficiently rewarded, leaving the remnant of good behaviour at the mercy of the more exciting bad. Unrewarding teaching, unimaginative learning methods and scant attention to pupils' productions are ways of weakening the incentive to co-operate.

**Charts and records**

Younger pupils benefit from having a visual reminder of their improvement target. This should relate the behaviour that is to be increased or decreased to something of interest to the pupil. Figure 6.1 shows examples of charts made by pupils, which had the incidental but important consequence of involving the pupils' peers in their reform. Coulby and Harper (1985) provide some other examples. For teenagers, such methods may be inappropriately juvenile. Some will find recording their classroom activity graphically, perhaps through a simple histogram, an interesting and instructive activity: pupils are often amazed at the amount of time they waste. This activity can be introduced to the whole class as a maths project and those with alarming results encouraged to continue monitoring their own progress.

Many schools use lesson record cards or report sheets for persistently disruptive offenders. These are ineffective with some pupils and are often difficult to fill in honestly and accurately. Typically, a pupil will behave in his or her usually disruptive way until close to the end of the lesson. Some may make no effort to behave but try to persuade a weary teacher to moderate the truth in exchange for the promise, likely to be unrealized,

10 points: ON TIME
              LISTENS TO TEACHER
              SHARES TEXTBOOK

20 points: COMPLETES LESSON
              COMPLETES WORK
              NO SHOUTING/INSULTS

Higgins scores 10 points every time Craig shouts or swears, leaves seat, distracts others.

*Figure 6.1* Examples of record charts

of co-operation next time. As the pupil moves through the day, succeeding teachers become reluctant to be the first to record total lack of co-operation; some may even suspect that their lesson is at fault and not the pupil.

Figure 6.2 shows an alternative. First, the card is specific, easier to fill in accurately, and a better basis for discussing the required behavioural changes with the pupil. Second, the types of behaviour required are mostly expressed positively. Third, and most important, it is weighted in the pupil's favour, since many of the listed types of behaviour are easily achievable. If the pupil gains nine or more ticks, a further two points are automatically earned. As each series of lessons is recorded, perhaps over a few days, the scores provide a clear measure of progress.

On time?
Went to proper place?
Neatly turned out?
Smiled or greeted teacher?
Done homework?
Properly equipped?
Paid reasonable attention?
Did most of work set?
Contributed to lesson?
Helped other pupil?

Helped give things out?
Helped clear away?
Answered question?
Accepted correction?
Finished set work?
Did not shout out?
Stayed to end of lesson?
Any other good points?
50% bonus points?
SCORE out of 20: _____

*Figure 6.2* Disruptive pupil's lesson record card

## Classroom climate

A positive classroom climate, where praise is regularly available, is recommended. Teachers who measure their own performance usually find that they issue more negative remarks than positive – in a ratio of about two to one. It is not particularly difficult to reverse this ratio, and to do so may help to increase the amount of praiseworthy behaviour, thus reducing the amount of space available to the unwanted. The effectiveness of the lavish use of praise is often presented as if it were a modern discovery but it has a longer history. Curtis (1963) quotes Ascham's sixteenth-century text: '... there is no such whetstone to sharpen a good wit, and encourage a will to learning, as is praise'. This advice has to be followed with discretion in the case of older pupils. Most primary school pupils are proud to please adults; most secondary school children respond better to praise when it is given privately, and not just because they wish to cultivate a rebellious image; many adults do not know how to accept praise and they find it difficult and embarrassing. Although it sometimes appears that some pupils offer little behaviour worth praising, close observation usually shows this not to be the case. Demanding pupils create this impression because during their periods of orderliness the hard-pressed teacher's attention is being given elsewhere. Observations by supporting colleagues not infrequently find that pupils who are apparently totally unco-operative are in fact behaving themselves for as much as one-third of the time. Hard though it may be to accept, these are most important opportunities to influence troublesome pupils. The same principle applies to pupils' work which is often too poor to be genuinely praised. Imaginative teachers can do their best: for example, some misspellings, like 'foggot' (forgot), improve the meaning of the original word. Rather than reacting only to errors and misbehaviour, the advice is to 'catch the pupil being good'.

When a disruptive pupil has been settled, or even excluded, another pupil sometimes steps into the role. This alerts us to the social characteristics of the classroom. It can rarely be the case that classrooms are wholly free of some degree of unwanted behaviour, if only because people's differing values produce gradations in the desirability of types of behaviour. This social phenomenon is described in Durkheim (1893/1933). Understanding and accepting this fact, and appreciating pupils' perspectives, are essential parts of learning to work with other people. In some classrooms there seems to be a need, whose source is difficult to identify, for an array of roles to be occupied (Hanko, 1985). The pupils and their teacher must reconcile their differing images of self, and their intentions, in an environment constrained by expectations and regulations from without. The resulting conflicts, negotiations and compromises constitute commitments to, and are the substance of, the classroom system.

Put simply, some classes seem to need a dunce, a clown, a scapegoat, a baby or a tyrant – someone to be excessively smart, or weak or tough (Hanko, 1985). A teaching programme or style that is restricted to telling or to free activity, a work programme that is drearily predictable or giddily indeterminate, and an evaluation scheme that is ambiguous or harsh may themselves make unwanted pupil roles and activities worth while. In extreme circumstances some pupils may feel unable to do any-thing to satisfy the teacher: the only possible way of finding success is to be the best at being the worst. Classroom observation is incomplete without considering these possibilities.

Using support teachers in the classroom is a recent alternative to the removal of pupils to the charge of a separate teacher (Bell and Best, 1986). This tends to avoid the dilution of curricula and expectations, focuses attention on the possible shortcomings of the ordinary classroom, and helps to prevent pupils and teachers becoming stigmatized in a separate room where the testing and assessment of one pupil become a substitute for the reform of curricula for all. Support teaching as a form of co-operative or team teaching requires planning. Roles need to be rotated to prevent one teacher becoming the leader and the other feeling de-skilled and unable, for example, to address the class in the absence of the dominant colleague (Denscombe, 1984). There are lessons for all schools in research in playgroups and nurseries reported by Bruner (1980): '. . . teachers, in fact, develop reputations for the particular services they supply and children come to them for those services . . . the children in a playgroup or nursery school may prevent the teacher from changing her role'. Resource-based learning helps to prevent polarization of teacher roles; the necessary block timetabling distributes discretion and authority to individual teams, enhancing the interest and feeling of significance in the work. The original problems are tackled in their original context; all pupils benefit irrespective of their needs; and a co-operative climate should lead to motivational, intellectual and social gains. For the teachers, such co-operation is both a source of personal support and an opportunity to develop competence in new subjects: a sort of classroom-based, rather than school-based, in-service development and training. The additional noise and movement create problems for teachers although it has been suggested that pupils are less troubled by it. Delamont and Galton (1986) point out that what counts as inappropriate movement is culturally specific and, by implication, alterable: Islamic and Jewish pupils, for example, may rock and chant when reading. Denscombe (1985) claims worries about noise derive largely from taking it as evidence of disorder in the traditional closed classrooms into which we cannot see. Quietness in classrooms is 'an impression to be sustained to outsiders who have meagre information on which to assess the extent of control exercised behind closed doors' (Denscombe, 1985: 11).

Individual teachers' expectations of pupils are often said to be a vital aspect of the classroom context (for example, DES, 1984) although the research literature is inconclusive. In a review of attempts to induce expectations, laboratory-type experiments and naturalistic studies, Rogers (1986) concludes that the evidence for the straightforward effect of expectations is lacking. However, there does seem to be support for the view that those teachers whose expectations are related to social class may influence younger children. It is also likely that artificial attempts to induce expectations may fail, not because teacher expectations are irrelevant, but because experimenters are unable to overcome the expectations and typifications that teachers already have. Hargreaves *et al.* (1975) construct a theory of typing involving the three stages of speculation, elaboration and stabilization. They say that teachers attend principally to appearance, conformity and ability when allocating or withholding the status of normality. Some classroom categories receive considerable acknowledgement in the organizational system and climate of the school and will be discussed in the next section. There seems little doubt that some pupils receive profane labels because of some teachers' preconceptions. Keddie (1971) recorded an example of pupil questions being accepted or rejected on the basis of their ability group.

Consideration of the classroom context, therefore, needs to include teacher attitudes and behaviour as well as those of the pupils. It is a universal phenomenon, and essential to thinking, for human beings to sort, categorize, type, label and to entertain expectations in relation to these classifications. The division of labour improves intellectual efficiency as it does any other: the world of experience, past, present and future, is too rich and complex to be apprehended in any other way. Left undisturbed and unchallenged, categorizing leads to ossification of routines, expectations and preferences; an autocratic classroom environment is more likely than a co-operative climate to allow one person's errors and prejudices to handicap those less powerful. Expectations and typifications may be self-confirming for pupils already vulnerable through other difficulties in their lives. Each antagonistic episode may be a small thing, local, insignificant and apparently leaving room for the pupil to improve and pull his or her socks up; each is a stitch in a tapestry depicting the distinctive nature of each pupil. Standing back, in what we imagine to be objective detachment, we view our product as a massive picture, too real, too substantial to be merely something of our own creation. We see the natural abilities associated with that sort of child, the type of behaviour to be expected from that sort of family; and are not our beliefs daily confirmed by the way the pupil reacts to the curriculum offered and the discipline we insist upon? Even we as its creators resist its influence with difficulty – it all hangs together too well. For those ignorant of its construction, it represents the true nature of things as they really are.

## THE SCHOOL

In one sense, pupils attend classrooms not schools. The different and particular features of group life in classrooms, compared with the briefer, shallower and more insubstantial school experiences, create a feeling of insulation between the two for both pupils and teachers. Nevertheless, school climate, culture or organizational arrangements constitute a context within which classrooms and their populations function. In classrooms, the official systems of the school co-exist with the unofficial peer-group systems of the pupils (Pollard, in Hammersley and Woods, 1984a).

For some, the school is necessarily a conservative force, condemned to reproduce cultural and social inequalities, and where the activities of the classroom are ultimately determined by the social relations of production (see Bourdieu's paper in Eggleston, 1974). Soder argues (in Barton and Tomlinson, 1982) for a direct link between the number of unemployed in an economy and the number (ideologically defined) in need of special education; it has been suggested by others that Warnock's apparent raising of the proportion of the population in need of special education was just in time to help blame some of the unemployed as victims of their own incompetence. As Soder says, the links 'can be difficult to find without in-depth analysis'. There is a sense in which troublesome pupils can be regarded as surplus to the political economy of the school: they produce nothing and do not consume the goods produced by others; but attractive comparisons are not evidence of correspondence.

Walker in Hammersley (1986) says that descriptions of classroom activities that cannot be related to the social structure and culture of society are conservative. For some, the relationship is seen as so complete that change, viewed as impossible, is not attempted – a conservative result. A school's organizational structure may be perceived as both immediate in its constraints and remote from our influence. It is commonly the case that social structure appears as objective and immutable (Berger and Luckman, 1971); yet social structures persist only with the support (active, passive or unintended) of their constituents. Change is always possible. Those people within a school who wish its organization to be other than it is are that part of the organization that is already changing. To believe that only thought is unconstrained, and that the economic and political system blocks progress, is only partly true – if true at all with respect to life in classrooms. That schools, that is, teachers, have some degree of autonomy is said to be widely accepted even by Marxists (Blackledge and Hunt, 1985: 114).

Structures are created and maintained by the aggregation of multitudin-
ous individual commitments, motives and objectives of people – and therefore cannot be forever free from change. Knowledge of this fact of social
life is the first step in gaining the power to cope with and control one's
social environment. Those enthusiastic for change need to remember that
changes have costs as well as benefits. For those content with things as
they are, the former will hide the latter from view. Writing of the role of
a consultant sociologist in a school, Reynolds (in Woods and Pollard,
1987) advises accepting a school's goals, not questioning them on the first
encounter. He suggests helping the school to become more effective in its
own terms and treating value issues as they arise, later in the consultancy.
In practice this may be a difficult act to maintain: giving people the advice
they are believed to want, while harbouring fundamental doubts, can drop
the consultant into a tangled web of patronizing deception.

A school's organizational ethos, distribution of authority and systems
of appraisal, as well as the rewards offered to both pupils and teachers,
are the subjects of, and influences on, perceptions, decisions and actions
– whether to comply, disengage or rebel. Eisner, discussing the contributions of educational radicals such as Holt and Kohl, comments: 'The
reward system of the school – the covert, muted one – speaks loudly'
(1985: 72). Cusick (1973) suggests that the remoteness of the organizational level of structure itself forces pupils to look to their peers to give
meaning and purpose to their lives in school. This will often involve not
attending to the work priorities of the teachers. The pupils may see the
teachers' agenda as a part of the organizational structure and distribution
of power. A feature in which pupils are dominated but otherwise uninvolved makes 'goofing off' a rational strategy (Everhart, 1983). The differ-
entiating and polarizing effects of streaming and banding upon pupils
have been documented (Hargreaves, 1967; Lacey, 1970; Ball, 1981). Bird
et al. (1981) have pointed out that these structural labels create more
problems for pupils than the temporary, and possibly inconsistent, labels
used in specific lessons. An attempt to find a statistical relationship
between such pupil-processing features was unsuccessful, however
(Galloway et al., 1985). Allocation to categories (stream or not stream)
does not capture the climate in which policies become practice – statistics
destroy information.

Teachers, too, are influenced by selection and appraisal processes of a
similar sort, but they are not easily researched. In an authoritarian school,
teachers may feel constrained to act so as to please the boss and against
their judgement, and, like their pupils, they may opt either to comply or
rebel (Hanko, 1985). Teachers cannot easily be self-critical, reflective
or sensitive to pupil needs if their performance is measured by a single
criterion – exam results or classroom silence, for example – and no
account is taken of their personal values and aims. Staff can be differen-

tiated and polarized, as Hargreaves and others found pupils to be. A critical atmosphere of assessment is not compatible with an honest and critical approach to self, others or situations. Eisner (1982) deplores the ill effects of the education system's preoccupation with, and valuing of, only the verbal and mathematical. He compares the situation to one where good chess players are unacknowledged because the only game that is played is poker. Becker (1952) wrote: 'All institutions have embedded in them some set of assumptions about the nature of the society and the individuals with whom they deal.' A social structure's available roles have psychological implications, for people are to some extent composed of the roles which they enact (Schostak, 1986). Pupil behaviour can be completely understood only if the school's differentiations and categories are identified and the related penalties and benefits taken into account. Central to schools' differentiation systems is ability: the criteria used; mode of identification; rewards or stigma attached; and rights to resources of space, time and personnel. How private, personal abilities become public property is an important influence on the attitudes and behaviour of both pupils and teachers.

School organization may influence a wider section of the pupil population than those who are openly troublesome. Tattum (1982) suggests that some disruptive pupils may represent the discontent of a larger but relatively silent group. As Bird et al. (1981) put it: 'Most disaffected behaviour could best be understood as an implied, if inarticulate, critique of schooling.' Willis (1977) has documented the extreme views of some pupils on the irrelevance of schooling to their lives. It may seem difficult to accept that these pupils speak for those who evidently fear and avoid them. Hargreaves (1967) and Lacey (1970) both found extreme pupils (Drac and Badman respectively) to be disliked and isolated. Nevertheless, it is likely that disruptive pupils express frustrations that are more widespread and possibly in an attenuated form. There is no particular reason why other pupils should thank them for inarticulately expressing fears and uncertainties that are widely shared.

Schostak (1983, 1986) has explored pupil frustrations and seems to propose radical upheaval as a solution. Reynolds (in Gillham, 1981, and a number of other papers) has claimed that a less coercive and more incorporative atmosphere, with low levels of institutional control, is likely to reduce disaffection and disruption. Rutter et al. (1979) appeared to find that schools organized and conducted on traditional lines were the more effective: for example, where there was an academic emphasis, a prompt start to lessons, homework set and marked and where heads ran 'a tight ship'. Rutter's book was much criticized, though it is worth noting that, compared with many studies, there was considerable work and detailed analysis on which to pounce (see, for example, Acton, 1980; Rutter et al., 1980; Tizard et al., 1980). A comprehensive collection of papers on these issues is edited by Reynolds (1985). Perhaps one source of the contradictions lies in the pupils themselves; they expect the traditional teacher to be in control but respond to being treated with flexibility and respect. Perhaps different pupils are being measured, or similar pupils at different times and in different circumstances. Conflicts among research findings are indices of the complexity of human affairs, in which, to paraphrase Edmund Burke, there is no certain truth and all our knowledge is but a woven web of guesses.

The school features which are associated with co-operative and orderly behaviour have not been identified to the satisfaction of all observers and researchers. Reid *et al.* (1987), in a comprehensive and detailed review of the school effectiveness literature, note that, although it is assumed the ineffective can be distinguished from the effective, there is no consensus on what constitutes an effective school. This does not mean we can ignore the significance of the school in the creation, maintenance and eradication of disruptive behaviour. Trying to understand necessarily requires us to distance ourselves from problems. As was argued in the context of pupil perceptions and motives, this is an important method of coping with problems which are otherwise felt personally: distance, in this sense, lends detachment.

The DES in its pamphlet (HMI Report No. 5) 'Education Observed' (1987) identifies some principles said to maintain high standards of behaviour and discipline. These are explicit and consistently applied policies, a positive climate, good teaching and quality relationships among pupils, teachers and the wider community. Rewards are said to outnumber sanctions, and these latter are applied with flexibility and discrimination. By contrast, policies are said to be firmly and consistently applied. Sound advice – but not easy to see how any school, except perhaps the most appallingly disorganized, could develop action from it. Reid *et al.* (1987) present a similar list, which includes effective leadership, happy and efficient staff, a concern for academic standards allied with empathetic pupil care, a curriculum accessible to all pupils and opportunities for all to participate in the running and organization of the school. Charlton and David (1993), in a more complete and comprehensive survey of research, condense research findings into eleven detailed points, including some which reach directly into the classroom: planned and punctual lessons, preventive management skills and respectful relationships.

These descriptions, as well as the generalized school types developed in Chapter 2, do not provide an explicit and unambiguous agenda for school reform. Resulting as they mostly do from school-level measurements, this is not surprising. Even if a list of factors could be agreed upon, the magnitude of their effects might be very small: perhaps 6 per cent in Rutter (1979), for example. For present purposes we need to know only which factors are possible influences upon pupil behaviour. In looking at each pupil, or group of pupils, it is possible to ask in each case which factors are significant. It is then a question of judgement, or possibly experiment, to discover whether the observations and enquiries are correct or not. The ways in which school factors enhance or handicap pupil progress and behaviour are often invisible to those who work in them and little clearer to a visitor. It is far from simple to adopt the standpoint of a stranger and not to see what is customarily there to be seen. Even when features contributing to disaffection have been identified, and there is consensus with respect to their influence, it is rarely a simple matter of removal and replacement.

It has been accepted for some time that the sort of streaming systems described by Hargreaves (1967) and Lacey (1970), where similar groups of pupils are together for much of their time in low-status classes, necessarily lead to a degree of disengagement, disaffection and, perhaps, open rebellion. Less rigid groupings, broad bands for example, seem to be less likely to produce polarized attitudes (Ball, 1981). Demands from without the school for standards and qualifications in knowledge of a certain sort (mostly knowledge about things) are best met, in many teachers' experience, by sorting pupils into homogeneous groups.

Delamont and Galton (1986) note that teaching pupils, through the covert curriculum, that they belong to different groups may subvert attempts to get pupils to work together in small groups. They found that young secondary pupils feared being put with a member of the other sex: Peter and Gita, seated together, were shamed and did not work. Allied to this may be an emphasis on a single, academic criterion for success. The content of assemblies, the pupils praised and indicated as models, the nature of teachers' encouragement in the classroom and the phrases used on reports all indicate to some pupils that they have failed. Many find that to turn their personal failure outwards, and blame the school for failing them, is a more satisfying way of accommodating their difficulties. In the exchange of punishment that follows, the uncomfortable role of the academic weakling may be swamped by the tough and powerful role of the disruptive hooligan. Paradoxically, the more successfully a school engenders a spirit of academic achievement, the greater will be the sense of betrayal felt by those least successful – confirmed when examination selections are made. The older the pupils, the more the hierarchy of authority, the stratification of knowledge and its separation from their lives becomes apparent, and the greater becomes its influence upon their thinking and action.

These academic responsibilities cannot be abandoned by schools but their influence can be moderated. Schostak (1983) notes that the term 'curriculum' derives from 'curricle', a chariot – a curriculum may be seen as a route chosen in the hope of gaining success. A variety of success criteria and a number of different curricular routes which are valued and defined as successful are ways of engaging a larger proportion of the pupil population in the school's activities.

Lacey (1970) describes two pupils who did not fit with the assumption that middle-class pupils tend to succeed and working-class pupils fail in the grammar school. Priestley was a middle-class drop-out interested in commerce and economics, which were two subjects not catered for in the school; Cready was a working-class success, whose fine singing voice had engaged him in the school via its choir. Had the music teacher dissolved the choir and begun an economics class, the school lives of the two boys might have been reversed. Pring (1976) mentions a pupil whose interest in electronics passed unnoticed by the school until it led him, through theft, into court. One essential consideration, therefore, is to ensure that the school offers a multitude of options in addition to its core curriculum. It is also necessary to give these options a high visible status with ample equipment, good rooms and senior staff; their value must be emphasized in actions.

Most secondary schools offer at least twenty options to years four and five but some make available as many as forty. Some schools make a particular effort to mix abilities and social classes in as many options as possible, thus blurring the distinctions associated with the subjects traditionally taught in homogeneous groups. The effort of producing such an extensive menu results in many teachers devising courses closely related to their own personal interests or expertise. For teachers to engage in activities alongside their pupils, and share real interest and enthusiasm, is one way of showing disaffected pupils that schooling is not artificial and irrelevant. The broader the menu, the greater the likelihood of giving and receiving satisfaction. There is a sense in which a disorderly class, or an abusive pupil, is an unrecognized talent, an unrewarded effort, a blocked ambition.

Where setting by ability is not minimized (by resource-based organization of learning, for example) it is possible to camouflage the hierarchy to some extent and for some of the time. Set numbering can be displaced by naming: theoretical maths, applied maths, vocational maths, maths studies, technical maths, craft maths, culinary maths are preferable to maths sets 1 to 7. The content and focus of the different maths groups might also reflect the interests of the pupils and enhance their motivation and achievements. It is important here, too, that those subject groups vulnerable to being dismissed as unimportant have their value confirmed by the allocation of staff, space and equipment.

From the first days in school, children begin to be transformed into types and categories of pupil: in playgroups common categories are 'noisy or quiet ones', 'big or small ones' and, of course, boys and girls. The categories in public use in the classroom, and supported and confirmed in school-wide practices, are available for pupil identity construction and for some pupils they are a source of conflict, a possible source of disaffection and a step on the route to disorder. As King (1978) found in infant schools, differing expectations are associated with the categories into which pupils are sorted by their teachers: girls can be trusted to hang their coats outside the classroom but boys cannot. Those girls and boys who find their teachers' typifications a poor fit may find themselves labelled 'really peculiar' (Sharp and Green, 1975) and in the embryo stages of a deviant career.

School organization with respect to pastoral care has a direct bearing on relationships between pupils and their tutors. The introduction of pastoral responsibilities into schools was, in part, a response to the belief that schools were growing in size and organizational complexity, becoming more goal-directed and impersonal. In contrast, many felt the ideal teaching relationship was more personal, concerned with individual needs and interests rather than organizational goals and valuing both education and pupils for their own sakes. For many young people, school is their first acquaintance with a social unit larger than their family. Relationships are less certain and emotions more thinly spread. Those whose domestic experience has been characterized by misfortune or chaos are in particular need of considerate supervision in school. The establishment of a bureaucracy of pastoral care is not a guarantee of its being practised. Since control of one group by another is a central feature of any administrative structure it is not surprising that pastoral systems become entangled and merged with discipline systems. This can shift their focus away from personal and affective concerns towards the goals of the school's senior managers. The particular problems of troublesome pupils are not inevitably foremost among their concerns.

Many schools arrange for tutors to retain responsibility for their groups as they progress through the year bands. This is intended to assist the development of relationships but is in itself insufficient. Tutoring in some schools is a nominal role with no discretion, responsibility or power attached. Tutors are often among the last to be informed of matters relating to individuals in their group.

Some schools ensure that relationships of trust have an opportunity to develop by devolving powers to tutors. The problems that could arise through weakness or inexperience can be pre-empted by using pairs of tutors with some groups; this reproduces in the pastoral sphere the benefits of support teaching within classrooms. Empathetic relationships develop, and tutors and pupils come to understand one another's perspectives and the constraints under which they operate. This can lead to conflict between teachers. A tutor may be regarded as too sympathetic to a pupil who may have grossly offended a colleague: to attempt to explain or even defend misbehaviour is readily viewed as disloyalty. Staffroom folklore reveres the headteacher who backs his or her staff, right or wrong; some heads present this as wise policy. In time of war it most certainly is. One aim of pastoral care, however, is to maintain the peace. After some crises it helps to make the peace terms explicit in a formal contract. Sometimes these are signed in a solemn session in the head teacher's office. The contract need not represent the school's final aim with respect to any pupil. It may be seen as a first achievable step: a negotiating baseline. An extreme example of a contract that some might view as a defeat for the school is printed below:

> The school agrees: not to demand homework or schoolwork; to allow the pupil to withdraw to the year area if in danger of losing self-control; to allow the pupil to consult and be accompanied by her tutor in any enquiry into any incident or report.

> The pupil agrees: to attend school regularly; to be on time for classes; to remain in the place indicated by the teacher; not to abuse, threaten or assault pupils; not to leave the school grounds at lunchtime.

Few demands were made upon an extremely troubled pupil. The school presented its concessions as the natural right of a person who was emotionally disabled – analogous to those made for pupils with physical disabilities. For the school in question it was a preferable alternative to exclusion and demonstrates what is possible even in extreme situations.

Graham (1988) mentions some American, pupil-led, radical alternatives to pastoral systems, such as the appointment of a mediator. A good pastoral system should pre-empt the need for this. The school as a whole enjoys benefits from ensuring that pupils' interests are well represented and from institutionalizing representation. First, it channels and controls pupil hostility, and with luck diminishes the impulse to violence; second, it wins time and allows all parties the chance to negotiate and compromise; third, it helps to persuade pupils who feel victimized that some adults can be trusted; fourth, it allows the tutor and the pupil to exchange real understanding in situations of crisis, far removed from the abstracted skills and processes of some personal and social education programmes. This is not to say that tutors should adopt the pupil's viewpoint. As with solicitors and their clients, representation does not preclude offering vigorous advice and reprimands. The tendency for some pastoral care lines of communication to become clogged and carriers of only bad news is documented in Spooner (1979), Best et al. (1983), Coulby and Harper (1985) and Galloway (in Reynolds, 1985). This can undermine the purpose of pastoral systems to the extent that they become viewed by pupils as another antagonistic, disciplinary instrument. The lateral distribution of authority and responsibility helps to remove the blockage.

## ACTIVITY 6.1: FIXING THE COFFEE MACHINE

The purpose of this exercise is to discover any aspects of your school environment unnecessarily conducive to troublesome behaviour. If any are identified, it does not follow that they ought to be altered; alterations, as well as existing arrangements, have costs and benefits for various pupils which must be taken into account. The exercise should increase understanding of some pupils' situations and therefore help in coping with them. The task is in two parts, the first of which was prompted by the analogy of society as a fruit machine (see Taylor's work, described in Furlong, 1985). The second part of the exercise is the difficult task of trying to look at your school in a detached way, as if a stranger, and through the eyes of a troublesome pupil. The more entertaining first part is to put you in a suitable frame of mind.

### Part 1

A school can be thought of as being in some respects like a coffee machine. Everyone has an equal opportunity to get a drink out of it, if they bring the correct change with them. Coffee machines do not serve all equally, however. Some do not get what they want and some get nothing – no money or faulty machine. Disappointed customers, or pupils, take one of several attitudes. They may continue to put money in without hope of success (plod through lessons, bored and without commitment). They may give up and refuse to use the machine (truants). They may try to wreck it to stop others using what they see as failing them (disrupters). Some may pretend to use the machine while quietly sipping their own drinks (some say these are mostly girls). Many will say they do not want coffee anyway, for in their neighbourhood everyone drinks tea.

The machine's minders, or teachers, have their own range of responses. Some want to make it more attractive and effective: put plants on it, see it is plugged in on time and not switched off early, assistants in uniform, a drink every time. Some want to get a new machine that dispenses different drinks. Others want to keep the present machine for some customers, and add a different one for the tea-drinkers. A few think they should settle for water. A few think we should discard the machine and go back to making our own coffee at home.

Consider how far your school fits or does not fit the analogy of a typical (faulty) coffee machine.

### Part 2

Some further questions to consider. Although this exercise focuses on the school, it can be adapted to analyse a department, a teaching team or a teacher and a single class.

1 What categories are used to describe, label, differentiate and allocate pupils? Think about the formal, official, system (for example, Fifth Year, A stream, TVEI band) as well as the informal, unofficial system (for example, the bouncy ones, the just-not-interested, the real troublemakers).
2 Briefly list the benefits, rewards, deprivations and rules, both formal and informal, associated with these categories and statuses (for example, mentions in assembly, free study time, warm part of the school). Do not ignore seeming trivialities. For example, if one class always has the job of chair-stacking after assembly, in what ways is this a benefit and in what ways a deprivation? How do the pupils, stackers and non-stackers, see it?
3 How do pupils learn of their category or interpret the school's arrangements? What things are communicated formally and what learned informally? Is the message transmitted the same as the one received?
4 Consider how a particular troublesome pupil or class experiences life in your school as you have analysed it under the above three points. Are there any unintentionally pejorative categories or deprivations? Is it possible to have non-evaluative categories at all? Does the communication system need attention? Are any changes needed, and are they feasible? Are those with the power to make changes convinced that changes are needed?

## ACTIVITY 6.2: THE CASE OF CARL, AGED 6

This exercise requires the pre-reading of a case study assembled from interviews and reports presented mainly as it was by the principal teacher involved. Part of the way through you are asked to pause and consider your feelings about the case before reading on.

Carl joined his new primary school halfway through the term, having moved from another city. First impressions were of a 'grubby, sturdy boy' who had little to say and was quiet for the first few days. The school was open plan and he began to wander, would not be occupied by anything offered him and rapidly became loud and disruptive. From the start his eating habits had attracted attention: rapid, omnivorous and with his fingers. He gathered food from other pupils' plates and from the waste bin – including banana skins. When crossed by pupils or teachers he bit and spat. The bites were severe enough to produce bleeding.

### Action 1

The school was accustomed to coping with difficult children and prepared to give Carl a fresh start. During the first week the headteacher from his previous school (more than 200 miles away) telephoned to apologize for the delay in passing on records and to say that the abrupt removal had been due to domestic violence; Carl was ungovernable and had an NTA to himself. The teachers, however, were not particularly interested in his records. They decided to ignore as much as possible: the open-plan, partly resource-based organization allowed a good deal of movement and noise, so Carl's wandering was not particularly disruptive. Fruit, bought with school funds, was used as a reward for co-operation. The tolerance did not include the biting and spitting, where intervention was instant.

## Result 1

The fruit reward had a slight effect but was limited to the mornings; by lunchtime it was all used, and after lunch he did not seem so hungry. The spitting continued in two or three tantrums a day, during which one or two people would be bitten. One side effect of Carl's fruit eating and spitting was to teach the staff a little chemistry: fruit acid saliva bleaches clothes. He began to strip in assembly and refuse to leave the hall afterwards. In one scene he totally wrecked an area of the school – the equivalent of a classroom – but a teacher succeeded in making him restore it during the lunch break.

## Action 2

Carl was referred to the Educational Psychological Service. The visiting psychologist approved the fruit rewards and ignoring regime, and suggested using time out and ensuring that 'cuddles' were not used to reward angry behaviour. He arrived at an opportune moment from the teachers' point of view: Carl was naked outside the staffroom. They watched with interest to discover how a psychologist dressed an unwilling child. Except for repeating 'good boy' as he worked, the technique was the familiar one of knee on chest and forcing arms and legs into garments.

## Result 2

The medical room was used for time out but this had to stop when Carl began kicking the window. As the school was single storey, and every area had an outside door, time out became locked out: when serious trouble started, Carl was put out of the door and all the other teachers locked their doors. Carl never attempted to run away from school. The policy began to produce other problems. His running around the building trying to get back in upset the teachers. Some felt that not only their teacher authority was threatened but also their natural, adult feelings for children. Carl was suspended from school and the statementing process began.

## Action 3

An extra NTA was appointed to ensure supervision of Carl at all times. Time out could now be safely in the medical room. The earlier regime of ignoring and using fruit and cuddle rewards continued. The boy's mother was encouraged to visit school and she happily joined in, helping clean cupboards and engaging in similar activities. Whenever Carl came near her, however, she told him to go away – sometimes using obscene language.

## Result 3

In the teacher's own words:

> He's calmed down a little – a bad scene once a week now – maybe three days' peace and three days' hell. With consistency we feel we have progressed. He doesn't undress near me because the first time he tried it I helped him off with his clothes. I just laugh or joke or sidestep him. I'm the sort of person who withdraws when I'm cross – maybe that helps. It's such a shame because he's such a lovely boy – bright, too, we think. There are two others in the family coming up from the nursery and we've heard that one of them is worse.

You should pause at this point and consider your own reactions to the information so far.

### A day or two in the mother's life

The following statement is the mother's account of the events leading up to her child attending hospital with a suspected skull fracture:

> My cheque did not come but I did not go phone as I had been up with Carl and his earache. I left it a day as sometimes it's in the next post but it wasn't. I left Carl in bed and took the two youngest with me to find a phone that was working – they're mostly vandalized round here. When I got through they kept me waiting and passing me from this department to that. I still hadn't got anybody to help when all my 10p coins ran out. So I just went back home trailing the kids, no money and no prospect of any.
>
> Carl was worse so I thought, I'll have to get a doctor. The woman next door offered to watch the two youngest while I took Carl down the clinic. I had no money left at all so she had to let me have the bus fare. I managed over the weekend by borrowing, and on the Monday I set off down the DHSS with the three kids. I didn't have an appointment of course so we just had to settle down and wait our turn. By the time I got to the front of the queue I was at my wits' end with

trying to keep the kids down and then I had to go through all the long list of details relevant to my claim because they didn't have my card. I didn't know whether to scream or cry.

It was nearly dinner time when I got my money – they even gave me some heating backdated that they'd refused me before. I thought it would be nice to give the kids a treat so we went into a fast-food restaurant, even though it's too expensive really. I let them choose something but Carl wanted a big, expensive ice-cream so I said no. When the burgers came he wouldn't eat his so I just left it in front of him. He was still going on about the ice-cream. Then he just pushed it off the table on to the floor. I just snapped. I lashed out at him and he fell over backwards and cracked the back of his head on the floor. I only went in there because I'd been on at them all day. I wanted to cheer us all up.

Discussion should cover these points:

1 How, if at all, did your feelings about this case change on reading the mother's account? What conclusions do you draw from your reactions?
2 Consider the personal skills and moral qualities needed by those living in poverty.
3 Reflect on the weaknesses, wastage and risks to which the poor are exposed.
4 Consider the experiences, knowledge, feelings and expectations that Carl carries into school.
5 What coping strategies are available to him?
6 List the appropriate personal qualities, expectations, understandings, perspectives and strategies conducive to success with pupils like Carl.
7 Consider aspects of school organization and ethos that would help or hinder pupils like Carl.
8 Finally, what has this exercise accomplished? Has it shifted the blame for individual venality to society? Has it shown how public issues are transformed into private, personal troubles? Has it altered your perceptions of, attitude to and capacity to cope with 'emotional and behavioural problems'?

**Comments on the exercise**

1 We often say that pupils' behaviour and effort is to be expected 'when you look at their homes': the implication and shared understanding is that chaos at home is confirmation of the futility of trying to educate or make progress with them. Many people will want to modify their opinion after reading the mother's story.
2 Thrift, effort and determination far beyond the average are required to survive in poverty. Some years ago, Matthew Parris MP tried and

failed to live for one week on the dole. The prime minister at the time was rumoured to have scorned his attempt and insisted that she could have managed without difficulty. No doubt she could. Anyone can do it for a limited period that has a certain end. The inclination to survive with dignity comes harder when there is no past to reflect on and no future to look forward to. The demands of children are not easy to resist and easily wreck efforts to be thrifty.

3 In these circumstances, spending scarce resources on a video and TV seems an understandable extravagance. So does leaving the children alone, or with an unvetted babysitter, in order to nip out for a quick drink. Money is similarly wasted on costly, TV-advertised toys, many needing batteries and most quickly broken. Overcrowding and shared beds may make some families vulnerable to unwarranted allegations of abuse, their hostile and unskilled reactions likely to act as confirming evidence from the viewpoint of some professionals.

4 Carl's experience of undependable, unpredictable, irritable adults may lead to caution or distrust of adults in school. He may be aware of material deficits with respect to clothes, toys, trips or accommodation.

5 Children may cope by withdrawing into themselves. Some indulge in wild or bizarre behaviour to distract themselves and others from their difficulties. Some children try both extremes, prompting the diagnosis that such grossly unpredictable behaviour must evidence deep neurological defects.

6 The teacher's account gives clues: impassive, reliable, not easily manipulated. She was detached enough to see a funny side to it all (for example, the acid saliva, the reception given the Ed. Psych.). She was able to ignore some of the behaviour and helped to extinguish it (for example, the stripping). In her final statement she shows her affection for the boy and her high expectations of his capability. It is common for teachers reporting cases to training groups to express a liking for troublesome pupils, and as often to seem surprised at this themselves. There is an example in Caspari (1976: 48). Kohl (1970) writes: 'I like defiant, independent and humorous people and my preferences naturally come out in my teaching.' Teachers like this are a considerable asset and are best viewed as the pupil's defence counsel in situations where aggrieved teachers may question a colleague's loyalty. Note also the lack of interest in the boy's records. This attitude, often the despair of administrators, is common among teachers who wish to make up their own minds before looking at other people's opinions. Novice teachers and students, however, are thirsty for prior information (see Wragg, 1984 and Chapter 2 of Calderhead, 1987).

7 School-wide practices and expectations can create problems for pupils who have no ready access to money nor a stable home life. Imagine the 'tight ship' ethos recommended by Rutter (1979) and some related

aspects: homework done, PE kit clean and complete, money for cookery and CDT or pupils have to do bookwork, endless letters asking for cash towards trips and treats. School refusal, theft and revenge begin to look like rational strategies in these circumstances. Note how the open or resource-based learning environment helped the school cope with Carl.

8 This is not an invitation to radical political action, although this case does flesh out the dry bone structure of school and society. The understanding it gives may spark some additional professional commitment to troublesome pupils which is the aim of this book. 'For we struggle not against flesh and blood, but against principalities, against powers, against the rulers of the darkness of this world, against spiritual wickedness in high places' (Ephesians 6:12).

## ACTIVITY 6.3: THE CASE OF ANN, AGED 15

This case parallels that of Carl but concerns an older pupil. As with activity 6.2 you are asked to pause and consider your own reactions before reading the final section.

1 A teacher's report on Ann's activities during a 40-minute lesson. The class was working from worksheets on English grammar and spelling exercises:

> Ann chose to sit near my desk at the front of the room. She spent a lot of time watching other pupils at my desk. She fooled around and talked to other pupils, then she got up and moved one boy's property away on to another desk. She returned to her place and asked a question about the work, but she did not put up her hand. She half stood and half knelt on her chair, drumming on the desk and gazing round the room, chewed her fingers and asked another question. I had given her at least three clear sets of instructions about what she was supposed to be doing by this point.
>
> She moved across the room and talked to another pupil. I challenged her and she said she was showing them how to do the work. The pupil began to say something but she told him to 'shut up' very fiercely. She went back to her place and fiddled with her pencil till it broke. She then spent several minutes fiddling about in the drawer looking for another one. Another question shouted out about her work. I ignored it. So far (20 minutes into the lesson) she had been instructed on what to do several times and praised twice when she was working – though she stopped work as soon as she was praised and flopped on the desk.
>
> She came out to my desk, taking a long tour round the room and managing to fall out with another girl. At my desk she continued to

frown threateningly at her. She left my desk and went up to another pupil and made some aggressive comment and then she threatened another boy with her fists but stopped short of hitting him. None of the pupils reacted aggressively. She came back to my desk and read through a passage with difficulty, but I prompted her and praised her effort. She went back to her desk and worked quietly for a few minutes. Another pupil got up to bring his work to me and she made a grab at him. She got up again and stood behind him at my desk making a noise with a rolled up worksheet.

She returned to her place after being asked to do so. For the final minutes of the lesson she slumped in her place looking very tired. Her eyes seemed dull and distant and her expression was care-worn. She chewed at her collar.

2 A teacher's report on an incident in a home economics lesson and Ann's behaviour over the following few days:

On entering the food technology room it was obvious that she was excited and high. I asked her straight away to moderate her language and control her behaviour so that we would all be able to work. I told her I would make arrangements for her to work elsewhere if she couldn't settle down. For about five minutes she seemed to try to control herself but then began flicking dough at people around the room.

I asked her again to behave and she shouted out: 'I wasn't effing doing any harm.' I realised that it was a downhill situation from there on, so I sent a pupil for another member of staff to get her out of the room. Before help came she had flipped and actually physically attacked me. Help arrived and she was removed with a torrent of violent, obscene abuse.

Next day I was ignored when I registered her in the morning but in the afternoon I had her again and she admitted that she had been in the wrong. I found it physically and emotionally exhausting just to be in discussion with her – even though it was a practical lesson with the kids getting on with their own work. She terrorizes other pupils to some extent, and I think I felt she was terrorizing me in a strange sort of way. Pupils have to comply with her demands or violence follows, and I suppose it was much the same for me – she wanted to talk and be contrite and I had to go along with it. There is always the possibility of verbal confrontation in the background that might escalate. She cannot accept ordinary discipline.

She was excluded for three days after hitting the headteacher. When she returned she was supposed to be getting ready for a period of work-experience. She refused to think about it. The last session at a catering company had been a disaster, with her having to leave for swearing and bad behaviour. They knew about her record and agreed to give her a chance to prove herself. She wouldn't wash her hands 'just because someone says so' and she called the supervisor 'a stupid effing bastard' and turned on the hose in the kitchen 'just for a bit of fun'.

The main problem, I think, is that she has no intention of working. She already gets all she wants through petty crime and intimidation – breaking into cars for the radios, taking videos from the flats. She told me that she did do a proper job once when the family was short. Her mother had sold the Family Allowance book to pay off a fine and she said that 'if her dad had found out he would have killed her'.

You should pause at this point and consider your feelings about this case: identify the pupil's motives, decide how you would react (short and long term) and evaluate the teachers' behaviour and policies as far as you can identify them. Some specific questions might include the following:

How would you respond to this pupil, day to day in the classroom?

What longer-term strategies or policies (behaviour, pastoral or classroom management, teaching and learning methods, curriculum) would you want to develop?

What feelings does the pupil's behaviour evoke in you?

Are these different from those of the teachers involved, and, if so, can you account for this difference?

3 This final section is a report by a teacher (some days later) on Ann's disclosures about a domestic incident on the previous evening:

On the evening in question the parents went out, leaving Ann and the other children in the house. Ann and her brother fell asleep on the sofa and when the parents returned the worse for drink at about midnight the father lost his temper and lashed out at Ann. The mother grabbed a knife and threatened to kill him if he touched her daughter. Father grabbed the knife and Ann ran out of the house and phoned the police from a call box.

She heard her mother screaming so she went back into the house to see her father threatening her mother with the knife and encouraging one of the dogs (a doberman) to bite her. Ann says the dog was shaking her mother 'like a doll'. She also says that her father picked up the small terrier and threw it against the wall 'to stop it yapping'. Ann says her father then punched her on the jaw.

Four police officers arrived and the younger children were taken to an aunt. Ann says her father told the police a false tale about what had happened with the dog and her mother wasn't believed.

Ann was too frightened to say anything because she thought her father would hit her again when the police had gone. The police took Ann and her mother to casualty and they came home in a taxi later.

Ann says she has had enough and refused to go home. She repeatedly stressed that she would not go home.

The headteacher contacted social services and the emergency desk checked with the police. Apparently, the police said the mother's and Ann's injuries were superficial and no further action was contemplated. The police said Ann should be reassured and sent home. She flatly refuses, as she says her father punched her and will do so again. The social services agreed to send someone up to the school to collect Ann and take her to a place of safety.

When Ann was informed of this she became tearful and still insisted she would never go home. She has asked that the home economics teacher go with her and this has been agreed to.

This report confirmed what many of the teachers already knew about Ann's domestic life and goes some way towards explaining their tolerance of her.

You might wish to reflect on these experiences and consider how they provide a framework of expectations which guide Ann's interpretation of her experiences in school. Perhaps this final document has caused you to modify your initial response to and feelings about this case.

What ways of coping are available to this pupil?

What qualities, understandings and strategies do teachers need?

## ACTIVITY 6.4: TRACKING PUPILS AND TEACHERS

This activity is often used with trainee teachers but is also revealing for experienced teachers and particularly useful in giving a fresh perspective to those who have worked in schools for a very long time. It is a good source of evidence for a staff meeting (or a seminar led by a trainee teacher in school).

There are two parts to the activity and they can be split between two people. First, follow a particular class or group through their timetable for one whole day. Note what opportunities exist to use a variety of learning methods, the standards expected, the assessment methods used, and look particularly at how the lower-attainers are catered for. Second, follow a teacher looking as before at how he or she modifies his or her requirements of pupils and paying particular attention to the range of tasks expected of him or her.

## Comments

It is not possible to say what this sort of exercise will reveal, but two common findings (across varied schools) are the disruption to pupils' sense of coherence and concentration by frequent changes of lesson, most marked where the timetable is substantially in 40-minute blocks; and the relentlessness of the school day for teachers and the weight of work and responsibility they have – observers are surprised at how often teachers miss coffee breaks. Where such stresses are encountered, or where a limited diet seems to be boring pupils, such facts need attention at school level. There will certainly be a relationship between bad behaviour and tedium, and between tedium and tired teachers.

# Chapter 7

# Putting learning into practice

Those who have taught many people to do what is right will shine like stars forever.

(Daniel 12: 3)

Those who do well at the labour of preaching and teaching shall be reckoned worthy of double stipend.

(1 Timothy 5: 17)

## SERVING STONE SOUP

On the fifth morning of the famine the villagers awoke to find a stranger among them. Relief had been promised but this person looked unsuited to the office. Perhaps he, too, was looking for nourishment? There is no food here, he was quickly told.

'I am here to help you', said the stranger, 'I can show you how to feed yourselves.' He held out three smooth stones. 'With these you can make a soup sufficient to feed everyone here.' Hunger and despair overcame the villagers' disbelief. Someone fetched a huge cauldron. Others filled it with water. A fire was lit beneath it. Then they waited.

The stranger dropped the stones into the simmering water. 'It won't take long now,' he said, sniffing at the steam. 'An onion would improve the flavour.'

'I have an onion,' said one of the villagers. 'You are welcome to it. It's of no use to me on its own.' Others murmured that they too had redundant onions. Soon not one but seven onions were produced and added to the pot.

The stranger continued to stir. 'A pity there isn't a carrot or two,' he said. Several people thought they had a carrot lying somewhere. They were found and added to the broth. The stranger continued to sniff and stir. He thought a potato would give it more body. Potatoes were produced. The villagers began to take the initiative, suggesting and offering various vegetables that remained in their larders, each in itself too small a thing to make a meal. The stranger decided that the soup was ready and, as he had promised, everyone was able to eat till they were full. The stranger himself joined in their feast and smiled at the praises and thanks lavished upon him by the grateful villagers. When all were fed, the stranger reached into the pot and held up the three stones for the astonished villagers to see.

'I will make you a present of these,' he said. 'If ever you find yourselves in distress again, just do as we have done today.' The delighted villagers congratulated each other on their good fortune. So overcome with happiness were they that they did not see the stranger slip away. As he set off along the road, he stopped and gathered three more stones.

## EVALUATING SHORT COURSES

This section and the next discuss some of the issues surrounding the assessment of in-service interventions in schools and will chiefly interest those responsible for planning and monitoring such work. Evaluation of one's own work is plainly vulnerable to criticism and error, but so also is any evaluation of anything. Evaluations, by definition, are judgements. To ask for an objective standard to which they can be referred is to ask for the values to be taken out, thus destroying what is distinctive about a judgement. An evaluation that is not infused with values – and therefore the possibility of disagreement – is not an evaluation but must be something else. Stenhouse, in Hamilton *et al.* (1977), claims that objectivity is possible in examining our own ideas and further that the only ideas we can examine objectively are our own. In opposition to this view, Scriven, in the same book, says that 'we would never accept an evaluation by a co-author of his own materials as meeting even the minimal methodological standards for objectivity' (Hamilton *et al.*, 1977: 133). Scriven defends a style of evaluation analogous to a consumer report. Courses are evaluated without contact with their authors and oblivious to their objectives: we buy good products not good intentions. Gomm, in Smetherham (1981), lists some of the strategies used to present evaluators' failures as successes of a different sort; the limitation of the brief, the shortage of time and resources and other problems may be listed to pre-empt criticism. Appropriate jargon may transform a bad job into a good one and the final report displays the qualities of the true star of the show – the writer.

It is an error to believe, however, that quantitative, evaluative representations are necessarily truer than qualitative: to prefer 'an ounce of data to a pound of insight' (Eisner, in Hamilton *et al.*, 1977: 90). The converse may also be the case. Eisner notes that quantities presuppose qualities and that the less expressive a description is, the truer it is taken to be: 'Yet if there is an absence of emotional or qualitative content, the description risks leaving out more of what is important in the classroom'

(Eisner, 1985: 158). Eisner compares preoccupation with quantitative data to ineffective attempts to improve football skills by attending only to the final score (Eisner, 1985: 179). McIntyre and Macleod, however (in Hammersley, 1986), find quantitative statements – 'quite a lot ... very rare ... we often heard' – in the work of 'Case Study' researchers. All evaluations necessarily use both qualitative and quantitative data. Attending to this fact helps to prevent errors and omissions, even though we may still be doing no more than adding one variety of theoretical findings to another (Atkinson and Delamont, in Hammersley, 1986). More than a century ago, these same qualitative and quantitative evaluation issues were raised during the operation of Robert Lowe's Revised Code, popularly known as 'payment by results'. In 1863, Matthew Arnold HMI complained of the restricted and rigid examination procedures constraining his work and compared them unfavourably with his former inspections: 'The whole life and power of a class, the fitness of its composition, its handling by the teacher were well tested ...' (quoted in Curtis, 1963: 262).

There probably can never be certainty in any evaluation work that the data are objective and valid. Writing on research into language use in classrooms, Stubbs notes that some researchers believe evidence may be justifiably gathered by selecting 'any feature of language which appears intuitively interesting' (in Adelman, 1981: 116). Glaser and Straus (in Hammersley, 1986: 55) state that researchers 'can easily find examples for dreamed up, speculative or logically deduced theory after the idea has occurred'. In seeking for confirming evidence for theory, rather than looking at data in search of theory, we are less likely to notice contrary examples. It is sometimes suggested that where the evidence is gathered on tapes and films, any sceptic may examine it to test the accuracy of the findings. This is seldom a feasible operation, and the existence of hundreds of hours of tapes and thousands of pages of transcripts may serve only to lend a spurious objectivity and authority to an evaluator's report.

Added to these pitfalls are others of a different sort. The observation by Eisner (1985) is seriously, if unintentionally, damaging to any claim that the course affected teachers' practice. Like other teachers, I tend to judge success by 'the extent to which students appear engaged, immersed, caught up, and interested in the activities of the classroom' (Eisner, 1985: 70). Even in the small-scale evaluation I have carried out, the quantity of data is too bulky to reasonably expect someone to spend time working through and checking them. A colleague examined a random sample of the data and sorted it into categories as a cross-check to my own. The selection was done in a simple and crude way: all the question and comment sheets and the interview reports were put in a pile, a nail was driven through and every sentence, phrase or comment thus pierced was selected for re-examination. Where the data is on paper, this method is a quick and effective way of generating a random sample. Some paragraphs of data give up only one sentence to the selection and this further helps to provoke fresh thought.

This technique drew attention to previously unnoticed items even before the selection was independently examined. When the open-ended comment sheets were treated in this way, six of the sixteen comments nailed did not fit into the categories used to discuss the data in the first draft of this chapter. Two suggested alternative ways of organizing the course and two commented on the teaching method. The other two comments were criticisms, passed over in the first trawl for categories into which to sort the information. One suggested that practical ideas for involving staff in formal discussions of problems were lacking; the other thought the suggested strategies needed uncommon confidence. Random sampling has one other benefit, in that all the data so selected can be quickly examined to test the claims made for them.

## THEORY AND PRACTICE

Eisner (1985) questions whether educational research can inform educational practice. He tried, unsuccessfully, to collect examples from university teachers. Most were unable to say how their personal work had been affected by research findings other than to claim that it functioned in the background. Woods and Pollard (1987: 11) argue that educational research has altered practice and claim that 'it can, in fact, transform one's view of life'. They mention the sensitivity to issues of race, gender and social class as well as streaming, school organization and the eleven-plus. For example, understanding the societal location and widespread prevalence of discipline problems is said to liberate teachers from 'false notions of personal inadequacy and blame'; the more common a problem is, the less likely it is that 'it is of the teacher's own making'. In Reynolds' own chapter of the book he lists the benefits of consultancy to a case-study school as more positive self-images among the staff; greater group co-operation with ability to share problems and anxieties; and greater initiative and 'line leadership', both within the school and in local education politics. Some of these benefits may not have been part of the intervention's explicit programme but one of the hidden consequences of being involved in educational discussion and having one's ideas treated seriously. To paraphrase Dewey, it is a fallacy to believe that teachers learn only one thing at a time. Some of the teachers' comments suggest that they learnt that working with troublesome pupils is as theoretically and intellectually demanding as any other teaching and that it can be fun. These aspects were not part of the original plan but they are undeniably important in lifting morale and generating a determination to persist and succeed. As Eisner (1982) argues, cognition is not restricted to the discursive and mathematical: affect and cognition are inextricable. Like all other information, emotions are encountered by minds.

Wilkin (in Woods and Pollard, 1987) notes that changes in practice need not be directly derivable from theory: practice may be affected by theory functioning in the background in an illuminative way. This latter may be one way of escaping the admission that theory and practice do not connect, and this seems to be the construction put upon similar comments received from faculty staff by Eisner (1985). His own impressions of teaching quality in university faculties are that the variance is as wide and the mean no higher in education than in other departments. He observes that those best informed about educational research 'seldom use the fruits of their labours either to make practical decisions or shape intellectual policy in the institutions where they work' (Eisner, 1985: 256). He suggests that research has followed practice (for example, in group work, open-plan schools, images of children) rather than initiated it. He mocks such commonplace findings as that 'time on task' is associated with gains in test scores. However, Rutter *et al.* (1979) severely weakened this sort of argument by listing 'obvious' findings that were not, in fact, among his team's conclusions. A problem is raised by Mac an Ghaill (in Woods and Pollard, 1987), who found some teachers claiming that awareness of the structural constraints upon their classrooms and the educational system had confirmed their feeling of powerlessness. However, interviews with the colleagues of these teachers seemed to show that the cognitive and affective components of the attitudes revealed to Mac an Ghaill did not match the behaviour observed by colleagues in school.

Eisner (1985) notes that even where research findings do seem to penetrate teachers' thinking, they do so in a vulgarized form bereft of qualifications, caveats and reservations about experimental design. Misunderstanding can go further still. Sometimes teachers on my course provided information which they believed illustrated a theme of the course but which, in fact, directly contradicted it. The importance of strict rules on school uniform was offered in support of Reynolds' notion of 'truce'. After discussing the need for staff to co-operate in respecting pupils' dignity, one teacher agreed and spoke approvingly of how his headteacher supported staff in dealing with miscreants: '. . . he really tears them off a strip and sorts them out, strips them down, strips them right down. . . '

American research reviewed by Eisner (1985: 261) showed that most experimental interventions in schools lasted little more than one hour. He comments that one cannot 'become familiar with the richness of classroom life' on such educational 'commando raids'. Changing people's attitudes, however, need not require extended intervention, as is often assumed by those mourning the passing of long, full-time courses for teachers. The trend, says Watson (1988), is 'towards short courses aimed at specific skills training and away from longer courses which allow time for reflection and change'. It is not the length of a course, however, but the nature of it that determines whether it will produce change or not. New perspectives are adopted in a moment and often following the introduction of a single piece of information. The longest of the courses from which this book is derived was nine sessions of two hours. Most of the school-based sessions were only three hours, and the minimum input has been just one-and-a-half hours. To these times must be added any sessions held by school staff after the courses, along the lines suggested, and with hand-out material for guidance.

## COMPLEXITY OF TEACHING

Teaching, whether of pupils in schools or teachers on in-service courses, is a highly complex activity. The difficulties encountered in assessing classroom effectiveness are doubled in attempts to assess the power of in-service training to alter classroom practice. Eisner speaks of the kaleidoscopic moments in teaching, the unexpected opportunities for explaining, demonstrating, signifying, and the difficulty of specifying objectives (as opposed to general direction) until after the lesson or programme is completed (in Hamilton *et al.*, 1977: 88–90). He makes much of the uniqueness of schools and the central importance of nuance to the quality of classroom life: 'the sense of engagement when a class is attentive will always elude the language of propositions ... yet it is precisely these qualities that the teacher must address' (Eisner, 1985: 256). Hamilton and Parlett describe the complexity and diversity of the learning milieu: a social, psychological, material, cultural, institutional network of interacting variables producing unique patterns of circumstances, customs, opinions and workstyles (Hamilton *et al.*, 1977: 11). As Eisner puts it, in arguing that propositional language is inadequate to the task of educational description and evaluation and defending his notion of connoisseurship: '... the simultaneity found in patterns of context is lost in the sequence of propositions' (Eisner 1985: 266).

This cannot permit anything to count as evaluation. Walker (in Smetherham, 1981: 148–51) points to the importance of taking note of personalities and offers a fictional account which he claims allows the signalling of 'ideas, meanings and significances'. This raises as many problems as it tries to solve, not least of which is the quality of the writing as a work of fiction in its own right. Jenkins' account (in Hamilton *et al.*, 1977) of Mr Bondine's lesson is also vulnerable to the charge that it is as partial and incomplete an account of the lesson as any behavioural or propositional description. Yet the Jenkins piece, witty and apparently effortlessly crafted, rings truer than that by Walker. It is not possible to say whether this is because it describes reality or not; Jenkins' fictional account of styles of innovator also has the ring of truth (OU course E283). To say that Jenkins is just a better writer is to rephrase the problem not to solve it. In passing, it must be noted that, unlike Jenkins, Mr Bondine judged the lesson a success. Partial representation is a problem in all accounts, however; statistics, whether simple or sophisticated, can disguise and misrepresent.

I have used this fiction technique in preparing some of the case studies used as exercises in the course. Also, as a method of eliciting information in interviews, I prepared a fictional account of participants' opinions of the course, giving the worst possible interpretation of it. This procedure has been used before (Hamilton *et al.*, 1977). These examples underline the importance of 'methodological self-awareness' and the need, in the 'unravelling and explication of mundane beliefs and actions', to suspend common sense not endorse it (Atkinson and Delamont, in Hammersley, 1986a). Evaluation in education has more in common with the evaluation of a marriage than the evaluation of a horse-training programme: it benefits from uncommon awareness and sensitivity.

## AIMS OF THE COURSE

Presenting repeated versions of the course led to some modification of its aims. I began to see the session on teacher skills as serving to inform teachers of my understanding of, and respect for, the ordinary teaching job; it was a display of credentials that made teachers more receptive to more contentious work later. I began to see the sessions on altering teachers' perceptions of classroom deviance as central to the popularity and effectiveness of the course; and the examples from my own experience of troublesome pupils seemed to have more importance than simply as illustrations of themes. As part of the emphasis on changing teachers' attitudes, I paid more attention to lifting morale through stressing the high level of professionalism inherent in teaching troublesome pupils.

I began to refer to theoretical work in more detail; for example, Dreikurs and Reynolds became seminar topics in their own right. The amusing anecdotes which had earlier served to keep tired teachers awake through evening sessions began to function as a 'hidden curriculum', which taught that working with troublesome pupils could be fun. Conveying enthusiasm became more difficult as the same material was faced time after time. It became necessary to change the order of presentation and especially to do fresh reading in search of a new idea or focus for repeated sessions.

To summarize, the focus of the course shifted from changing skills to changing perceptions and attitudes. It was my assumption, and part of the teaching, that in interpersonal relationships a change of attitude is in itself a change of behaviour. That is to say, viewing an aggressive pupil as making an unskilled attempt to find a trustworthy and indestructible adult necessarily altered that pupil's experience of adults; being restrained by an adult who understands your problem is a different experience from being restrained by one who sees you as simply evil. In a chapter of Woods and Pollard (1987: 162), Reynolds sees his role as a school consultant as one of changing behaviour, from which, through reinforcement, change in attitudes, values and perceptions will follow. There is no necessary reason for this distinction and it is difficult to visualize how this would happen in practice. It is similarly difficult to understand his other suggestion, that methods and means can be made more effective without regard to aims and ends. How problems are perceived, and therefore the teacher's experience, is a product of the individual's internal system as well as the qualities of the environment. The qualities of the environment are multiple. Which features are salient, and the meaning attached to them, partly depends upon each particular act of perception. Eisner (1985) refers to the concept of 'anticipatory schemata' developed by Neisser (1976); these schemata influence the form our experience takes. Perception is constructive, an anticipatory cognitive event, an active seeking not a passive receptive mould (Eisner, 1982: 41, 49). 'What we experience depends in part on what nets we cast', and the nets we cast are the nets we weave.

It follows that what people learn from their experience is in part a function of what they have already learned; how they look at the world influences what they see and the meanings they attribute. Eisner (1982: 37) points out that when we say that some people fail to learn from experience we may be failing to recognize that 'the experience we assume they are having, from which they might learn, they in fact are missing'. It is also the case that what people may believe experience has taught them, they have in fact taught themselves; travel does not broaden closed minds. It was the aim of the course to get teachers to look for a range of possible significances in their classrooms and to be willing to see some things differently.

## EVALUATION DATA

Teachers seemed to look for, and sometimes to find, a number of things in the course: some found new ideas or practical approaches; some found reassurance that their present practice and performance were legitimate; others found that their problems were insignificant in relation to some of the cases introduced on the course; a number had particularly valued the opportunity to share ideas with others without being able, apparently, to specify what they had found worth while.

It soon became clear that teachers distinguished learning of explicit rules and procedures from learning in a nebulous, but nevertheless valued, way from experience – in this case vicariously through case studies and examples. This response is an illustration of Smythe's (1987: 3) claim that professional knowledge – derived from cases – cannot always be codified; we display skills, embedded in practice and inseparable from it, we cannot adequately describe. Some distinguished between those aspects of the course that had helped them personally and those that they thought useful procedures for beginners. In general, there was a tendency to value explicit rules and pieces of advice for use with inexperienced (and inexpert) teachers and to value more diffuse experiential learning for themselves. Some of the value attributed to the section on pupils' motives and strategies appears to have been due, at least in part, to the plenitude of examples used to illustrate the themes. Berliner (1987) emphasizes that experts are distinguishable by their ability to learn by reflection upon experience; the ability to follow rules is insufficient. Clark and Yinger (1987) conclude from their research into teachers' planning that expert teachers solve problems by drawing on a repertoire of practical knowledge that generates exemplars such as case studies or significant examples.

Much of teachers' activity is not appropriately described as problem solving. Bromme (1987) suggests that the analogy with medical diagnosis corresponds to reality only in certain limited circumstances; remedial teaching is one such. Generally, however, teachers' attention is said to be focused on the lesson as a whole – its content, the likely pupil response and the need to maintain 'instructional flow'. There is here a parallel with Jackson (1968): teachers' thinking is in the form of a sandwich with reflection enclosing a thick filling of interactive spontaneity. This phenomenon has been discussed with respect to student teachers by Mardle and Walker (in Woods, 1980b); college-based analyses of pupil problems make no impact on common-sense understandings in the classroom. The authors suggest that teacher training begins in infancy and continues throughout schooling, with only a brief and temporary disturbance during formal teacher training. Trainee teachers make use of theory only when it is congruent with existing (that is, prior to teacher training) beliefs. However, Lacey (1977) noted occasional situational influences upon students' decisions in acknowledging their beliefs: for example, some might argue points to annoy other members of the group. Clearly, the absence of theory from practical activity is a barrier to improving classroom responses. In assessing the worth of in-service work it is necessary to distinguish between perceiving the material as relevant at the time of delivery and finding it so back in the hurly-burly of the classroom.

In interviews and on comment sheets, a large number of remarks, both spoken and written, expressed inexplicit thoughts about the course as a whole: such comments as good, useful, enjoyable or 'Dodgy ground. Depends on relationships too much.' The sessions on pupil motives and strategies were most frequently remarked upon as having been valuable. In the view of one headteacher, this particular topic had made a difference to teachers' staffroom discussion following a half-day session held in his school:

> I have noticed that discussion of pupils has been much more analytical. I'm thinking in particular of what I would call hard members of staff – they've not been so ready to dismiss kids – it's certainly affected their way of thinking and that's very good I think ... very professional.

Perhaps the hard persona he referred to was a defence against the feeling of being under attack. When the unwanted behaviour is viewed differently, the need for defence disappears. The nature of the cases used to illustrate this particular topic, and the examples given from the literature, had persuaded some that their own problems were minor. A primary school head wrote: 'The wide range of examples helped us to put our own problems into a more sensible perspective.'

The next most frequent comment indicated that the course had been reassuring in some way:

> Ideas I've been developing over fifteen years [about motives]... it's a good feeling to know they are correct. It was useful to know that the way I operate with difficult situations is generally accepted as being effective for more extreme cases.

These comments express the feeling that teachers' ways of working, perhaps developed in isolation, are supported by the literature. It may also be that the course's claim that professionalism consisted to some degree in being able to avoid habitual, common-sense punitive responses was a morale booster in a time of morale attack; 1987/1988 saw teachers' contracts, the National Curriculum 'consultative document', repeated criticism in the press and Parliament of the quality of teachers, and unfavourable comparisons with a supposedly dynamic and enterprising industrial sector.

Teachers generally felt that the approaches proposed were practical: 'down to earth – real world'. Remarks about practicality were often accompanied by comments upon cases mentioned. Some commented upon the benefits to be derived by exchanging experiences with others and adding to their own repertoire of experience: 'Helpful to hear the views and difficulties encountered by others – we are not on our own!'

Many teachers found the contrasts between experienced teachers' reactions and those of students enlightening. Students' comments were introduced to illustrate the range of responses possible and to show course members that much of what they took to be common sense was in fact a type of specialized, professional knowledge. The strategies of the inexperienced startled some of the teachers. Reminding them of their own early errors confirmed their present expertise and further supported their confidence in their professionalism. A boost to morale may help teachers to cope irrespective of the precise advice and information accompanying it. Many thought that establishing school-based study groups was likely to be the most important outcome for them. 'I feel I have got something very positive to offer the school's INSET programme.'

## THE DEVELOPMENT OF UNDERSTANDING AND COPING IN SCHOOLS

Knowledge has scant effect upon practice if introduced piecemeal. One enthusiast for change on a school staff is unlikely to be any more effective than inviting an expert to visit, pronounce and depart. A school that wants to reappraise its strategies with disaffected pupils, that wants to gain the capacity to control problems in context, must organize. As Dreikurs (1957) says, it is not always possible to consider a child in terms of underlying causes when confronted by difficulties in action in the classroom. The way to learn to see things differently, so that one is no longer confronted by the inexplicable, is through discussion of cases with fellow professionals. The first step is to fix a series of meetings for the express purpose of discussing one or two individual cases. It is best to build these meetings into the school's training timetable and not wait until crises have occurred; the stressful atmosphere following a serious disruptive incident is not the best climate to begin thinking dispassionately about a problem. A time limit of an hour or so concentrates the discussion and encourages members to look for agreement. Open-ended meetings may stray into pessimistic generalizations about the modern world; one pupil's case must be discussed in its context and not used as an illustration of 'what things are coming to'. It is sometimes helpful to listen to members draw parallels with their own feelings of anger, attention seeking or revenge in situations where they are ignored, rejected or demeaned. Probably three meetings covering three pupils make a safe start. The principal headings used in this course provide suitable items for the agenda of such meetings. Sometimes information will be available; sometimes the meeting will expose gaps to be filled. A sample agenda is reproduced at the end of this chapter. Thorough exchange of perceptions, opinions and information should lead to an agreed, whole-school policy; and it should alter teachers' anticipatory schemata, what they expect, perceive and comprehend in the classroom.

Discussions allow anxiety to be shared, worries faced, strengths and weaknesses acknowledged. The pupil's behaviour is seen in the whole context of his or her personal, domestic and school circumstances and the intractable becomes redefined as vulnerable; understandings, perceptions and expectations alter. We learn to respond professionally and to set aside our 'untutored selves' (Kahn and Wright, quoted in Hanko, 1985). Hanko quotes a teacher who claimed that she had come to like difficult pupils through working in the group. This is reminiscent of Kohl's comments (see the notes to the exercise for Chapter 6). Learning to separate untutored responses from professional responsibilities is to accept that tackling deviant behaviour is as much part of a teacher's professional task as it is for police, barristers, priests and parents. It is true that teachers recognize that 'success at their job necessarily involves a capacity to establish and maintain classroom control' (Denscombe, 1985). However, Doyle reports the finding, with respect to problem pupils, that teachers 'did not always see the solving of these problems as part of their duties as classroom teachers' (Wittrock, 1986: 423). Planned sharing through open talk not only removes this misperception but as Dyke (1987) puts it: 'The simple act of "wondering why" creates the space for something new to happen.'

It is not always possible to alter all the circumstances that are thought to be inducing or contributing to a pupil's troublesome behaviour. There may be good reasons for retaining them irrespective of their effect upon an individual pupil. A secondary school cannot drop examinations nor ignore curriculum legislation, but where unmodifiable factors are identified this knowledge becomes part of the understanding. Similarly, a nursery class reading programme cannot be abandoned in the face of parental opposition even if it does frighten one or two pupils into phobia or rage. Focusing on the behavioural problems, as we have in this book, does not mean that the educational functions of school can be discarded; we think of the emotional and intellectual spheres as separate but it is a mistake to regard them, in school life, as separate and competing. Teaching maths and correcting exercise books are ways of demonstrating concern and regard for a pupil; and emotional therapy is an inescapably intellectual enterprise – everything, as it were, goes in through the mind. Identifying disturbing features focuses attention on fundamentals: there is a whole world of difference between being labelled as a child with emotional and behavioural problems who cannot read, and being labelled as a child who cannot read, with behavioural problems in consequence. One will receive potentially helpful attention; the sort of attention given to the other may well make the matter worse.

Those who take the lead in introducing staff training and discussion programmes need to take care not to slip into the role of outside expert, lecturing teachers on their responsibilities. To be of value, meetings must generate information and leave the teachers in control and committed to tackling the problem (Hanko, 1985: 63). The chair or meeting-convener must encourage open discussion and honesty by his or her own non-judgemental attitude and by gently preventing others from competitive contributions; the common staffroom claim, 'she's all right for me', must become data for consideration not implied criticism of colleagues.

Meetings can be convened with hidden agendas. For example, a request for in-service work on the contribution of school ethos to behavioural problems can sometimes be an attempt to compel some staff to obey a contentious school policy: wheel in the expert and hit the staff with that version of the Rutter report that made the popular papers. Hanko (1985: 140) suggests that 'one accepts the teachers' views of their difficulties as the essential and only possible starting point in a mutual pooling of expertise'. This is essential but far from easy, and sharp clashes of view on both particular and general matters, compounded by differences in status, can make even the most turbulent class seem docile by comparison. One way of keeping the meeting on task is to be open about the disagreements and the feelings engendered by them: to accept them as the reality, without approval or disapproval, inviting members to account for them and share other points of view. It is useful to remember that many of the features of group life in classrooms can appear in problem-focused meetings. A judgemental atmosphere will force teachers defensively into fixed roles; defensive communication does nothing for our problems and creates fresh ones of its own.

With experience, it may be possible to include consideration of teachers' needs: for example, to be recognized as competent and to feel valued. As groups grow in confidence, the feelings of teachers can be discussed with less fear of offence being taken. Teachers sometimes communicate more than they realize. For example, a teacher who had made a number of witty interventions during a course chose to introduce a case giving him concern. This case concerned a pupil who was said to seek constant attention – 'the class clown' – and the teacher's response had been such things as making him stand in the corner. The group quickly identified the incorrect strategies and proposed a better approach. When discussion turned to why the teacher was so concerned about such trivial behaviour, some suggested, in the light of his earlier contributions and the manner of his presentation, that perhaps he saw unwanted aspects of himself in this pupil. His instant response was a mocking, cock-a-snook gesture – thus neatly confirming the group's diagnosis. Hanko (1985) gives examples of how, 'with lightness of touch', it is possible to find some of the reasons for being upset by behaviour in ourselves: coming late to complain about the problem of lateness, hyperactively describing a hyperactive pupil, and failing to prepare a case presentation on a pupil who refuses homework.

Another problem which might seem a nice one to have is a too rapid improvement in a pupil's behaviour. Dramatic changes are sometimes claimed. Hanko (1985) mentions teachers who come to meetings having prepared to open the discussion on a pupil giving trouble but who say: 'Strangely enough, the case I was going to present, he was okay today.' She warns against expecting instant effects to last if the effort that produced them is instantly abandoned. Caspari (1976: 52) notes that it is difficult to pinpoint what is happening in such cases. The effort of understanding alters the perception, and the resulting change in teacher attitude improves the pupil's experience of school life. Where problems seem to vanish abruptly, it may be an instance of W. I. Thomas's rule, which paraphrased is: a threat defined as unreal is unreal in its consequences. Hanko (1985: 53) says it is unclear how far benefits to the child are due to teachers having 'a better understanding of his needs or to the support which they themselves received in relation to their own concern about handling him'.

Our habit of deference to experts sometimes causes us to regard insights as a gift from without, and teachers fall back into the belittling role of receivers of advice from superiors. Sometimes, after what seems an ineffectual if explorative meeting, a course leader will be thanked for his or her helpful advice; having given none, this can be startling. The meeting leaders must resist the temptation to take the credit for, assuredly, there will be blame to allocate in due course. Discoveries, insights and solutions, where they occur, are communal productions arising from the strengths of the group. To see them any other way is to return to the arid enterprise of importing dead knowledge from outside. Dead knowledge, as Whitehead said, does not keep any better than fish.

## CONCLUSION

Let us return to some of the issues we began with. This book has addressed a problem that it has declined to define definitively and has possibly disappointed those who hoped that a definition of good and bad behaviour would clarify issues and suggest a remedy. The government's Enquiry Into Discipline In Schools put this as its first question when it began taking evidence in 1988. Sometimes the request seems to be accompanied by the hope that knowing the thing's name will deliver some power over it. It is not possible to produce a definition that is both helpful and satisfies all teachers – leaving aside the agreement of outsiders and parents. Teachers differ in what they find acceptable or serious and in what they feel they can cope with and control. As we have seen, some regard rudeness as part and parcel of everyday life and correct it without allowing it to halt their lessons or unduly upset them; others regard it as the thin end of a wedge and may send a pupil out of the room to a senior teacher. Those who are able patiently and tolerantly to use skill, stealth and what I have termed 'disarming strategies' seem to feel more competent and actually to be more successful in winning co-operation in the long run; those who always react confrontationally and coercively are most stressed, more likely to aggravate situations and more likely to be pessimistic about the future. Definitions serve no useful purpose and statistics gathered on the basis of them are unreliable. The more experienced and competent the teacher, the more likely he or she is to question and challenge attempts to present examples of 'serious incidents'. Confident teachers see hope and possible strategies in any incident described to them; some worried teachers find every sort of behaviour threatening. Behaviour in school is too complex to be bounded by definitions. As in a friendship or marriage, a definition of what is right or good depends on the parties to the definition and its value is limited: when things are going well no one thinks of it; when a crisis occurs, definitions are not uppermost in people's minds.

Evading the question of definitions evades the question whether disruption is getting worse or not, and the ambiguous results of surveys were discussed in the first chapter. Of the many cases I have discussed, with more than 3,000 teachers over several years, few have been assaults – and often those presented were not regarded as counting as assaults by some of the teachers present. Many teachers feel there is more rudeness and inattention but there seems to be little reliable evidence that circumstances have changed much in the past twenty years or so. There are some teachers less able to cope than others – as there always have been and, by definition, always will be – but they are neither numerous nor totally beyond help.

To ask for the causes of troublesome behaviour is another deceptively simple question. Disruptive incidents or confrontations arise when certain factors are present on both the pupil's and the teacher's side. Causes may be found in the people involved, their families and friends, and their classroom and school circumstances. For example, a pupil from a family living on unemployment benefit, who is accustomed to undeserved anger and punishment from unhappy and pessimistic parents, and who is aware of his relatively deprived home life, may withdraw into silence or choose to work out his or her frustration on a teacher by open defiance. The type of lesson and the mood of his or her peers may amplify or mask whichever strategy the pupil adopts. Further, the teacher may understand the pupil's motives and problems and may react in a cool, dispassionate manner, accepting the unwanted behaviour and selecting a more appropriate moment to improve it. Another teacher, ignorant of the pupil's circumstances and unobservant of behavioural clues, might view the unwanted behaviour as a personal insult. An unrewarding exchange, accompanied by attempted coercion, might lead to what will later be described as an assault.

The 'discipline problem' is best understood as a part of the communication, debate and dispute between school and society. Those predisposed to blame schools and teachers for the imagined or real ills of society argue illogically from single incidents to 'widespread disorder'. Some teachers, and in particular their unions, hope to present their job as more deserving of sympathy and salary by claiming that pupil behaviour is ungovernable. The 'discipline debate' is one aspect of an ideological dispute between those who think teachers are venal and those who think they are undervalued. The discipline issue is similar, therefore, to the professionalism issue. The word 'profession' has become an ideological tool in a struggle between some teachers and some of their employers. Teachers are sometimes told that they are professionals: they should, therefore, selflessly serve the community, refrain from challenging policy and abandon the right to strike. On the other hand, teachers may assert that they are professional: they should, therefore, be given autonomy, have their advice followed by ministers and be highly paid. It has become a futile exercise to try to give a yes/no answer to the once popular question – is teaching a profession? Similarly, it has become futile to hope for yes/no answers to questions in the discipline debate.

The solution, if there is one, lies elsewhere. I believe that teachers must rebuild confidence and restore personal esteem from within. We need to accept that our responsibilities are much greater than the simple ideal of teaching docile pupils in pleasant surroundings, revered by parents and lavished with resources and emoluments by governments. Problems and privations have always been a part of normal life as they always will be. It needs to be understood that teachers can no more abolish trouble-some behaviour than the police can abolish crime or doctors banish illness. We need to learn to cope as best as we can but most of all to learn that the overwhelming majority of teachers are already performing at maximum human efficiency. It may be objected that I seem to be ignoring the specialist agencies expressly established to assist teachers with troublesome pupils and sometimes to relieve them of the burden. Do not other professionals turn to experts when they meet difficulties in their work? Certainly the psychological and social services can be a useful resource but they are not professional experts in the matter of teaching. The study of psychology and two or three years' teaching experience is no substitute for twenty years of reflective practice in the classroom (as we approach the end of the century, more than two-thirds of the teaching profession have more than twenty years' experience in their jobs). The real experts to turn to are our colleagues, even if their expertise consists only in the ability to engage the trust and attention of just one trouble-some individual. That is what our job is about and competence in it is no small thing.

In short, teachers need to acquire increased confidence and changed attitudes to difficult behaviour: to see it as tractable, as something to be tackled dispassionately, as part of their job and not just as grit in the machine. The fact that so many experienced and competent teachers single out reassurance as one of the most valuable results of in-service training supports the view that the 'discipline problem' is as much to do with ideology as reality. As for the role of government and other outsiders, anything that lifts the morale and confidence of the profession will reduce the complaints from teachers about unruly behaviour. Perhaps we cannot expect too much in that respect. The responsibility for our professional development must be our own.

## ACTIVITY 7.1: THE BEST OF ALL POSSIBLE SCHOOL SYSTEMS

Leibnitz, crudely summarized, argued that because God made the world it must therefore be the best of all possible worlds. The view that it seemed to have sizeable defects must therefore be imperfect. Much the same sort of attitude influences discussions on educational systems. If our favoured political party introduced a measure, it must be for the best – irrespective of the problems and injustices that seem to arise.

Suppose that you knew nothing about yourself or your own children other than that they would attend schools and you would teach in one. Imagine (in a type of thought-experiment invented by John Rawls) that 'a veil of ignorance' covers such details as your children's abilities and interests, and your own too. Imagine that you have a choice of countries in which to reside, but the choice must be made before you know whether you will be a brilliant teacher of technology or a struggling instructor in basic French; you must also choose before you know whether your children will be precocious geniuses or severely intellectually disabled. What would you hope to find in the country you chose? Think about the macro and the micro level. What sort of an educational system? What type of school organization? What sort of learning and assessment methods? What sort of people attracted to teaching, and what sort of training for teachers?

### Comments on the activity

Some people find this activity difficult and threatening. As if they recognize, but will not admit, the contradictions in their favoured plan, they leap immediately to rationalizations. (I want a fiercely competitive and differentiated system because the country needs to reward talent; I want compulsory attendance at state comprehensives and less emphasis on the academic side because we need to learn to love each other as equals.) This activity always brings us face to face with our own values and shows how educational issues are fundamentally moral issues. Most people find their way back to their adopted position – but perhaps that does not matter too much as long as the journey there is long enough to pick up some understanding of other possibilities.

## ACTIVITY 7.2: DISCIPLINE POLICIES AND PREVENTING BULLYING

This activity, although worth reflecting on individually, can be carried out only in conjunction with pupils, parents and colleagues. No comments follow, as guidance is given here.

The prevention of bullying should not be seen as just another policy to bolt on to the school's pile of documents and plans. Preventing bullying should be an outcome of the process of formulating a behaviour policy and its implementation and review. Pupils need to be involved – and parents too – from the outset. As well as rules, policies should address the range of opportunities available for pupils to develop responsible attitudes. The school's ethos in the fullest sense should also be considered.

The task can be tackled in three main stages. First, negotiate with each class five or six positively framed rules. These rules should be collated and a definitive shortlist compiled. This is best done through school councils or specially convened meetings of class representatives. Resist the temptation to improve the rules to the point where the pupils do not recognize their own contributions. The negotiation phase is crucial if the pupils are to have the opportunity to learn through discussion. It should not be approached in the pseudo-exploratory, Socratic manner, where all the answers are held by the teacher. Sharing the construction of the policy ensures that all participants learn socially acceptable behaviour from the outset. If this vital first stage is short-circuited by a committee of staff, both pupils and teachers are deprived of the chance to learn.

Second, look at aspects of the school's provision that bear directly on behaviour. Review the opportunities the school offers for pupils to develop a sense of self-discipline and responsibility. Good behaviour is not just about conformity; we also hope for positive contributions and evidence of pupil initiative. Look, too, at the attendance rates and recording procedures. Pupils know they are not valued if attendance and punctuality are disregarded. Overhaul the pastoral systems that support and guide pupils and ensure their health and welfare. This will include everything from alleviating learning difficulties to helping pupils with post-school choices.

Third, consider the contribution of the wider school ethos. Does the school actively promote the social and moral development of pupils, and how is this monitored? Does an equal opportunity policy exist, and are real efforts made to enhance pupils' cultural understanding, are pupils and parents involved and is progress monitored? Does the school address the spiritual needs of pupils? This is not answered by providing whole-school assemblies only – though properly and imaginatively conducted they can help. Are opportunities made and taken throughout the curriculum? However irreligious British adults may be, few are unmoved by some aspects of music, art, technology or world events in the past or present.

The school's ethos is tied up with its methods of teaching, learning and assessment. Do these activities indicate teachers' high expectations of pupils? Do they show that pupils' contributions and views are valued and treated with sensitivity?

Where bullying has become an issue, all these aspects need review. As DfE circular 8/94 says: 'Many pupils experience bullying at some point.' The evidence is that even in well-run schools, there is usually some sort of bullying going on, and almost by definition it is secret and persistent. The people who supervise pupils at lunch, therefore, need to understand their role. Bullying may be normal but it is not an acceptable part of school life; unintended encouragement or reinforcement must be avoided; active monitoring is needed as well as assiduous action in response to complaints. Staff must act 'and importantly be seen to act' (DfE, 1994). Some schools have adopted ways of letting pupils inform on bullies anonymously. These can be suggestion boxes about the school or even just letting it be known that information is welcome. While I was interviewing a headteacher in his room (in preparing this book) a note suddenly appeared under the door: 'Theares going to be a fihgt on the field tonight.'

The same open discussion that should characterize rule-formation is needed for bullying. Openness is the enemy of any activity that needs secrecy. Formal teaching is often necessary and opportunities exist in the National Curriculum already: for primary pupils, parallels can be drawn with the plight of slaves in the ancient world; for secondaries, the rise of the Nazis might be studied in preparation for study of post-war Britain.

Bullies evoke, in the main, the sort of feelings that identify their motives as power and revenge (in terms of the work in Chapter 4). The particular cases of bullies will need to be addressed in addition to the school-wide policies; they will need the sort of attention that any other troublesome pupil needs. In some cases, the victims of bullies can themselves have problems that have contributed to their vulnerability, and they too may be the focus of review. A suggested checklist of items to consider in opening investigations on any troublesome pupil, bully or not, follows.

1 Retrieve and identify pupil motives or reasonable strategies.
   Mirrors, parallels; avoid re-enacting.
   Identity display, testing, attention seeking, power and revenge.
   Sources of hostility and avoidance strategies.
2 Classroom and teacher factors.
   Skills, varied teaching and learning styles.
   Unintended discrimination or undervaluing.
   Group roles.

Behaviour: identify and measure, predisposing and confirming circum-
stances, unintended rewards.
Catch the pupil being good.
Priorities, charts, records.
3 School.
Categories and differentiations.
Pupil experience of rewarding or stigmatizing labels.
Roles, routes and choices available.
Shadow or imagine the pupil's experience.
Contracts.
4 Domestic context.
Family roles, purposes, experiences.
Dependable and reliable adult, hostility.
Avoid reproducing or re-enacting domestic fears in school.
5 Shared understandings. Redefine the intractable; alter perceptions and
attitudes.
Share anxieties, recognize strengths.
Sense of scale, worry in advance.
Professional vs untutored responses.
Agreed whole-school policy.

## ACTIVITY 7.3: IMPROVING PLAYGROUNDS

Supervision of playgrounds is probably the least popular of a teacher's
duties. Policing the boundary between the necessary, but turbulent, activities of play and conflict can be very stressful and irritating. Formulate a
plan of action for improving playground behaviour. Think about the
skills, attitudes and understandings required of all the personnel involved,
including the lunchtime supervisors. Consider policy changes at every
level: from altering the times of breaks, direct teaching of play activities
or making clubs available to developing the capacity of teachers and
supervisors to manage conflicts, ensuring there are effective systems of
communication.

### Comments on the activity

School policies on behaviour and discipline should address the management of behaviour during breaks and ensure consistency of standards: for
example, explicit teaching of the rules and of games for younger children.
Improving the environment is an obvious step where facilities are poor:
this encompasses the planting of trees, provision of equipment and seats,
as well as zoning the more energetic activities to protect those who want
quiet.

Lunchtime supervisors have a thankless task when they are poorly supported, and attention should be given to their needs. Many need guidance on what is actually permitted; some see their role as preventing almost any vigorous activity and this can gratuitously inflame situations. Members of the Elton Committee witnessed just such an incident during their tour of schools (DES, 1989). The conflict management techniques explained in Chapter 5 might help. A ready method of contacting senior teachers (and form teachers too, if possible) is necessary. Supervisors should have some of their paid time extended before and beyond the pupils' break. They can then chat to teachers and be seen to do so by pupils, some of whom might think that supervisors are not part of the school's staff. The phrase 'she's only a supervisor' is said to be used even by some parents.

A set of tips might also be helpful. One primary school worked out the following on a training day.

*How to keep control in the playground*

Attend to those who behave well, especially if they are sometimes troublesome. Try to catch them when they are being good and encourage games and join in if you can.

Try to ignore the naughty unless they are seriously troublesome or doing harm to another person or damaging property. Deal with trouble by making as little fuss as possible.

Don't nag. State the rule and leave it at that if you can. Don't let children wind you up or make you angry.

Don't make wild threats. Try a joke or a simple statement that you will speak to their teacher later. (Make sure you do!)

Praise children who avoid trouble and never let them retaliate. Remember, you are here to see that everyone is happy. You are not a sentry!

Detailed and useful advice for primary schools can be found in Blatchford (1989).

## ACTIVITY 7.4: HOW MUCH CAN TEACHERS DO?

A school's outcomes, whether examination results, truancy statistics or levels of discipline, are a consequence of several factors. If we were concerned about truancy, for example, we might write an equation of the following form for a particular class:

$a + b + c + d =$ attendance rate

In this equation $a =$ the teacher's contribution in terms of maintaining pupils' motivation; $b =$ the pupil's contribution, which might be such things as his or her personal talents and disposition; $c =$ the contribution of the school's ethos, which would include the effect of colleagues through their support for rules and standards, and the influence of other pupils through their example; d = the contribution of the environment and social composition of the school's catchment.

The task is to put a percentage figure on each of a to d. This activity can be extended to include other outcomes, and the number of factors increased, and even interactions among them included in the equation. The point of the exercise is to expose the limitations of each component as an explanatory factor and to develop a realistic focus in planning change. For example, teachers cannot be 100 per cent blamed or praised for poor attendance or examination results, and neither can the school's environment.

## Comments

Evidence accumulating through inspections of schools suggests that it is not too difficult to achieve attendance rates in the 90 to 95 per cent range for schools in comfortable suburbs, and these schools usually meet or exceed the national averages in examinations. Schools with the poorest results in examinations and attendance rates below 90 per cent are mostly those serving poor districts, where entitlement to free meals is above the national average. There are important points to consider: schools with apparently similar catchments can vary by 100 per cent in examination outputs, and by even more in terms of exclusion figures. The controversial statistics are the uncertain relative strengths of teacher-effectiveness and schools' catchments and intakes. Plowden's research in primaries and Rutter's in secondaries support a figure of around 6 per cent for teachers and maybe 40 per cent for domestic factors. Interestingly, W. Edwards Deming (Neave, 1990), a tireless advocate of realism in relation to workers' responsibility for product quality in industry, suggests a similar figure. Even if it is as simple as this, 6 per cent is not insignificant – and it ignores the contribution made by the organizational system to which each teacher's work contributes an increment. For the pupils who form part of the 6 per cent improvement, the improvement might well be 100 per cent.

It is difficult to resist the argument that some schools are seriously disadvantaged in the drive to improve their average standards because of the disproportionate weight of social problems that their pupils bring to them. It has been claimed that publishing league tables will accelerate the trend towards a system for the well-off and another for the poor. My view is that things will not get worse. Some parents have always selected schools wholly on social class grounds without reference to results at all. League tables have given such people a rationalization for their class-related choices.

Fashions change. Perhaps a new generation of parents will react against narrow, petty middle-class views of education as exclusive and cloistered, and we will see the educational equivalent of the search for natural simplicity that we have seen in other areas of life. Parents will want the children's social and educational experience to be as free from artificial preservatives as their breakfast; as unbleached and wholesome as whole-wheat flour; as plain and fresh as their pine floors and furniture; and full of the richness and bustle of a dock-side flat in a city centre. The inward-looking neighbourhood watch will give way to active community involve-ment. Perhaps the timid confines of mock-Georgian housing estates will be abandoned as people move to the vibrant and cosmopolitan hearts of our cities, where real life, like real bread and real education, has the rough bits left in.

## ACTIVITY 7.5: HELPING A TROUBLED COLLEAGUE

This final activity asks you to consider how you would help a teacher who was experiencing the sort of problems and evidencing the sort of needs described in the confidential diary here. Identify development needs in terms of skills, attitudes, knowledge of subject and knowledge of children. Consider how you and the school might respond.

### Monday

Deep depression. The start of my third week in this school and I am bound to say I do not look forward to it. Teaching in this school seems to me to depend on control and nothing else. I am a maths and biology joint honours graduate with six years' experience in a first-class school, but it seems to count for nothing with these children. They don't even bother to learn my name. I do wonder about the wisdom of the staff policy in appointing me without warning me how much things have changed in the eight years I've been out of the system rearing a family. I do feel let down in terms of training in such important things as mixed-ability and low-ability teaching, not to mention teaching ethnic minorities which make up more than half the school. I don't know why I say teaching – it's a management and containing exercise here. Non-existent resources, no motivation, no interest in knowledge that is vital to their futures. No one offers to help set up the equipment, so work has to be rushed. Writing up experiments is a joke. They can't even understand the corrections: 'A sentence must have a verb.' 'Miss, what's a verb?'

**Tuesday**

Downright defiance and abuse in the biology practical because I wouldn't let a boy go to the toilet. It was only five minutes into the lesson and I didn't care for his tone of voice. Whatever happened to raising hands before speaking? The children just seem to think they can wander in and out at will and I have to shout just to be heard above their din. The head of faculty arranged for me to observe one of the senior pastoral teachers with one of my most difficult classes – he helps out in the maths department apparently. He kept them quiet with a lot of toadying as far as I could see, but the quality of the teaching was atrocious. I don't know whether he was overawed (not being a maths graduate and having me in the room) but he confused the x and y axes on a graph he was demonstrating. This got him into a mess after about five minutes. He turned to me and said: 'Well, what shall I do now?' I resisted the temptation to say 'Resign you fool' and showed him what he had done wrong. I was surprised the pupils continued to sit there and listen.

**Wednesday**

A quieter day. Mostly maths groups today, which are easier to control than biology, as they can just be set to do exercises from the book. A lot of absence for some religious festival or other. I feel sorry for the few good pupils – the quiet Asians and the intellectually brilliant Poles and the beautiful Chinese girls. They're from good families, though some of them are what I would call middle-of-the-road clever children rather than very bright. I don't know what their parents are doing sending them to a school like this. Probably they couldn't see anything wrong. I didn't myself when I came to look round, I must admit. I know now of course – all those quiet classes have been paid for by letting them have an easy ride. The standards are atrocious as you can tell just by listening to the pupils' conversation and the dreadful handwriting to be seen on the work displayed on the walls. Seems to me letting so much of the work be done on computers is hiding the underlying poor quality. They have no sense of style or expression – not even basic grammar.

**Thursday**

Paper planes and chewed up paper balls completely wrecked the theory lesson. It's bad enough having them eating and chewing – some of them set out their food and coke cans on the benches but don't think about books or pens. No theory, no practical, so they will have to copy

from the board again. I suppose this is what happens when you try to
be friendly. I should have gone in tough from the start with all that
artificial teacher-authority stuff. A very unpleasant encounter with a
girl who had drawn an obscene picture in one of her exercise books.
It was her history book – I was checking through her bag as I suspected
her of taking my felt markers. She cheekily claimed the teacher had
let them do it, and started to tell me about what happens before you
get a baby, so I sent her out to the head immediately. Unbelievably, it
later transpired that it was true. The head of history lets some of them
do a project on Egyptian hieroglyphics as part of their study on the
ancient world. He assured me that there really is one glyph that means
'before' that looks like a man's private parts. For Egyptian scribes, the
fact that intercourse comes before life suggested the sign, and they
were not what he called squeamish about such things. He had no regard
for the embarrassment I had been subjected to and seemed to treat
the whole affair with undue levity – making some cheap remark that the
sign for 'after' would have been a cigarette if the Egyptians had known
about tobacco.

### Friday

Assembly for the year group I'm attached to and do most of my
teaching in – year 7. A very colourful affair with a band, but I don't
know that it had much to do with the sort of issues normal assemblies
are concerned with. Surprised to see that one of my most uncontrollable
boys played an instrument, and the standard seemed very acceptable
overall. I suppose in this sort of non-academic activity that sort of child
will do quite well. After another week of chaos I'm absolutely
exhausted and totally drained. Is this really what I was so expensively
trained for?

### Comments on the activity

If nothing else, this case exemplifies the need for induction for teachers
returning to their profession after a break.
Missing skills: there are apparently gaps in preparation (of equipment)
as well as a limited repertoire of teaching methods. Rather confrontational
and invasive rather than cool and detached.
Unhelpful attitudes: apparently not very well disposed to pupils she views
unfavourably and through some stereotypical (though positive) categories
('quiet Asians', 'good families', 'middle-of-the-road clever', and so on).
She may well hold some even more worrying negative stereotypes not
disclosed here that would seriously impede her ability to fulfil her professional responsibilities.

Knowledge of subject: seems to be confident here, but this confidence may have contributed to the apparent impatience with pupils' less perfect understanding.

Knowledge of children: seems rather out of touch with children who are on the edge of adolescence.

Possible action: some of the identified needs might be addressed in an induction programme and by allocating time to an experienced member of staff to act as mentor. Where unhelpful and unsympathetic attitudes to pupils are at fault, the task of development is much harder. Perhaps the selection procedure should have been more rigorous so that a more suitable person could have been appointed or help and advice offered before damage to relationships was done.

# Further reading

There are several general overviews and introductions. Laslett and Smith (1984) is a brisk, succinct guide which benefits from experience with pupils in schools for the maladjusted. Robertson (1981) is good on classroom skills. The original research on which much classroom management is based is to be found in the mammoth American Education Research Association's publication edited by Wittrock (1986). Wragg (1984) reports on British work. Reid *et al*. (1987) is a handy encyclopaedia of research on effective schools. Cheesman and Watts (1985) is a cheerful introduction to the behavioural approach. Readers attracted by the work in Chapter 4 would enjoy Dreikurs (1957), Balson (1982) and Stott (1982). Hanko (1985) is very helpful for those intending to lead discussion groups, as is the *Journal of Educational Therapy* (26, Chesterfield Gardens, London, NW3 7DE). Teachers considering this area for a higher degree will find Furlong (1985) useful.

# References

Acton, T. A. (1980) 'Educational criteria for success: some problems in the work of Rutter, Maughan, Mortimore and Ouston', *Educational Research* 22: 3.

Adelman, C. (1981) *Uttering, Muttering: Collecting, Using and Reporting Talk for Social and Educational Research*, London: Grant McIntyre.

Angyalfi, S. (1994) *The Historical Development of Jewish Special Education*, Leeds: Leeds Metropolitan University.

Atkinson, P. and Delamont, S. (1977) 'Mock-ups and cock-ups', in M. Hammersley and P. Woods (1984a).

Baddeley, G. (1992) *Learning Together through Talk*, The National Oracy Project, Key Stages 1 and 2, London: Hodder & Stoughton.

Ball, S. J. (1981) *Beachside Comprehensive*, Cambridge: Cambridge University Press.

Balson, M. (1982) *Understanding Classroom Behaviour*, ACER.

Barnes, D. (1976) *From Communication to Curriculum*, Harmondsworth: Penguin.

Barnes D., Britton, J. and Rosen, H. (1969) *Language, the Learner and the School*, Harmondsworth: Penguin.

Barton, L. and Tomlinson, S. (eds) (1982) *Special Education and Social Interests*, London: Harper & Row.

Bastide, R. (1972) *The Sociology of Mental Disorder*, London: Routledge & Kegan Paul.

Becker, H. S. (1952) 'Social class variations in the teacher–pupil relationship', in R. R. Cosin, I. R. Dale, G. M. Esland and D. F. Swift (eds) *School and Society*, London: Open University and Routledge & Kegan Paul.

——(1963) *The Outsiders*, New York: Free Press.

Bell, P. and Best, R. (1986) *Supportive Education*, Oxford: Blackwell.

Bennett, H. (1992) *Teacher Appraisal: Survival and Beyond*, Harlow, Essex: Longman.

Berger, P. and Luckmann, T. (1971) *The Social Construction of Reality*, Harmondsworth: Penguin.

Berliner, D. C. (1987) 'Ways of thinking about students and classrooms by more and less experienced teachers', in J. Calderhead (1987).

Bernstein, B. (1961) 'Social class and linguistic development: a theory of social learning', in A. H. Halsey *et al.* (1961).

——(1971) 'On the classification and framing of educational knowledge', in M. F. D. Young (ed.) *Knowledge and Control*, London: Collier-Macmillan.

Best, R., Ribbens, P. M. and Jarvis, C., with Oddy, D. (1983) *Education and Care*, London: Heinemann.

Beynon, J. (1985) *Initial Encounters in the Secondary School*, Lewes: Falmer.

Bibby, P. (1994) 'Powerless to act', *Times Educational Supplement*, 29 April 1994.
Bird, C., Chessom, R., Furlong, V. J. and Johnson, D. (1981) *Disaffected Pupils*, Middlesex: Brunel University.
Blackledge, D. and Hunt, B. (1985) *Sociological Interpretations of Education*, London: Croom Helm.
Blatchford, P. (1989) *Playtime in the Primary School*, Windsor, Berks: NFER–Nelson.
Blishen, E. (1980) *A Nest of Teachers*, London/Lewes: Hamish Hamilton.
Booth, T. and Coulby, D. (1987) (eds) *Producing and Reducing Disaffection*, Milton Keynes: Open University Press.
Bourne, J., Bridges, L. and Searle, C. (1994) *Outcast England: How Schools Exclude Black Children*, London: Institute of Race Relations.
Brennan, W. K (1979) *The Curriculum for Slow Learners*, Schools Council Working Paper, 63.
Brice-Heath, S. (1986) 'Questioning at home and at school: a comparative study', in M. Hammersley (ed.) (1986b).
Brody, H. (1994) *The Healer's Prayer*, New Haven, CT: Yale University Press.
Bromme, R. (1987) 'Teachers' assessments of students' difficulties and progress in understanding the classroom', in J. Calderhead (1987).
Brophy, J. E. and Evertson, C. M. (1976) *Learning from Teaching*, Boston: Allyn & Bacon.
Bruner, J. (1980) *Under Five in Britain*, London: Grant McIntyre.
Bull, S. L. and Solity, J. E. (1987) *Classroom Management: Principles to Practice*, Beckenham: Croom Helm.
Calderhead, J. (1984) *Teachers' Classroom Decision Making*, London: Holt, Rinehart & Winston.
——(1987) (ed.) *Exploring Teachers' Thinking*, London: Cassell.
Caspari, I. (1976) *Troublesome Children in Class*, London: Routledge & Kegan Paul.
Charlton, T. and David, K. (eds) (1993) *Managing Misbehaviour in Schools*, London: Routledge.
Cheesman, P. L. and Watts, P. E. (1985) *Positive Behaviour Management*, London: Croom Helm.
Chessum, R. (1980) 'Teacher ideologies and pupil disruption', in L. Barton, R. Meighan and S. Walker, *Schooling, Ideology and Curriculum*, Lewes: Falmer.
Chisholm, B., Kearney, D., Knight, G., Little, H., Morris, S. and Tweddle, D. (1984) *Preventive Approaches to Disruption*, London: Macmillan.
Cicourel, A. V. (1968) 'Police practices and official records', in R. Turner (ed.) *Ethnomethodology*, Harmondsworth: Penguin.
Clark, C. M. and Yinger, R. J. (1987) 'Teachers' planning', in J. Calderhead (1987).
Cohen, L. and Cohen, A. (1987) (eds) *Disruptive Behaviour*, London: Harper & Row.
Cooper, P. (1993) *Effective Schools for Disaffected Students: Integration or Segregation*, London: Routledge.
Corrigan, P. (1979) *Schooling the Smash Street Kids*, London: Macmillan.
Coulby, D. and Harper, T. (1985) *Preventing Classroom Disruption*, London: Croom Helm.
Coupe, J. and Porter, J. (1986) *The Education of Pupils with Severe Learning Difficulties*, London: Croom Helm.
Cronk, K. A. (1987) *Teacher–Pupil Conflict in Secondary Schools*, Lewes: Falmer.
Curtis, S. J. (1963) *History of Education in Great Britain*, Foxton: Cambridge University Tutorial Press.

Cusick, P. A. (1973) *Inside High Schools: The Students' World*, New York: Holt, Rinehart & Winston.

Cuttance, P. (1985) 'Frameworks for research on the effectiveness of schooling', in D. Reynolds (ed.) *Studying School Effectiveness*, Lewes: Falmer.

Davies, B. (1984) 'Friends and fights', in M. Hammersley and P. Woods (1984b).

Davies, J. G. V. and Maliphant, R. (1974) 'Refractory behaviour in school and avoidance learning', *Journal of Child Psychology, Psychiatry* 15: 23–3.

Davies, L. (1984) *Pupil Power: Deviance and Gender in School*, Lewes: Falmer.

Davies, R. (ed) (1994) *The Kenneth Williams Letters*, London: HarperCollins.

Delamont, S. (1976) *Interaction in the Classroom*, London: Methuen.

Delamont, S. and Galton, M. (1986) *Inside the Secondary Classroom*, London: Routledge & Kegan Paul.

Denscombe, M. (1985) *Classroom Control: A Sociological Perspective*, London: George Allen & Unwin.

DfE (1992) 'Exclusions: a discussion document', London: Office for Standards in Education.

DfE (1994) 'Pupil behaviour and discipline', Circular 8/94, London.

DES (1975) *Survey of Violence, Indiscipline and Vandalism in Schools*, London: HMSO.

——(1978) *Behavioural Units*, London: HMSO.

——(1980) *Truancy and Behaviour Problems in Some Urban Schools*, London: HMSO.

——(1984) *Education Observed 2*, London: HMSO.

——(1987) *Education Observed 5: Good Behaviour and Discipline in Schools*, London: HMI report.

——(1989a) *Discipline in Schools: Report of the Committee of Enquiry Chaired by Lord Elton*, London: HMSO.

——(1989b) *Standards in Education: The Annual Report of HM Senior Chief Inspector of Schools*, London: HMSO.

——(1990) *HMI in the 1990s, The Work of HM Inspectors*, London: HMSO.

——(1992) *Education in England*, London: HMSO.

Dewe, P. J. (1985) 'Coping with work stress: an investigation of teachers' actions', *Research in Education* 33: 27–40.

Docking, J. W. (1980) *Control and Discipline in Schools*, London: Harper & Row.

Doyle, W. and Carter, K. (1986) 'Academic tasks in classrooms', in M. Hammersley (1986a).

Dreikurs, R. (1957) *Psychology in the Classroom*, London: Staples Press.

Driver, R. (1983) *The Pupil as Scientist*, Milton Keynes: Open University Press.

Dunkerley, D., and Salaman, G. (1986) 'Organisations and bureaucracy', in M. Haralambos (ed.) *Developments in Sociology* II, Ormskirk: Causeway Press.

Durkheim, E. (1893/1933) *The Division Of Labour In Society*, London: Free Press.

Dyke, S. (1987) 'Psycho-analytic insight in the classroom: asset or liability?', *Journal of Educational Therapy* 1(4): 43–64.

Edwards, D. A. and Furlong, V. J. (1978) *The Language of Teaching*, London: Heinemann.

Eggleston, J. (1974) (ed.) *Contemporary Research in the Sociology of Education*, London: Methuen.

Eisner, E. (1982) *Cognition and Curriculum*, New York: Longman.

——(1985) *The Art of Educational Evaluation*, Lewes: Falmer.

Emanuel, R. B. (1990) 'Counter-transference: a spanner in the works or a tool for understanding', *Journal of Educational Therapy* 3(2): 3–12.

Everhart, R. B. (1983) *Reading, Writing and Resistance*, Boston, Mass.: Routledge & Kegan Paul.

Evertson, C. M. and Emmer, E. T. (1982) 'Effective management at the beginning of the school year in junior high classes', *Educational Psychology* 74(4): 485–98.

Finlayson, D. S. and Loughran, J. L. (1975) 'Pupils' perceptions in high and low delinquency schools', *Educational Research* 18(2).

Fontana, D. (1985) *Classroom Control*, London: Methuen.

Furlong, V. J. (1985) *The Deviant Pupil*, Milton Keynes: Open University Press.

Galloway, D. (1985) *Schools, Pupils and Special Educational Needs*, Beckenham: Croom Helm.

Galloway, D., Ball, T., Blomfield, D. and Seyd, R. (1982) *Schools and Disruptive Pupils*, London: Longman.

Galloway, D., Martin, R. and Wilcox, B. (1985) 'Persistent absence from school and exclusion from school: the predictive power of school and community variables', *British Educational Research Journal* 11(1).

Galvin, P. and Singleton, R. (1984) *Behavioural Management*, Windsor: NFER.

Galvin, P., Mercer, S. and Costa, P. (1990) *Building a Better Behaved School: A Development Manual for Primary Schools*, London: Longman.

Gannaway, H. (1984) 'Making sense of school', in M. Hammersley and P. Woods (eds) (1984b).

Garfinkel, H. (1967) *Studies in Ethnomethodology*, Englewood Cliffs, New Jersey: Prentice Hall.

Gathorne-Hardy, J. (1977) *The Public School Phenomenon*, London: Hodder & Stoughton.

Gillborn, D., Nixon, J. and Ruddock, J. (1993) *Dimensions of Discipline, Rethinking Practice in Secondary Schools*, London: Department for Education.

Gillham, B. (ed.) (1981) *Problem Behaviour in the Secondary School: A Systems Approach*, London: Croom Helm.

Gillingham, J. (1993) *Richard the Lionheart*, London: Weidenfeld & Nicholson.

Goffman, E. (1968) *Asylums*, Harmondsworth: Penguin.

Gordon (ed.) (1983) 'Is teaching a profession?', Bedford Way Paper, London: Institute of Education.

Graham, J. (1988) *Schools, Disruptive Behaviour and Delinquency*, Home Office Research Study, 96, HMSO.

Gray, H. and Freeman, A. (1988) *Teaching Without Stress*, London: Paul Chapman Publishing.

Gray, J., McPherson, A. F. and Raffe, D. (1983) *Reconstructions of Secondary Education: Theory, Myth and Practice Since the War*, London: Routledge & Kegan Paul.

Grunsell, R. (1985) *Finding Answers to Disruption*, London: SCDC.

Hall, E., Woodhouse, D. A. and Wooster, A. D. (1984) 'An evaluation of in-service courses in human relations', *British Journal of In-Service Education* 11(1): 55–60.

Halsey, A. H., Floud, J. and Anderson, C. A. (1961) *Education, Economy and Society*, London: Collier-Macmillan.

Hamilton, D., Jenkins, D., King, C., MacDonald, B. and Parlett, M. (1977) (eds) *Beyond the Numbers Game*, London: Macmillan.

Hammersley, M. (ed.) (1986a) *Controversies in Classroom Research*, Milton Keynes: Open University Press.

——(1986b) *Case Studies in Classroom Research*, Milton Keynes: Open University Press.

Hammersley, M. and Woods, P. (1984a) *Classrooms and Staffrooms*, Milton Keynes: Open University Press.
——(1984b) *Life in School*, Milton Keynes: Open University Press.
Hanko, G. (1985) *Special Needs in Ordinary Classrooms*, Oxford: Basil Blackwell.
Hargreaves, A. (1978) 'The significance of classroom coping strategies', in M. Hammersley and P. Woods (1984a).
Hargreaves, D. H. (1967) *Social Relationships in a Secondary School*, London: Routledge & Kegan Paul.
——(1980) 'Teachers' knowledge of behaviour problems', in G. Upton and A. Gobell (eds) *Behaviour Problems in the Comprehensive School*, Cardiff: University College.
——(1982) *The Challenge for the Comprehensive School*, London: Routledge & Kegan Paul.
Hargreaves, D. H., Hestor, K. H. and Mellor, J. M. (1975) *Deviance in Classrooms*, London: Routledge & Kegan Paul.
Her Majesty's Stationery Office (1977) *The Pack Report*, London: HMSO.
——(1989) *Discipline in Schools, Report of the Committee of Enquiry Chaired by Lord Elton*, London: HMSO.
——(1993a) *Handbook for the Inspection of Schools*, Office for Standards in Education, London: HMSO.
——(1993b) *Access and Achievement in Urban Education*, Office for Standards in Education, London: HMSO.
Hewott, F. M. and Blake, P. R. (1973) 'Teaching the emotionally disturbed', in R. M. W. Travers (ed.) (1973)
Hoghughi, M. (1978) *Troubled and Troublesome*, London: Burnett Books.
Holman, P. G. and Coghill, N. F. (1987) *Disruptive Behaviour in School*, Bromley: Chartwell-Bratt.
Hughes, J. N. (1988) *Cognitive Behaviour Therapy*, Oxford: Pergamon.
Jackson, P. (1968) *Life in Classrooms*, New York: Holt, Rinehart & Winston.
James, G. (1994) *Obfuscation Eschewed: The Concept of Evanescence in Resource Management*, Leeds Metropolitan University Monograph.
Johnstone, M. and Munn, P. (1987) *Discipline in Schools: A Review of the Literature*, Edinburgh: Scottish Council for Research in Education.
Jones-Davies, C. and Cave, R. V. (1976) *The Disruptive Pupil in the Secondary School*, London: Ward Lock.
ILEA Research and Statistics Group (1986) *The Junior School Project*, London: ILEA.
Keddie, N. (1971) 'Classroom knowledge', in M. F. D. Young (ed.) *Knowledge and Control*, London: Collier-Macmillan.
Kemeny, H. (1993) *Learning Together Through Talk*, The National Oracy Project, Key Stages 3 and 4, London: Hodder & Stoughton.
Kimball, B. A. (1994) *The True Professional Ideal in America*, London: Blackwell.
King, R. (1978) *All Things Bright and Beautiful?*, London: Wiley.
Kohl, H. (1970) *The Open Classroom*, London: Methuen.
——(1986) *On Becoming a Teacher*, London: Methuen.
Kounin, J. (1970) *Discipline and Group Management in Classrooms*, New York: Holt, Rinehart & Winston.
Kyriacou, C. and Sutcliffe, J. (1977) 'Teacher stress: a review', *Educational Review* 29(4): 299–306.
——(1978) 'A model of teacher stress', *Educational Studies* 4(1): 1–6.
——(1979) 'Teacher stress and satisfaction', *Educational Research* 21(2): 89–96.
Lacey, C. (1970) *Hightown Grammar*, Manchester: Manchester University Press.

——(1977) *The Socialisation of Teachers*, London: Methuen.

Laing, A. F. and Chazan, M. (1986) 'The management of aggressive behaviour in young children', in D. P. Tatum (ed.) *Management of Disruptive Pupil Behaviour in Schools*, Chichester: Wiley.

Laslett, R. (1977) *Educating Maladjusted Children*, London: Staples Press.

——(1982) *Maladjusted Children in the Ordinary School*, Stratford: National Council for Special Education.

Laslett, R. and Smith, C. (1984 and 1992) *Effective Classroom Management*, London: Croom Helm.

Lawrence, J., Steed, D. and Young, P. (1977) *Disruptive Behaviour in a Secondary School*, London: University of London.

——(1984) 'European voices on disruptive behaviour in schools: definitions. concerns, and types of behaviour', *British Journal of Educational Studies* 32(1).

Lloyd-Smith, M. (1984) (ed.) *Disruptive Schooling*, London: John Murray.

Longworth-Dames, S. M. (1977) 'The relationship of personality and behaviour to school exclusion', *Educational Review* 29: 163–7.

Lovey, J., Docking, J. and Evans, R. (1993) *Exclusion from School: Provision for Disaffection at Key Stage 4*, London: David Fulton.

MacLure, M. and French, P. (1980) 'Routes to right answers: pupils' strategies for answering teachers' questions', in P. Woods (ed.) (1980a).

McManus, M. (1987) 'Suspension and exclusion from High Schools: the association with catchment and school variables', *School Organization* 7(3).

——(1990/1) *Foundation for Life Series* (*Work and Leisure; Home, Family and Health; You and Your Community*), London: Hodder & Stoughton.

——(1995) 'The use of Ofsted reports as data for investigating the relationship between school factors and exclusion' (forthcoming).

Mardle, G. and Walker, M. (1980) 'Strategy and structure: a critique of teacher socialisation', in P. Woods (ed.) (1980b).

Marland, M. (1975) *The Craft of the Classroom*, London: Heinemann.

Marsh, P., Rosser, E. and Harre, R. (1978) *The Rules of Disorder*, London: Routledge & Kegan Paul.

Marshall, S. (1963) *An Experiment in Education*, Cambridge University Press.

Martin, N. C. (1976) *Writing and Learning Across the Curriculum*, London: Ward Lock.

Mead, G. H. (1934) *Mind, Self and Society*, Chicago: Free Press.

Mehan, H. (1979) *Learning Lessons: Social Organisation in Classrooms*, Cambridge, Mass.: Harvard University Press.

Mercer, N. and Edwards, D. (1981) 'Ground rules for understanding', in N. Mercer (ed.) *Language in School and Community*, London: Edward Arnold.

Meyenn, R. J. (1980) 'School girls' peer groups', in P. Woods (ed.) (1980a).

Mortimore, P., Davies, J., Varlaam, A., West, A., Devine, P. and Mazza, J. (1983) *Behaviour Problems in Schools*, London: Croom Helm.

Musgrove, F. (1979) *School and the Social Order*, Chichester: Wiley.

Nash, R. (1973) *Classrooms Observed*, London: Routledge & Kegan Paul.

National Curriculum Council (1989) *Curriculum for All: Special Needs in the National Curriculum*, London: HMSO.

Neave, H. R. (1990) *The Deming Dimension*, Knoxville, Tennessee: SPC Press.

Neisser, U. (1976) *Cognition and Reality: Principles and Implications of Cognitive Psychology*, New York: W. H. Freeman.

Pack, D. C. (1977) *Truancy and Indiscipline in Schools*, Edinburgh: Scottish Education Department.

Partington, J. A. and Hinchcliffe, G. (1979) 'Some aspects of classroom management', *British Journal of Teacher Education* 5(3): 231–41.

Pearson, G. (1983) *Hooligan: A History of Respectable Fears*, London: Macmillan.

Phillipson, M. (1976) *Sociological Aspects of Crime and Delinquency*, London: Routledge & Kegan Paul.

Pik, R. (1987) 'Confrontation situations and teacher support systems', in L. Cohen and A. Cohen (eds) (1987).

Pollard, A. (1984) 'Goodies, jokers and gangs', in M. Hammersley and P. Woods (1984b).

Porter, R. (1990) *Myths of the English*, Cambridge: Polity Press.

Posner, G. J. (1980) 'Promising developments in curriculum knowledge presented to American Education Research Association', quoted in Y. Sheeran (1988) 'A sociocultural approach to children's writing', M. Phil. thesis, University of Leeds.

Pring, R. (1976) *Knowledge and Schooling*, London: Open Books.

Reid, I. (1986) *The Sociology of School and Education*, London: Fontana.

Reid, K. (1986) *Disaffection from School*, London: Methuen.

Reid, K., Hopkins, D. and Holly, P. (1987) *Towards the Effective School*, Oxford: Blackwell.

Reynolds, D. (1985) (ed.) *Studying School Effectiveness*, Lewes: Falmer.

Reynolds, D. and Sullivan, M. (1979) 'Bringing schools back in', in L. Barton and R. Meighan (eds.) *Pupils and Deviance*, London: Nafferton.

——(1981) 'The effects of school: a radical faith restated', in B. Gillham (ed.) *Problem Behaviour in the Secondary School*, London: Croom Helm.

Rigg, B. (1994) 'Exclusion from secondary schools', thesis submitted for the in-service B. Ed., Leeds Metropolitan University.

Robertson, J. (1981) *Effective Classroom Control*, Oxford: Blackwell.

Rogers, C. (1961) *Freedom to Learn*, New York: Holt, Reinhart & Winston.

——(1986) 'Teachers' expectation and effects', in M. Hammersley (ed.) (1986a).

Rose, L. (1991) *The Erosion of Childhood: Child Oppression in Britain 1860–1918*, London: Routledge.

Rutter, M., Maughan, B., Mortimore, P., Ouston, J. and Smith, A. (1979) *Fifteen Thousand Hours*, London: Open Books.

——(1980) 'A response to the discussion papers', in B. Tizard *et al.* (1980).

Schostak, J. F. (1983) *Maladjusted Schooling*, Lewes: Falmer.

——(1986) *Schooling the Violent Imagination*, Lewes: Falmer.

Schostak, J. F. and Logan, T. (1984) *Pupil Experience*, London: Croom Helm.

Schutz, A. (1972) *The Phenomenology of the Social World*, London: Heinemann.

Sharp, H. and Green, A. (1975) *Education and Social Control*, London: Routledge & Kegan Paul.

Silcock, P. (1993) 'Can we teach effective teaching?', *Education Studies* 45(1).

Smetherham, D. (1981) *Practising Evaluation*, Driffield: Studies in Education Limited.

Smythe, J. (1987) (ed.) *Educating Teachers: Changing the Nature of Pedagogical Knowledge*, Lewes: Falmer.

Sockett, H. (1983) 'Towards a professional code in teaching', in P. Gordon (ed.) *Is Teaching a Profession?*, Bedford Way Paper 15, University of London.

Speck, W. A. (1993) *A Concise History of Britain 1707–1975*, Cambridge: Cambridge University Press.

Speer, A. (1970) *Inside the Third Reich*, London: Weidenfeld & Nicholson.

Spooner, D. (1988) *Lay Stone on Stone*, Leeds: The Gerbil Press.

Spooner, R. T. (1979) 'Pastoral care and the myth of never ending toil', *Education* 2 February 1979: 251–2.

Stenhouse, L. (1975) *An Introduction to Curriculum Research and Development*, London: Heinemann.

Storr, A. (1968) *Human Aggression*, Harmondsworth: Penguin.

Stott, D. H. (1978) *Helping Children with Learning Difficulties*, London: Ward Lock.

——(1982) *Helping the Maladjusted Child*, Milton Keynes: Open University Press.

Stubbs, M. and Delamont, S. (eds) (1976) *Explorations in Classroom Observation*, London: Wiley.

Sturt, M. (1967) *The Education of the People*, London: Routledge & Kegan Paul.

Tattum, D. P. (1982) *Disruptive Pupils in Schools and Units*, Chichester: Wiley.

——(1986) (ed.) *Management of Disruptive Behaviour in Schools*, Chichester: Wiley.

Taylor, A. J. P. (1969) *War by Timetable*, London: Macdonald.

Tickle, L. (1984) 'One spell of ten or five spells of two', in M. Hammersley and P. Woods (1984a).

Tizard, B., Burgess, T., Francis, H., Goldstein, H., Young, M., Hewison, J. and Plewis, I. (1980) *Fifteen Thousand Hours: A Discussion*, University of London.

Topping, K. J. (1983) *Education Systems for Disruptive Adolescents*, London: Croom Helm.

Travers, R. M. W. (1973) (ed.) *Second Handbook of Research on Teaching*, Chicago: Rand McNally.

Tyldesley, J. (1994) *Daughters of Isis: Women of Ancient Egypt*, London: Viking.

Wagner, A. C. (1987) 'Knots in teachers' thinking', in J. Calderhead (1987).

Waller, W. (1965) *The Sociology of Teaching*, New York: Wiley.

Ward, C. (1994) 'Self-help and sustainability', *Royal Society of Arts Journal* June: 54–66.

Watson, J. (1988) 'One-year courses: the teachers' views', *British Journal of Special Education* 15(2).

Welton, J. (1982) *Meeting Special Needs*, Bedford Way Paper 12, University of London.

Werthman, C. (1963) 'Delinquents in schools', in B. R. Cosin (ed.) *School and Society*, Milton Keynes: Open University Press.

Wheldall, K. and Merrett, F. (1984) *Positive Teaching: The Behavioural Approach*, London: George, Allen & Unwin.

Wideen, M. F. and Andrews, I. (1987) (eds) *Staff Development for School Improvement*, Lewes: Falmer.

Willis, P. (1977) *Learning to Labour*, Farnborough: Saxon House.

Wills, D. (1945) *The Barns Experiment*, London: Allen & Unwin.

——(1967) (first published 1941) *The Hawkspur Experiment*, Harmondsworth: Penguin.

Wilson, A. (1987) *The Developmental Psychology of the Black Child*, New York: Africana Publications.

Wittrock, M. C. (1986) (ed.) *Third Handbook of Research on Teaching*, New York: American Education Research Association/Macmillan.

Woodhouse, D. A., Hall, E. and Wooster, D. A. (1985) 'Taking control of stress in teaching', *British Journal of Educational Psychology* 55: 119–23.

Woods, P. (1980a) (ed.) *Pupil Strategies*, London: Croom Helm.

——(1980b) (ed.) *Teacher Strategies*, London: Croom Helm.

——(1983) *Sociology and the School*, London: Routledge & Kegan Paul.

——(1984) 'Teaching for survival', in M. Hammersley and P. Woods (1984a).

Woods, P. and Pollard, A. (1987) (eds) *Sociology and Teaching*, London: Croom Helm.

Wragg, E. C. (1984) *Classroom Teaching Skills*, London: Croom Helm.
——(1987) *Teacher Appraisal: A Practical Guide*, London: Macmillan.
——(1993) *Primary Teaching Skills*, London: Routledge.
York, R., Heron, J. M. and Wolff, S. (1972) 'Exclusion from school', *Journal of Child Psychology and Psychiatry* 13: 259–66.

# Index